6502
APPLICATIONS BOOK

RODNAY ZAKS

SYBEX

U.S.A.:
2020 Milvia Street
Berkeley, CA 94704
Tel: (415) 848-8233
Telex: 336311

EUROPE:
18 rue Planchat
75020 Paris, France
Tel: (1) 370 32 75
Telex: 211801

The programs presented in this book have been designed for their educational value, and checked out with care. However, they are not warranted for any purpose.

Every effort has been made to supply complete and accurate information. However, Sybex assumes no responsibility for its use; nor any infringements of patents or other rights of third parties which would result. No license is granted by the equipment manufacturers under any patent or patent rights. Manufacturers reserve the right to change circuitry at any time without notice.

In particular, technical characteristics and prices are subject to rapid change. Comparisons and evaluations are presented for their educational value and for guidance principles. The reader is referred to the manufacturer's data for exact specifications.

Library of Congress Card Number: 78-73740
Library of Congress Cataloging in Publication Data
Zaks, Rodnay.
6502 applications book.

(Microcomputer programming series)
Bibliography: p.
Includes index.
1. 6502 (Computer)--Programming. I. Title.
II. Series.
QA76.8.S63Z35 001.6'42 78-73740
ISBN 0-89588-015-6

Printed in the United States of America

ACKNOWLEDGEMENTS

Many persons have contributed to the checkout, development or improvement of these programs. Special acknowledgements are due by the author to: Pierre Le Beux, Daniel David, Jaff Lin, Eric Martinot, Tricourt, and to Eric Novikoff (ASM65 assembler).

The following persons have also contributed valuable comments on the final draft of the manuscript, and their contribution is gratefully acknowledged: John McClenon, Doug Trusty, Phil Hooper, Daniel David, Robert Chitsum, and John Smith.

The following companies have provided access to valuable information or resources at an early date, and their contribution is gratefully acknowledged: Rockwell International, Synertek Systems, Apple.

The listings of Chapter Four, part 1 have been produced on a Rockwell System 65. The listings of part 2 have been produced with the ASM65 assembler listed in Appendix A.

Art Credits:
Daniel Lenoury (Cover Design)
Barry Janoff and Renate Woodbury (Technical Art)

Crayton,
Happy programming!
Best wishes on your special day!
December 24th 1979
Heidi

OTHER BOOKS IN THIS SERIES:

- *Programming the 6502 (ref C202)*
- *6502 Games (ref G502)*

PREFACE

This book presents practical application techniques for the 6502 microprocessor. It assumes an elementary knowledge of microprocessor programming on the level of the preceding book in this series (Reference C202: *Programming the 6502*). Understanding how to program the microprocessor chip itself (the 6502) is only a prerequisite for the actual programming of a microprocessor board connected to real devices. The next problem is to learn how to write actual application programs involving the input/output ports and other facilities available in a real system. This book addresses itself to this problem. It will present the techniques and programs required for typical applications, using the actual input-output chips available on a board.

The programs presented in this book will require a minimum of actual hardware to be effectively implemented. The user is therefore encouraged to practice the concepts and techniques presented here on actual hardware. A realistic description of possible applications boards will be presented. The programs are applicable to any 6502-based microcomputer board such as the KIM, the SYM, the AIM 65, or others. Many programs can be run directly on one or more of these boards while others will require some changes. However, the concepts and techniques are common to all.

The application programs presented in this book will allow the reader to build a complete home alarm system, which includes fire detection and other features, an electronic piano, a motor speed regulator, an appliance or hobby-train controller, a time-of-day clock, a simulated traffic control system, a morse code generator, an industrial control loop for temperature control, including analog-to-digital conversion, and more.

This book is intended to teach all the basic skills required to apply the 6502 to real life applications. It is preceded in our 6502 series by "C202 - *Programming the 6502*," and followed by "G402 - *6502 Games.*"

CALL FOR PROGRAMS

While reading this book, you will find many useful or interesting programs. Many of you will want to develop other novel application programs using the 6502. If you should find improvements for programs already in this book or if you should develop new interesting programs, let us know. All our books are constantly updated and expanded. One of your programs might get published in a subsequent edition or another book. Write to the author at the following address:

Rodnay Zaks, Ref. D302
Sybex Inc.
2020 Milvia Street
Berkeley, CA 94704

Also if you have suggestions for additional programs which you would have liked to see included in this book, let us know, and we might be able to accommodate your request in a subsequent edition.

TABLE OF CONTENTS

TABLE OF ILLUSTRATIONS

CHAPTER 1

INTRODUCTION

When learning how to program, understanding the operation of the microprocessor itself is only the first problem which must be solved. This is the problem addressed by our book, ref C202, *Programming the 6502.* The next problem is to learn how to program effectively, using input/output devices connected to the microprocessor board. This is the purpose of this book. Naturally, no book can completely cover all possible devices. A selection, therefore, has been made among the important input/output devices usually connected to a 6502, and application programs are presented, which are likely to fit a majority of applications.

First, you will learn how to effectively program a PIO, the parallel input/output chip. You will learn to use polling or interrupts. You will learn to generate pulses, measure delays, and control actual input/output devices such as switches, relays, or more complex devices such as a digital to analog converter, a motor, and others. You will also learn how to use more complex input/output chips such as a *programmable timer.* Additional interfaces will be presented for simple devices, so that you may actually build an applications board and practice on it.

In order to learn programming effectively, you are strongly encouraged to practice. It is indeed the only real way of becoming a proficient programmer. In order to practice, you will need a microcomputer board such as the KIM, the SYM, the AIM65, or any other 6502 board. Because all boards normally provide at least one PIO (often 2), and at least 2 timers (sometimes more), all programs presented in this book should run on any of these boards with minor variations, if any.

The additional hardware which you will need in order to run specific programs will be discussed in Chapters 4, 5 and 6. It is minimal and easily obtainable. In particular, you will find in Chapters 4, 5 and 6 the description of suggested applications boards which can be constructed from common components at low cost. It will allow you to run the programs in the chapter, using your microcomputer board and the applications board. It is suggested that you consider building it in order to practice.

However, it is not indispensable. You will learn all the basic techniques by merely reading the book. If you wish to grow from there, then actual practice is strongly recommended.

Connecting Your Microprocessor to the Real World

Connecting the microprocessor itself to the real world first involves building a basic microprocessor board, then connecting it to actual devices. Both hardware and software interfaces will be required to connect actual devices to the board. This book will present in detail both the hardware components and the programs required for the most commonly used devices. In order to design industrial programs normally involving expensive devices such as traffic signals, simulated devices will be used on the applications board, using LED's for example. If the program were to be applied to a real traffic system, only the interface hardware would usually be changed. The program would remain essentially identical. The skills you will learn are, therefore, applicable to real life situations.

The Pedagogy

When reading this book, you will usually "learn by doing." Each program will be presented in detail: its purpose, its flow-chart, the hardware interface, the devices, the program itself, and the complete analysis of the techniques used. Each chapter is essentially self-contained. For example it is not necessary that you understand all the PIO features of Chapter 2 to read Chapter 3. However, sequential reading is recommended for a complete understanding. The contents of Chapter 2 introduce all the usual parallel I/O chips used in a 6502 system, from the 6520 to the 6532. Since all existing 6502 boards to date use these standard chips, this chapter should be read by all those who are not familiar with them.

Chapter Three presents the "Standard 6502 Board", and some well-known variations: KIM, SYM, AIM65 (others exist). Most examples presented in the book will run directly on a SYM, and with simple changes, on a KIM, or other boards.

Chapter Four introduces the basic application techniques for connecting simple devices: relays, switches, speaker. The first applications board will be used for applications ranging from a Morse generator to a telephone dialer.

Chapter Five presents more complex home and industrial applications. The second applications board will be used for applications ranging from simulated traffic control and analog-to-digital conversion to a complete home burglar alarm or an electronic piano.

In Chapter Six actual low-cost peripherals are connected to a microcomputer board: from paper-tape-reader to keyboard and printer.

Finally, a summary and synthesis are presented in Chapter Seven.

You will also find in Appendix A a complete assembler for the 6502, written in BASIC, to facilitate your development of complex programs requiring an assembler.

You will find on the next page a Standard Programming Form designed to facilitate writing your 6502 programs.

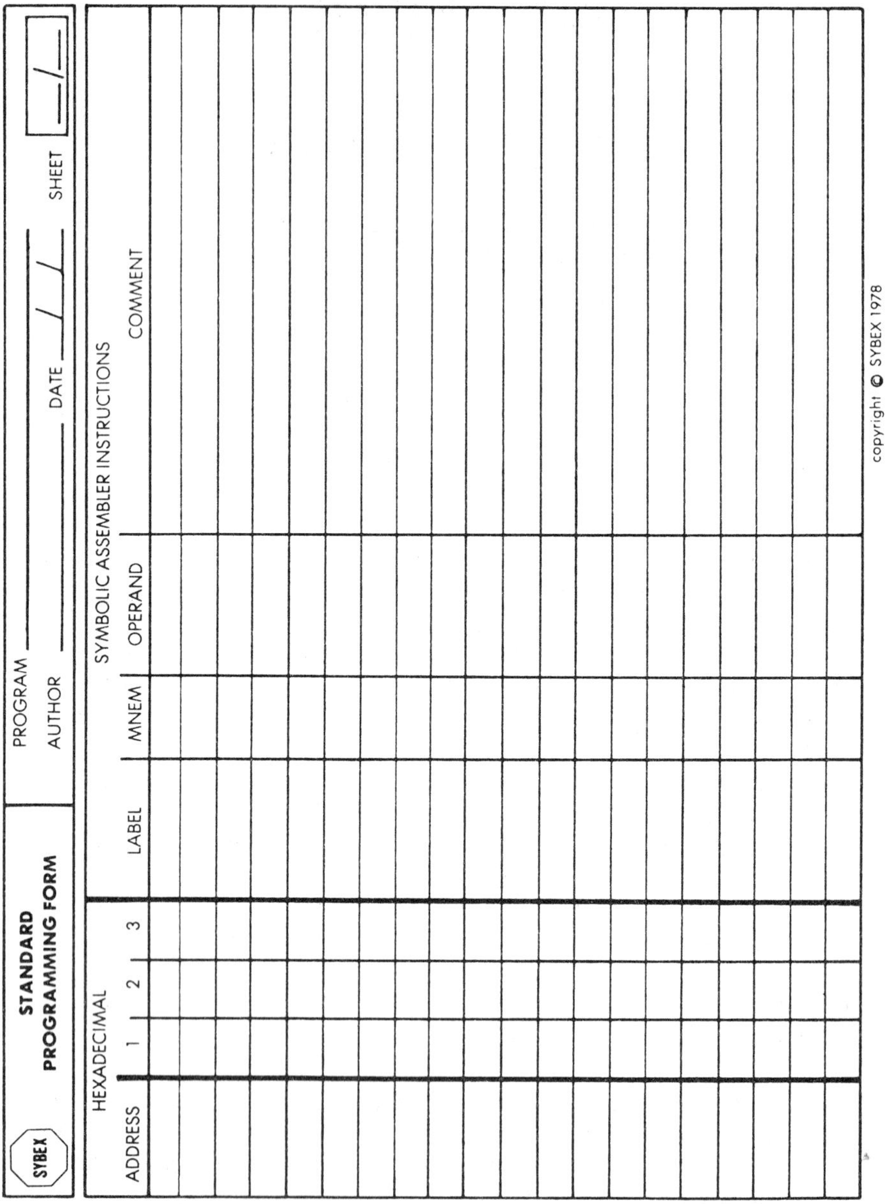

Fig. 1-1: Standard Programming Form

CHAPTER 2

THE INPUT OUTPUT CHIPS

INTRODUCTION

In this book, we will connect a variety of input-output devices to a 6502 board in order to realize practical microcomputer applications. It is therefore essential to understand the input-output resources of a 6502 system. The reader who is not familiar with the basic terms or with the basic techniques (such as "polling") is encouraged to review them in the previous volume of this series, reference C202 (*Programming the 6502*).

In this chapter, we will review systematically the parallel input-output chips used on nearly every 6502 board to provide the required input-output facilities. It is indispensable to understand at least how a "PIO," such as a 6522 works, before proceeding to the application chapters. The exact details of the timer operation or other exotic resources (such as a shifter) are not essential in a first reading and could be skipped. Also, the exact details and formats of the various registers inside the 6520, 6522, 6530, and 6532 are not important to memorize. They are provided here as a reference for the following chapters.

It is therefore suggested that you read carefully at least one of the sections on a PIO such as the 6520 or the 6522, without trying to remember all the details, but focussing on the way they operate. Nearly every application will make use of a PIO, i.e. of one of the chips presented in this section.

In addition to these chips, most microcomputer boards will provide some other specialized input-output interfaces, such as a cassette interface or a CRT interface. The interested reader is referred to the manufacturer's literature or to the reference book C207 (*"Microprocessor Interfacing Techniques"*) for details on these specific interfaces.

BASIC DEFINITIONS

This section is a reminder of the terms we will use in this chapter.

The three essentiai input-output facilities on nearly every microcomputer board, are the "PIO," the "UART," and the "timer. Let us examine them:

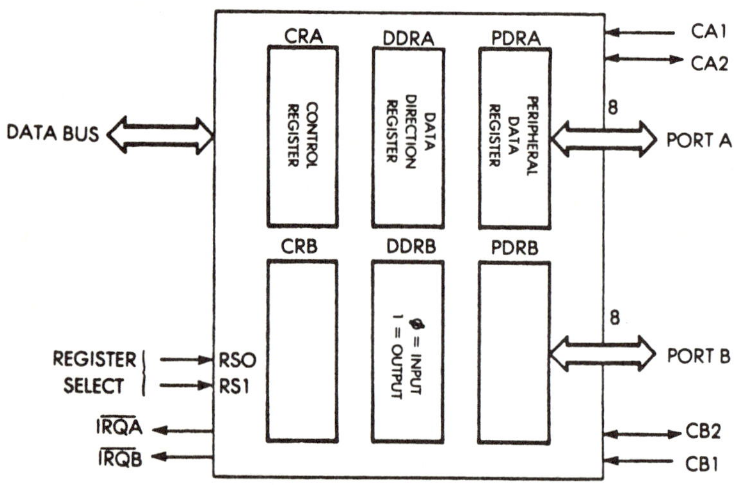

Fig. 2-1: Typical PIO

The PIO

The "PIO" or "parallel input-output chip," is a component which provides at least two parallel eight-bit ports. In a PIO, the use of each line of each port is usually programmable in direction. The direction of each line is usually determined by the contents of a "data-direction register" associated with each port. Whenever a specific bit of the data direction register is "0", for example, the corresponding line on the port will be an input. Prior to using the PIO, the programmer will first have to load the contents of the data-direction register of each port, in order to define in which direction the lines will be used. Specific additional constraints may be imposed by manufacturer such as restricting lines to be programmable in direction in groups of four, or else assigning special functions to some bit positions such as bit six and bit seven. Some of these restrictions will be encountered in the chips presented in this chapter. The internal block diagram of the "standard PIO" is shown in Fig 2-1. The two buffers for port A and port B appear on the right of the illustration. The data-direction register associated with each port appears to the left of these buffers. Additionally, two control registers are provided in this simplified diagram. The control register is required to specify the function of the control signals which are provided by this PIO. In particular, it must determine and control the "hand-shaking" procedure, and whether the control signals will trigger flags or interrupts, and also whether a low-to-high transition, or a high-to-low transition, should be used for example. Typically, the programmer will have to specify the contents of the control register prior to making any use of the control lines supplied by the component. Also the programmer will look up the contents of the control register to determine whether an internal interrupt or other special condition has been detected (status information).

In addition to the two data ports, a PIO should also supply control lines to allow automated hand-shaking with a peripheral. These control lines are shown on the right side of the standard PIO of Fig 2-1, and are labeled respectively CA1, CA2 for port A, and CB1, CB2 for port B.

As an example of a hand-shaking procedure, the external peripheral might supply a "DATA READY" signal on CA1. The microprocessor would then respond with a "DATA REQUEST" signal on CA2. Additionally, when a "data ready" signal is received on CA1, it should be flagged in the control register, and an interrupt request might be generated externally in order to alert the 6502 to this event. This is a typical simple example of the control sequence required for effective hand-shaking. Much of this procedure is automated inside the standard PIO, and the options are defined by the contents of the control register. The specific details will be presented for each of the PIO's we will describe, beginning on page 20.

The Timer

A basic requirement in most practical applications is the ability to generate specific *delays*. Delays can be measured by software techniques or else by hardware timers. As long as no interrupts are used in the system, delays can usually be generated conveniently by software loops (see reference C202 for details). However, in more complex situations, or in situations where interrupts may occur, it is desirable to use one or more external hardware timers to generate or measure fixed delays.

Using the Timer on Output

In its simplest form, a hardware timer is a counter equipped with a register (8 bits or 16 bits). When used in output mode, the timer's register is loaded with a given value by the program. It is then given a "go ahead" signal and it starts counting. Most timers will use the system clock, but not necessarily (usually a one MHz clock=one-microsecond pulses). The number placed in the counter's register will be decremented by one for every successive clock pulse. If the value placed in the register was N, the contents of the counter will have decremented to zero after N pulses, that is after N microseconds, assuming one-microsecond pulses. Whenever the counter decrements to zero, a signal will be generated which will set a status flag in the timer chip and/or generate an external interrupt. Depending on the precision required, the program will either poll timer devices or else accept interrupts. Typical programs will be presented in this chapter.

If the timer were equipped with a single 8-bit register, it could count only from one to 256. The maximum delay would only be 256 microseconds with a standard clock. This delay is too short for most applications. Naturally, it would be possible to use the interrupt generated at the end of the 256 microseconds to update a memory location, then test whether this memory location had reached a specific value. However, this would result in inaccurate time measurement and a somewhat cumbersome process. Therefore, a timer which is equipped with an 8-bit register would be insufficient. Two techniques are used to overcome this limitation. Conceptually, the simpplest one is to use a 16-bit register for the counter. The counter may then count from 1 to 64K, i.e., from one microsecond to 65,536 microseconds or approximately 65 milliseconds. This is indeed sufficient for most applications. However, this technique requires that the timer be loaded in at least two operations, since the data-bus is only 8-bit wide. First, the program must load one half of the register, then it must load the other half, an inconvenience.

The other technique to generate delays over a wide range is to use internal divide circuits within the timer. Such a timer will then appear to the programmer as a device equipped with perhaps four registers. For example, if the first register is used, then the delay generated will be expressed in clock units (1 microsecond typical). If the second register is used, then the delay unit will be 8 times the clock cycle; in the third one the timing unit will be 64 times the clock cycle, and in the next one the timing will be 1,024 times the clock cycle (or approximately one millisecond, assuming a 1 MHz clock). This approach is somewhat more convenient to the programmer and offers the possibility of loading the timer in a single operation, yet using it over a wide range. However, the internal complexity of the device is increased.

Using the Timer On Input

A timer may be used on input to measure the duration of an external pulse, or else the time elapsed between two successive pulses. In this case, the initial contents of the timer counter are zero and the counter will increment its internal register with each timing interval. Once the delay has been measured, a flag will be set by the device or else an external interrupt may be generated, and the program will be responsible for reading the contents of the counter register which indicate the external event duration.

Pulse Trains

A timer may be used not only to generate or measure a pulse, but also to generate or count a train of pulses. Whenever a delay is generated or measured for a pulse, the timer mode is usually called a "one-shot" mode. When a train of pulses is generated, it is often called a "free-running" mode. Additionally, a number of options can be provided to specify whether a high-to-low transition or else a low-to-high transition of the signal should be used to activate or stop the timer, or else whether levels should be considered rather than pulses. Additionally, the timing and logical value of interrupt flags can be specified. Further, the conditions under which the internal status is set and reset are usually programmable. Because of the large number of possible variations, each timer device tends to have a strong personality and needs to be studied in detail before being used.

The UART

"UART" stands for "Universal Asynchronous Receiver Transceiver." The essential function of the UART is to perform serial-to-parallel, and parallel-to-serial conversions. Additionally, the standard UART provides a number of options usually required for serial communications with external devices such as parity (checking, inhibition or generation) and start and stop bits. The conversion is performed by an internal shifter. Such a shifter may also be incorporated in some input-output chips.

Actual 6502 Input-Output Devices

Virtually every 6502-based board will require at least 2 PIO's and one timer. These functions will be typically provided by a combination of 6520 and 6530 chips or by a combination of 6522 and 6532 chips. The 6520 and 6530, which will be described below, are the original input-output chips which were introduced by MOS Technology. The 6502 is now manufactured by several other manufacturers, such as Synertek and Rockwell, and additional support chips have been introduced, such as the 6522 and the 6532. Still other support chips will probably be introduced in the future.

At this time, however, the most important chips are the 6520, the 6530, the 6522, and the 6532. These four essential input-output chips will be described now.

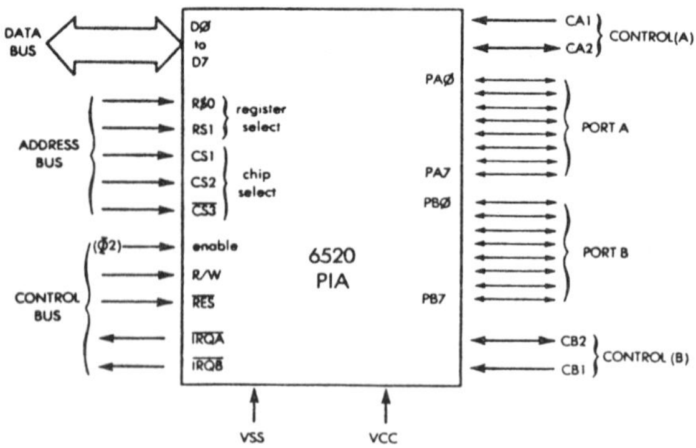

Fig 2-2: The 6520 PIA

THE 6520 (PIA)

The 6520 is almost a pure "PIO," as we have defined it. it has been designed as a pin-for-pin replacement for the Motorola M6820, and has been called by the manufacturer a "peripheral interface adapter" or "PIA." The signals of the 6520 are shown on Fig 2-2. Its internal architecture is shown in Fig 2-3.

Referring to Fig 2-3, it can be seen that this device provides two parallel input-output ports, port A and port B. Each port is equipped with a buffer. However, the two ports are not quite identical, and the buffer really works only as an output buffer, not as an input one. A data-direction register ("DDR") is available for each port, and specifies the direction of each line of the port. A value "0" in this DDR specifies an input, and a value "1" specifies an output. The choice of conventions stems from a safety consideration: whenever a "RESET" is applied, the contents of all registers will be zeroed and

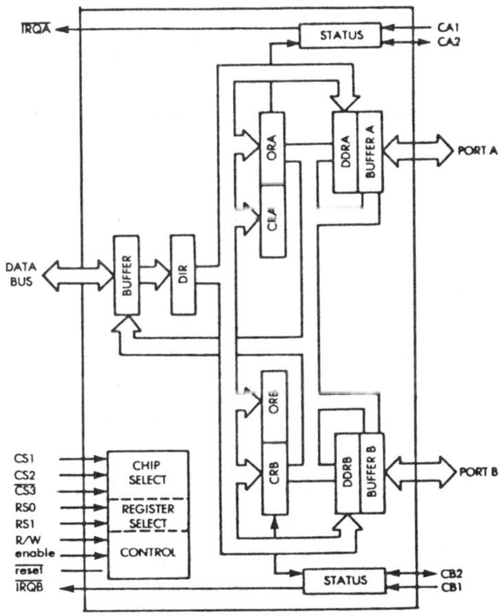

Fig 2-3: 6520 Internal Architecture

the data-direction register will become all zeroes. As a result, all lines will be configured as *inputs*; this is the safe way to start a system. No external pulse can be generated until the program has started execution.

Additionally, each port is equipped with two registers, the *control register* and the *output register*. The data sent by the 6502 to the device are gated to the *output register* (ORA) of the specified port, where they are held. The function of the *control register* (CRA) will be explained below. It specifies the role of various control options and contains status information for each port.

Finally, each port is equipped with two external control lines, labeled CA1, and CA2 for port A. CA1 is a monodirectional line from the device to the 6520. CA2 is a bidirectional line, which may be used either as an input or an output.

The two ports are logically equivalent and symmetrical, as indicated on Fig 2-3. However, practical differences exist. In particular, the drive capability of port B is superior to port A, and the role of the control signals is not completely symmetrical.

Looking now at the left of Fig 2-3, or at Fig 2-2, the data bus connects the internal buffer of the 6520 to the system data bus. Two interrupt requests may be generated by the device, if so specified by the contents of the control registers for port A and B; they are respectively IRQA and IRQB. Finally, three chip-select inputs must be specified for the device, and are labeled CS1, CS2, and CS3. This design was used by Motorola in order to allow the convenient direct connection of up to 8 separate devices to the data bus, without the necessity of an external address decoder. In practice, the high number of chip-select inputs on the chip may have resulted in a disadvantage which will be pointed out below (one register-select missing). Two register-select inputs are provided, and connected to the address bus. They are labeled RS0 and RS1. This means that the 6520 device appears to the programmer as *four* memory locations. This may seem surprising since we have just determined (see Fig 2-3) that there are four registers per port, i.e. a total of *eight registers*. How can one address 8 registers with only 4 addresses? This is a problem brought about by the pin number limitation of the device. One bit of the control-register, bit 2, is used to multiplex between the two sets of registers. When bit 2 of the control register is equal to "0," the data-direction for that port is selected. When it is "1," the peripheral-interface buffer is selected.

Finally, three more control lines are available: "R/W" (read or write), "enable" (usually phase two of the clock), and finally "reset."

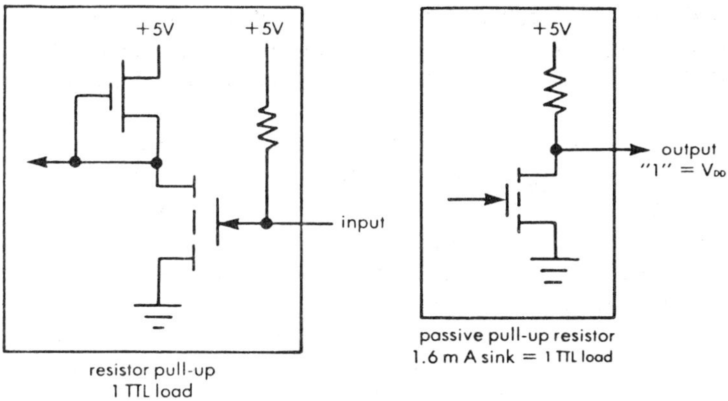

Fig. 2-4: Buffer A

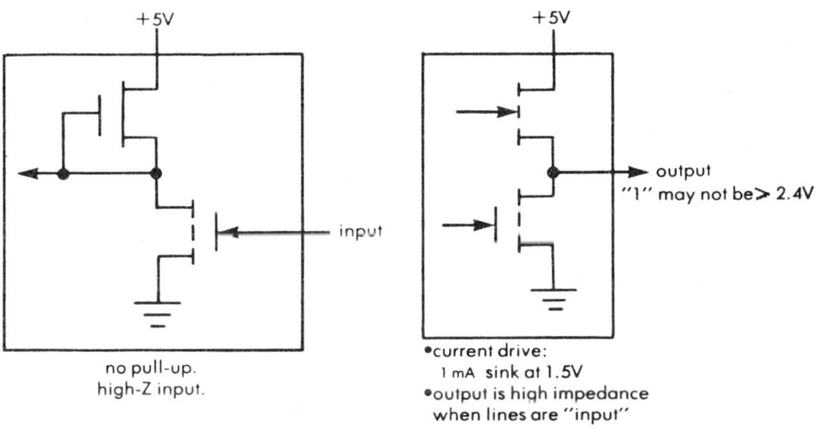

Fig. 2-5: Buffer B

Differences between Port A and Port B

Port A and port B, even though they are logically equivalent, are physically dissimilar. The buffers of port A use *passive pull-ups.* They can sink 1.6 mA, making the buffers capable of driving a standard

TTL load. On port B, the buffers are *push-pull* devices (see Fig 2-4 and 2-5). Since they are *active* devices, the logic "1" voltage may not be higher than 2.4 volts (versus V_{DD} in the case of port A). However they have a superior current drive (1mA at 1.5v), so that they can be directly connected to LED's, or to Darlington transistor switches. Finally, when port B is used as *input*, the output buffer enters a *high-impedance* mode, so that the input will have a high impedance (more than one Megohm). The details of the port A buffer are shown on Fig 2-4, and the details of the port B buffer are shown on Fig 2-5.

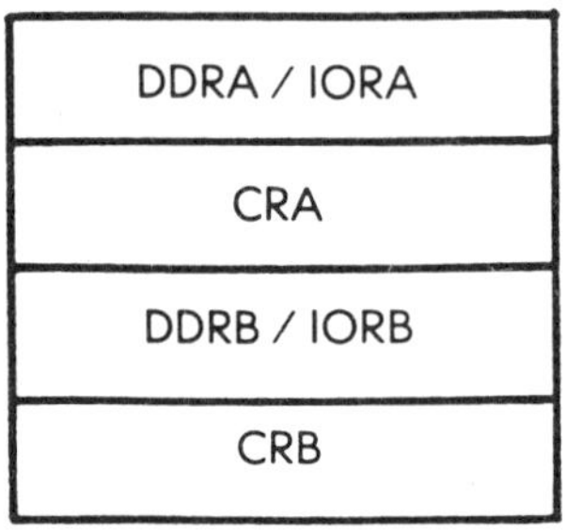

Fig. 2-6: 6520 Memory Map

The Internal Registers

Let us consider now in more detail the specific resources and peculiarities of the 6520. First, as we have already noted, the 6520 is equipped with 6 internal registers: the two buffers (which share the address of the output register), the two data direction registers, and the two control registers. However, because of the pin number limitation, only two register-select pins are available on the device, called respectively RS0 and RS1. The resulting 6520 memory map is shown on Fig 2-6. It shows that registers DDRA and IORA for example, share the same logical memory address. The control-register is addressed independently. The 6520 differentiates internally between the DDRA and the IORA by the value of bit 2 of the control register. The register selection is presented on Fig 2-7. Whenever bit 2 of the control register is "0," the DDR is selected. Whenever it is "1," the IO register or buffer-register, is selected. The control register is the only register which can be addressed directly by RS0 and RS1 since it is logically necessary to specify the contents of this control register prior to accessing the other registers.

RS1	RS0	CRA-2	CRB-2	REGISTER SELECTED
0	0	1	-	BUFFER A
0	0	0	-	DDRA
0	1	-	-	CRA
1	0	-	1	BUFFER B
1	0	-	0	DDRB
1	1	-	-	CRB

Fig. 2-7: 6520 Register Selection

This scheme implies that the initialization of this device is somewhat more complex than it should be, and that, if the program should need to access successively the DDRA and the IORA, additional instructions must be inserted to modify the contents of bit 2 of the CRA every time. This is indeed inconvenient.

The Control Register

The contents of the control register are shown on Fig 2-8. It has already been pointed out that bit 2 of this register performs a special function: it differentiates between the DDR and the IOR register for that port. The other bits within the register provide control options for the two control lines available on each port, and 2 bits are reserved for status or interrupt information. The control register A functions are controlled by bits 3, 4, and 5 and are shown on Fig 2-9.

7	6	5	4	3	2	1	0
IRQ1	IRQ2	CA/B2 control			DDRA/B select	CA/B1 control	

Fig. 2-8: 6520 Control Registers

CRA BIT 5	4	3	MODE	EFFECT
1	0	0	Handshake on read	•CA1 interrupt input transition sets CA2 high. •Read Port A instruction sets CA2 low.
1	0	1	Pulse output	•Read Port A data sets CA2 low for one cycle (= acknowledge to device).
1	1	0	Manual Output	sets CA2 low
1	1	1	Manual Output	sets CA2 high

Fig. 2-9: 6520 CA2 Control

CRB BIT 5	4	3	MODE	EFFECT
1	0	0	Handshake on write	•CB1 interrupt input transition sets CB2 high. •Write Port B data sets CB2 low.
1	0	1	Pulse Output	•Write Port B data sets CB2 low for one cycle (= acknowledge to device).
1	1	0	Manual Output	sets CB2 low
1	1	1	Manual Output	sets CB2 high

Fig. 2-10: 6520 CB2 Control

The functions of the two control lines of port B are controlled by bits 3, 4, and 5 of its control register and shown on Fig 2-10. Bits 0 and 1 provide interrupt control for the CA1 and CB1 inputs. They are shown on Fig 2-11.

CR BIT 1	CR BIT 0	ACTIVE TRANSITION OF INPUT SIGNAL	IRQ OUTPUT
0	0	negative	disable (high)
0	1	negative	enable (will go low when CRA bit 7 set by CA1/CB1 transition)
1	0	positive	disable (high)
1	1	positive	enable (as above)

Fig 2-11: Interrupt Control (CA1, CB1 Inputs)

Using the 6520

After a "Reset" has been applied, the contents of all the registers will be zero. The 6520 must, therefore, first be initialized to specify the input and output configurations on both its ports. The control options of the control register must also be specified and the 6520 should normally be left with a "1" in bit position 2 of the control register, so that the IOR register can be accessed directly by the 6502.

A typical sequence is:

```
LDA    #$0F        "00001111" = 4 INPUTS, 4
                   OUTPUTS
STA    DDRA        CONFIGURE DIRECTION
LDA    #CONTROL    CONTROL OPTIONS:
                   BIT 2=1 TO ADDRESS
                   IORA
STA    CRA
```

INPUT-OUTPUT

Sending data out on port A would be accomplished by the following two intructions (assuming CRA-bit 2 ="1"):

```
LDA    #DATA  OR ELSE LDA $20 (FROM
                   MEMORY)
STA    IORA
```

Reading an input connected to the 6520 is accomplished by:

```
LDA   IORA
STA   $20        SAVE IT IN MEMORY
```

We are saving here the contents of the accumulator immediately in memory location 20 (hexadecimal). However, this line is not indispensable. In many cases, we will simply read the contents of IORA in the accumulator and then perhaps check their value but not necessarily store them.

6520 Warnings

In addition to the dissimilarities between port A and port B, some specific features of the control functions should be remembered. In particular, bits 6 and 7 are cleared on A or B if 6 is input and if reading. Also, to clear bit 7, one *reads* port B data. The CB2 handshake, unlike the CA2 handshake, is for *writing* B data (CA2 operates for *read or write*). Finally, bit 6 or 7 may cause an interrupt.

Polling the 6520's

The simplest way to poll several 6520's is to check the status of bits 6 and 7 of the control register. When both bits 6 and 7 are "0," the device does not require any service. If either bit is "1," an internal interrupt has been generated, and service is required.

Technique 1

In order to identify quickly which one of four devices has requested service, a sequential table access technique may be used, provided the addresses of the 4 devices are sequential in the memory. Address n will be allocated to CRA1, address n + 1 to CRB1, address n + 2 to CRA2, address n + 3 to CRB3, etc. The program can then make use of the indexed indirect addressing feature and is shown below:

```
START   LDX   #8            INDEX
NEXT    LDA   (BASE-1,X)    ACCESS NEXT CR
        BMI   SERVICE       IRQ ON?
        DEX                 X=X-1
        BEQ   START
        BNE   NEXT
```

```
BASE   -WORD CRA 1  PIO #1  PORT A
       -WORD CRB 1          PORT B
       -WORD CRA 2  PIO #2  PORT A
       -WORD CRB 2          PORT A
       -WORD CRA 3  PIO #3  PORT A
       -WORD CRB 3          PORT B
       -WORD CRA 4  PIO #4  PORT A
       -WORD CRB 4          PORT B
```

Fig. 2-12: Identifying the PIO

Index register X is set to the initial value "8" and will be successively decremented by 1, every time we go through the polling loop. The accumulator is loaded with the contents of the last enrty in the table first:

```
LDA    (BASE-1, X)
```

If bit 7 was set (bit 7 is the sign bit or "N" flag), a branch will occur to the service routine:

```
BMI    SERVICE
```

If the N flag was not set, X is decremented, and the next CR is checked:

```
DEX
BEQ    START   RESTART IF X=0
BNE    NEXT    GO ON IF X IS NOT 0
```

Improvement: would switching the last two instructions speed up the program?

Technique 2

Within each CRA, two status bits must be checked: bits 6 and 7. The "BIT" instruction of the 6502 has been created for this specific purpose. It is a nondestructive comparison which will check the contents of bits 6 and 7. The program for polling the 6520's appears on Fig 2-13.

```
BIT    CRA
```

```
              BMI    IRQA7
              BVC    NOTA1
IRQA6         . . .             A2 IRQ FOUND (Bit 6)
  :
IRQA7         . . .             A1 IRQ FOUND (BIT 7)
  :
NOTA1         BIT    CRB        SAME FOR PORT B
              BMI    IRQB7
              BVC    NEXT2
IRQB6         . . .             B2 IRQ FOUND (BIT 6)
  :
IRQB7         . . .             B1 IRQ FOUND (BIT 7)
  :
NEXT2         BIT    ...        NEXT 6520
               :
```

Fig. 2-13: Identifying the Ports

The "BIT" instruction is used to test whether either bits 6 or 7 are a "1". This is performed by:

```
BIT     CRA
```

We must then test whether bit 6 or 7 was set to "1." The BIT instruction sets V flag and the N flag, so that these two flags can now be tested;

```
BMI     IRQA7      BIT 7 = 1
BVC     NOTA1      NO INTERRUPT FOUND
```

If none of the flags were set, a branch will occur to NOT A1, where the CRB will be checked. Bit 7 is tested with the BMI instruction. If bit 7 was one, the sign bit N will have been set, and the routine at address IRQA7 will be executed.

Otherwise, bit 6 was the bit that was set and the routine at address IRQA6, following the BMI, will be executed.

This sequence can be executed for any number of 6520's. Note that this procedure gives higher priority to A7 than A6.

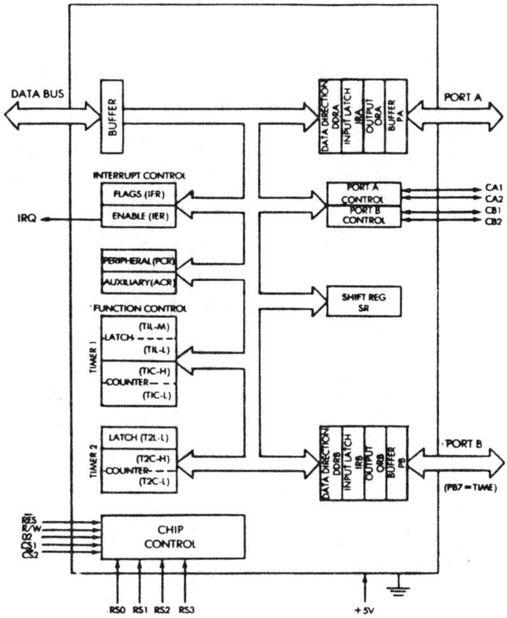

Fig 2-14: 6522 Internal Architecture

THE 6522

The 6522, introduced by MOS Technology, and also manufactured by Rockwell International and Synertek, is the successor device to the 6520.

The 6522 chip, called the VIA (Versatile Interface Adapter), is a PIO-timer-shifter combination. It is equipped internally with 16 registers which are shown on Fig 2-14. The corresponding memory map is on Fig 2-15.

Four sets of registers can be distinguished as to their function:

1. The PIO registers (addresses 0 through 3, plus address F).
2. The timer registers (two timers, addresses 4 through 9.
3. The shift register (address A).
4. The control registers (addresses B through E).

These four sets will now be examined in detail to explain the capabilities of the 6522.

00	ORB (PB0 TO PB7)	I/O data, port A	
01	ORA (PA0 TO PA7)	used for control-affects handshake	
02	DDR B	data direction registers	
03	DDR A		
04	T1L-L/T1C-L	counter-low	timer 1
05	T1C-H	counter-high	
06	T1L-L	latch-low	
07	T1L-H	latch-high	
08	T2L-L/T2C-L	latch-low counter-low	timer 2
09	T2C-H	counter-high	
0A	SR	shift register	
0B	ACR	auxiliary	function control
0C	PCR (CA1,CA2,CB2,CB1)	peripheral	
0D	IFR	flags	interrupt control
0E	IER	enable	
0F	ORA	output register A (does not affect handshake)	

Fig. 2-15: 6522 VIA Memory Map

RS3	RS2	RS1	RS0				
0	0	0	0	00	ORB	+ handshake	PARALLEL I/O
0	0	0	1	01	ORA		
0	0	1	0	02	DDRB		
0	0	1	1	03	DDRA		
0	1	0	0	04	T1L-L(W)/T1C-L(R)	+ clear T1 Int Flag (R)	TIMER T1
0	1	0	1	05	T1C-H(R)/T1L-H + T1C-H(W)	+ T1C-L T1L-L + clear T1 Int Flag (R)	
0	1	1	0	06	T1L-L		
0	1	1	1	07	T1L-H	+ clear T1 Int Flag(W)	
1	0	0	0	08	T2L-L(W)/T2C-L(R)	+ clear T2 Int Flag(W)	TIMER T2
1	0	0	1	09	T2C-H	+ T2C-L T2L-L + clear T2 Int Flag(W)	
1	0	1	0	0A	SR		SHIFT
1	0	1	1	0B	ACR		CONTROL
1	1	0	0	0C	PCR		
1	1	0	1	0D	IFR		
1	1	1	0	0E	IER		
1	1	1	1	0F	ORA	no handshake	PARALLEL I/O

Fig. 2-16: 6522 Registers

The PIO Section

The PIO Section provides two 8-bit bidirectional ports. Each port is equipped with an input/output register. They are called respectively ORA and ORB for port A and port B. They are shown on Fig 2-14. Each register is associated with a direction register, respectively DDRA AND DDRB. Whenever the corresponding bit of the data direction register is set to "1" the line connected to the OR will be an *output.* Whenever the data direction bit is "0", the corresponding line will be an *input.* The polarity has been chosen so that all lines are iniput when a "reset" is applied.

There is an asymmetry in this PIO: Port A is equipped with two OR registers, with and without the handshake feature.

Using the PIO

Before using the PIO as input or output, the data-direction registers must be loaded with the proper value to configure the corresponding bits of the I/0 registers as input or output. As an example, let us configure here Port A as an output and Port B as an input.

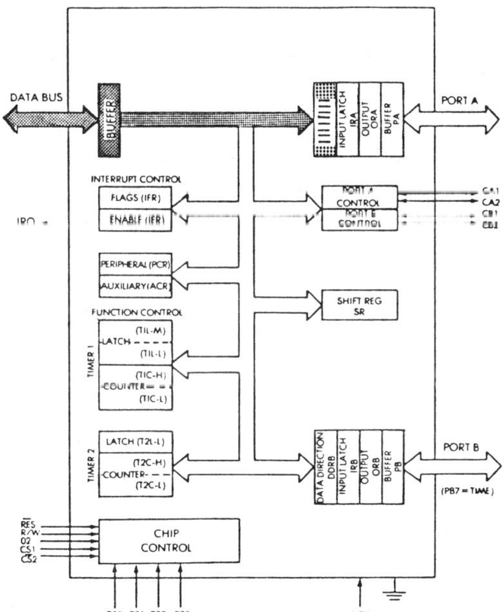

Fig 2-17: Using the 6522: STA DDRA

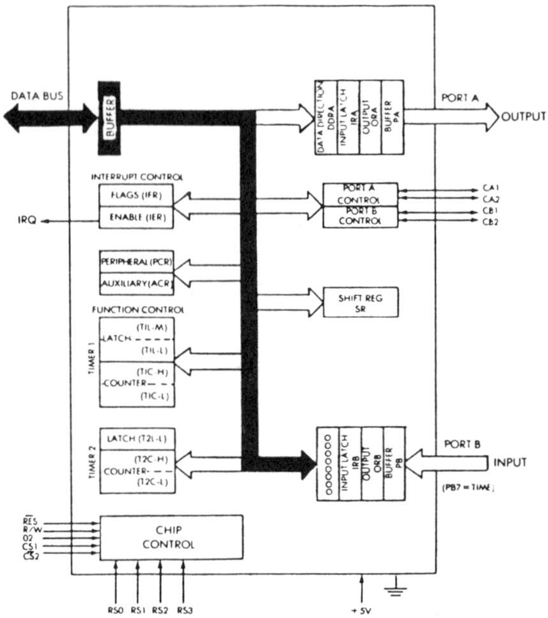

Fig 2-18: Using the 6522: STA DDRB

```
LDA    #$FF     "11111111" = OUTPUT
STA    DDRA
LDA    #0
STA    DDRB     B is INPUT
```

(see Fig 2-17 and 2-18)

Let us now output the value "00000001" on Port A (see Fig 2-19):

```
LDA    #$01     "00000001"
STA    ORA
```

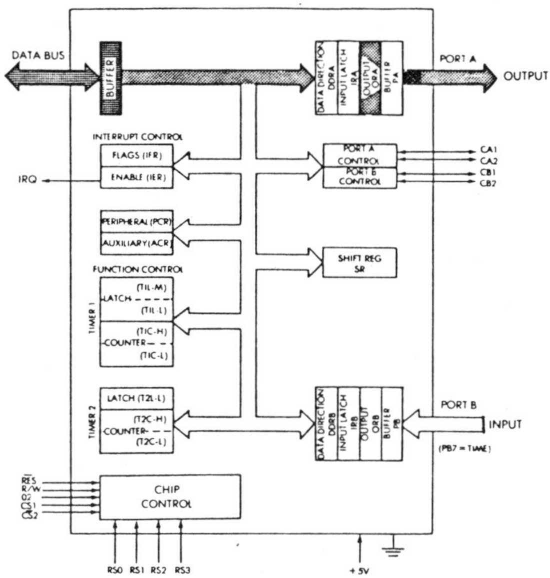

Fig 2-19: Using the 6522: STA ORA

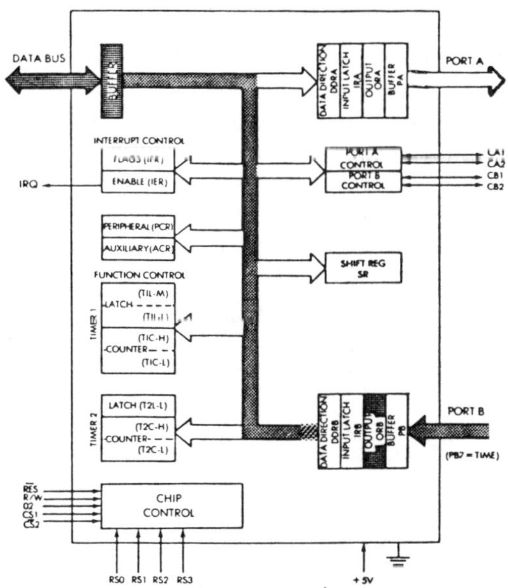

Fig 2-20: Using the 6522: LDA ORB

Finally, let us read the value of Port B into the accumulator (see Fig 2-20).

```
LDA    ORB
```

Whenever using the OR registers, it is usually necessary to check a *status* signal to make sure that the device being spoken to is *ready* to listen or to transmit. This is call *handshaking.* The operation of the control signals required to implement it will be explained now.

The Two Control Signals (Peripheral Control Register)

Each port is equipped with two control lines, named CA1, CA2, and CB1, CB2 (see Fig 2-14, on the right side). For example, before sesnding data to a printer device, such as a Teletype, the microprocessor must ascertain that the printer is not busy, and is ready to accept the next character. This will be accomplished by a *handshaking* procedure.

Whenever the printer is no longer *busy,* it is *ready* to accept the next character, and it will send a pulse or a level transition to the 6522. This level transition, or pulse, must be detected and latched by the device, then tested by the program. The signal will be transmitted to one of the two control inputs, CA1 or CB1.

The 6522 allows great flexibility in specifying the nature of the signal coming in or out.

It is possible to specify whether a *high-to-low* (or "negative") transition (a falling edge) or a *low-to-high* (or "positive") transition (a rising edge) will trigger the internal interrupt flag. This is specified by bit 0 (for CA1) and bit 4 (for CB1) of the *peripheral control register* (PCR). "0" corresponds to the high-to-low transition, and "1" corresponds to the low-to-high transition (see Fig 2-21).

7	6	5	4	3	2	1	0
CB2 control			CB1 control	CA2 control			CA1 control

Fig. 2-21: Peripheral Control Register

7	6	5	4	3	2	1	0
IRQ(R) EN(W)	T1	T2	CB1	CB2	SR	CA1	CA2

Fig. 2-22: Interrupt Flag Enable Register (IFR/IER)

CR BIT 1	CR BIT 0	ACTIVE TRANSITION OF INPUT SIGNAL	IRQ OUTPUT
0	0	negative	disable (high)
0	1	negative	enable (will go low when CRA bit 7 set by CA1/CB1 transition)
1	0	positive	disable (high)
1	1	positive	enable (as above)

Fig. 2-23: Control Lines Function (ACR)

Once the nature of the signal has been specified, it becomes possible to test it.

Checking status: It is possible to detect whether a transition has occurred by testing the contents of bits 1 or 4 (for CA1 and CB1 respectively) of the *interrupt-flag register* (IFR) (see Fig 2-22). This bit will be "0" as long as no signal has been received, and will become "1" once the appropriate transition has been detected. After reading a "1" status, it must be possible to *reset* it so that one can move on to the detection of the next event. This will be accomplished either by writing a "1" into the appropriate bit position of the register, or else by reading, or writing, the corresponding input/output data register.

PCR3	PCR2	PCR1	Mode
0	0	0	CA2 Negative Edge Interrupt (IFRO/ORA Clear) Mode—Set CA2 interrupt flag (IFRO) on a negative transition of the input signal. Clear IFRO on a read or write of the Peripheral A Output Register (ORA) or by writing logic 1 into IFRO.
0	0	0	CA2 Negative Edge Interrupt (IFRO Clear) Mode—Set IFRO on a negative transition of the CA2 input signal. Reading or writing ORA does not clear the CA2 interrupt flag. Clear IFRO by writing logic 1 into IFRO.
0	1	0	CA2 Positive Edge Interrupt (IFRO/ORA Clear) Mode—Set CA2 interrupt flag on a positive transition of the CA2 input signal. Clear IFRO with a read or write of the Peripheral A Output Register.
0	1	1	CA2 Positive Edge Interrupt (IFRO Clear) Mode—Set IFRO on a positive transition of the CA2 input signal. Reading or writing ORA does not clear the CA2 interrupt flag. Clear IFRO by writing logic 1 into IFRO.
1	0	0	CA2 Handshake Output Mode—Set CA2 output low on a read or write of the Peripheral A Output Register. Reset CA2 high with an active transition on CA1.
1	0	1	CA2 Pulse Output Mode—CA2 goes low for one cycle following a read or write of the Peripheral A Output Register.
1	1	0	CA2 Output Low Mode—The CA2 output is held low in this mode.
1	1	1	CA2 Output High Mode—The CA2 output is held high in this mode.

Fig. 2-24: PCR Detailed Operation (courtesy: Rockwell)

PCR7	PCR6	PCR5	Mode
0	0	0	CB2 Negative Edge Interrupt (IF3/ORB Clear) Mode—Set CB2 interrupt flag (IFR3) on a negative transition of the CB2 input signal. Clear IFR3 on a read or write of the Peripheral B Output Register (ORB) or by writing logic 1 into IFR3.
0	0	1	CB2 Negative Edge Interrupt (IFR3 Clear) Mode—Set IFR3 on a negative transition of the CB2 input signal. Reading or writing ORB does not clear the interrupt flag. Clear IFR3 by writing logic 1 into IFR3.

Fig. 2-25: Continued - PCR Detailed Operation

0	1	0	CB2 Positive Edge Interrupt (IFR3/ORB Clear) Mode—Set CB2 input signal. Clear the CB2 interrupt flag on a read or write of ORB or by writing logic 1 into IFR3.
0	1	1	CB2 Positive Edge Interrupt (IFR3 Clear) Mode—Set IFR3 on a positive transition of the CB2 input signal. Reading or writing ORB does not clear the CB2 interrupt flag. Clear IFR3 by writing logic 1 into IFR3.
1	0	0	CB2 Handshake Output Mode—Set CB2 low on a write ORB operation. Reset CB2 high with an active transition of the CB1 input signal.
1	0	1	CB2 Pulse Output Mode—Set CB2 low for one cycle following a write ORB operation.
1	1	0	CB2 Manual Output Low Mode—The CB2 output is held low on this mode.
1	1	1	CB2 Manual Output High Mode—The CB2 output is held high in this mode.

Fig. 2-25: PCR Detailed Operation (continued)

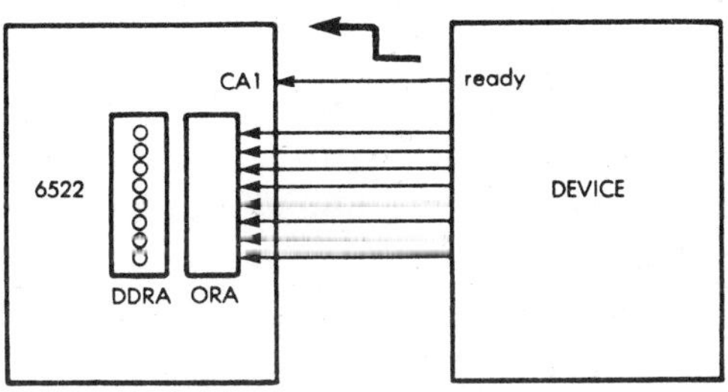

Fig. 2-26: Reading Data When Ready

A Simple Input Example

Let us specify a low-to-high "ready" transition from the peripheral, and an input configuration on Port A (see Fig 2-26). Whenever the data is ready, it will be read into the accumulator. The program is:

```
LDA   #0
STA   DDRA   SET INPUTS
```

```
        LDA   #1
        STA   PCR    CA1 INTERRUPT LOW-TO-
                     HIGH
WAIT    LDA   IFR    READ INT FLAGS
        AND   #$02   00000010  MASK BIT 1
                     FOR CA1
        BEQ   WAIT   READY?
        LDA   ORA    READ DATA IN
```

Improvement: Can you modify the two instructions "LDA IFR AND #$02" to improve efficiency?

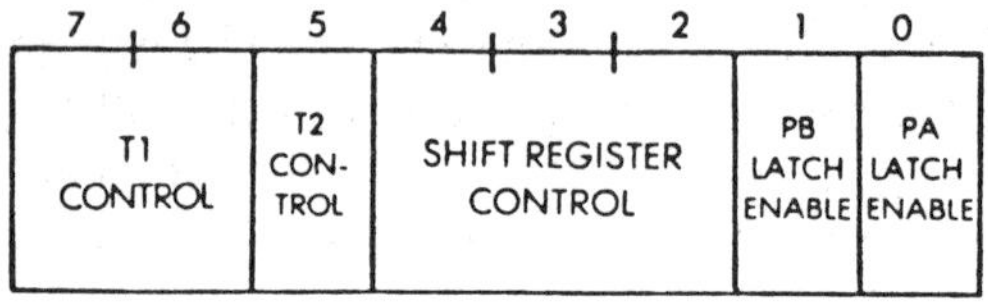

Fig. 2-27: 6522 - Auxiliary Control Register

Latching the Input/Output

The input and output of the 6522 are not symmetrical. Outputs are always *latched.* This is why the input/output register is called OR (*output* register). *Inputs are not necessarily latched.* This is specified by bits "0" and "1" (respectively port A and port B) of the auxiliary control register (ACR). Whenever these bits are "0," no latching occurs on input. Whenever these bits are set to "1," the inputs are latched (see Fig 2-27). When an input is not latched, the program is actually reading the value of the input lines connected to the port it is reading. When the inputs are latched, the latch is enabled by the active transition of CA1 or CB1, depending on the port used. The value is then preserved in the latch register until the next pulse is received on the control line. *Danger:* on *output,* the program reads the latch controls, which may or may not be the same as the contents of OR.

Sending a Control Signal Out

CA2 or CB2 are used to provide a control strobe (see Fig 2-14).

Since these lines are bidirectional, they must be configured for output by setting the peripheral control register bit 3 or 7 respectively (for A2 or B2) (see Fig 2-24).

The nature of the signal can be specified to be either a level or a pulse. "0" in bits 2 or 6 respectively (for A or B) corresponds to a *pulse*. "1" corresponds to a *level*. Whenever a level is specified, it is possible to specify either a positive value or a negative value. This is accomplished by setting or clearing bits 1 and 5 respectively (for A2 and B2) (see Fig 2-24).

Finally, when a pulse is generated, its duration can be controlled with bits 1 and 5 (respectively for A2 and B2) of the control register. Whenever the bit is set to "0," a single cycle strobe will be generated. Whenever this bit is set to "1," an output pulse will be generated, which will remain low from the time the OR register is accessed (read or write) until the next signal transition on CA1 or CB1.

Summary of Control Output

A pulse of virtually any duration and polarity can be specified. It can be used to poll an external device (interrogate it), to acknowledge a data transfer, to move on to another device connected to the same line, or to control the state of the device (on, off, or other option).

A summary of the peripheral control register bits is shown on Fig 2-21, and the details are shown on Fig 2-24 and 2-25.

	7	6	5	4	3	2	1	0
IFR	IRQ	T1	T2	CB1	CB2	SR	CA1	CA2
IER	set/ clear control							

Fig. 2-28: Interrupt Registers

Interrupts

Interrupts are controlled by two registers, the interrupt enable register (IER), and the interrupt flag register (IFR). The registers are shown on Fig 2-28. They share the same memory address. One is an input register, the other an output register.

The interrupt flag register IFR is an input register. Each bit position from 0 to will be set whenever an interrupt is detected on any of the external lines (CA1, CA2, CB1, CB2), on the shift register (SR), on any of the two timers (T1 and T2). Bit 7 is set whenever any other bit is set in the register.

The interrupt enable register (IER) will enable or disable interrupts from any of the sources. The bit positions in IER match the ones of IFR (see Fig 2-28). Whenever a bit position is "0," the corresponding interrupt is *disabled* and will not be sent. Whenever it is "1," it is *enabled,* and if an interrupt occurs, it will be recorded. It becomes then possible for the program to read the contents of the IFR register and test any relevant bit to determine whether an interrupt has occurred. In order to set or clear conveniently any of the IER bits, bit position 7 of IER is used in conjunction with a read or write signal and the contents of the data bus are then copied into the IER register. If IER bit 7 is "0", each "1" will clear an enable flag. If bit 7 is "1", each "1" written into IER will set an enable.

Example: Let us enable CA1 and CA2 interrupts, and disable all others (see Fig 2-28):

```
LDA   #$7C    "01111100" = CLEAR BITS
              2 TO 6
STA   IER
LDA   #$83    "10000011" = ENABLE BITS
              0 AND 1
STA   IER
```

Exercise 2-1: *Write a program to enable CB1 interrupts, and disable others.*

Exercise 2-2: *Disable CB1 and CB2, leaving others unchanged.*

Identifying the Interrupt

Whenever several interrupts can occur simultaneously, i.e., whenever several bits of the IFR are used, the program will have to check the contents of IFR and determine which interrupt has occurred. The order in which it checks these bits will determine the priority of the corresponding interrupt. For example, if an interrupt from T1 has highest priority, then this is the bit which should be checked first. The simplest way to check the contents of IFR is to shift its contents right or left by one position and check the value of the bit which falls off (into the Carry bit) by testing the carry bit. This technique assigns priorities in a right-to-left or left-to-right manner to the signals of Fig 2-28.

Exercise 2-3: Look at Fig 2-28. List the devices in order of effective priority, assuming that the contents of IFR are shifted left by the polling program.

Naturally it is also possible to check for combinations of interrupts by checking the values of specific bits in the IFR register. For more details on interrupts and polling, refer to Chapter 3 of ref. C202.

The Timers

The 6522 is equipped with two *interval timers.* These timers can be used as inputs or as outputs.

When used as an *output,* a timer may generate either an output signal or a train of pulses.

When used as an *input,* a timer will measure the duration of a pulse, or else will count the number of pulses received. When generating or reading a pulse of set duration, the timer is said to be in "*one-shot*" mode. Either timer 1 or timer 2 of the 6522 can be used in this manner.

When used to generate or to count a continuous train of pulses, the timer is said to be in a "*free-running mode.*" Only timer 1 may be used in this manner.

Prior to using any timer in output mode, its counter register must be loaded with a value: when generating pulses, the counter will either contain the number of clock pulses to be generated, or the duration of the pulse.

When using the timer on input, its register must be cleared. When counting pulses, it will contain the number of pulses so far. When sensing a pulse, it will contain its duration.

Timer 1 versus Timer 2

Timer 2 may be used on input to count pulses applied to PB6 of IORB (see Fig 2-14). When used on output, it can only generate a pulse of set duration on PB6. It cannot generate a train of pulses. Either one of these two modes is selected by bit 5 of the auxiliary control register (ACR) (see Fig 2-27). "0" corresponds to the one-shot mode, and "1" to the pulse-counting mode.

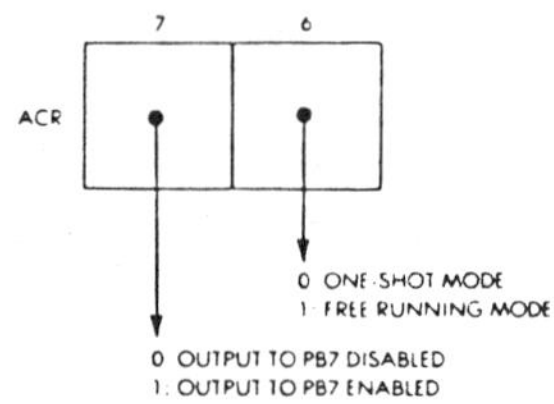

Fig 2-29: 6522: Auxiliary Control Register Controls T1 Modes

Timer 1 is different from Timer 2 and offers additional possibilities. It has four operating modes which are shown on Fig 2-29. It can be used either in one-shot mode or in free-running mode. Additionally, it may either enable or disable an output on PB7. The mode is specified by bit 6 of the auxiliary control register. It is "0" for one-shot operation and "1" for free-running mode.

Bit 7 specifies whether PB7 is enabled or disabled. When "0," PB7 is disables, when "1," PB7 is enabled (see Fig 2-30).

ACR 7 OUTPUT ENABLE	ACR 6 FREE RUN ENABLE	MODE
0	0 (ONE-SHOT)	Generate time out INT when T1 loaded PB7 disabled.
0	1 (FREE RUN)	Generate continuous INT PB7 disabled.
1	0 (ONE-SHOT)	Generate INT and output pulse on PB7 everytime T1 is loaded. = one-shot and programmable width pulse.
1	1 (FREE RUN)	Generate continuous INT and square wave output on PB7.

Fig. 2-30: 6522 - Auxiliary Control Register Selects Timer 1 Operating Modes

Loading the Counters

Each timer uses a 16-bit counter. The low part must be loaded first and the high part must be loaded next. Loading the high part of the counter automatically clears the timer interrupt flag and starts the timer running. Timer 1 is also equipped with a true 16-bit latch, while Timer 2 is not. This enables Timer 1 to operate continuously, in "free-running" mode; the latch is automatically transferred to the counter when the counter reaches zero. For Timer 1, the values of the latches may be read or written without affecting the counters. This is used to generate waveforms of arbitrary complexity.

The details of timer addressing are shown on Fig 2-31.

	ADDRESS	WRITE	READ
TIMER 1	- - 04	T1L-L	T1C-L/ + clear T1 int flag
	- - 05	T1L-H + T1C-H + T1 L-L ►T1C-L + clear T1 int flag	T1C-H
	- - 06	T1L-L	T1L-L
	- - 07	T1L-H + clear T1 int flag	T1L-H
TIMER 2	- - 08	T2L-L	T2C-C + clear T2 int flag
	- - 09	T2C-H T2L-L ►T2CL + clear T2 int flag	T2C-H

Fig. 2-31: Timer Addressing

Real Duration

The actual waveform from Timer 1 is shown on Fig 2-32. Note that the real duration is the value of the count ("N") plus 2, or the value of the count plus 1.5. In order to obtain a more exact timing, the user should therefore load in the counter register the desired number of periods minus 2.

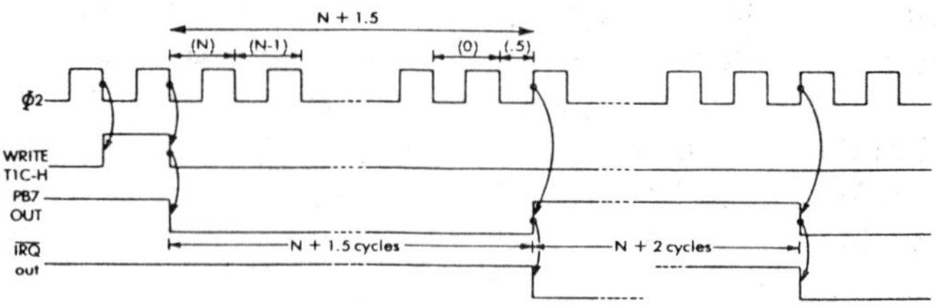

Fig. 2-32: Timer 1 in Free Running Mode

The Shift Register

The shift register is provided for serial-to-parallel or parallel-to-serial conversion. The shifting speed can be controlled by three time sources: Timer 2, Phase 2 of the clock (Φ2), and an external clock. The external timing source is specified by bits 2 and 3 of the auxiliary control register (see Fig 2-27). Bit 4 of the auxiliary control register specifies input or output. The complete table showing the function of these bits appears on Fig 2-33.

ACR4	ACR3	ACR2	Mode
0	0	0	Shift register disabled.
0	0	1	Shift in under control of Timer 2.
0	1	0	Shift in under control of Ø2 pulses.
0	1	1	Shift in under control of external clock pulses.
1	0	0	Free-running output at rate determined by Timer 2.
1	0	1	Shift out under control of Timer 2.
1	1	0	Shift out under control of the Ø2 pulses.
1	1	1	Shift out under control of external clock pulses.

Fig. 2-33 Shift Register Control

On output, the user will load the shift register. This will automatically start the timing and shifting process. Whenever 8 bits will have been shifted out of the register, the interrupt flag (bit 2 of the interrupt flag register) will be set automatically. It can then be tested by the program.

On input, the shift register must be initialized to some value such as "0" in order to start the timing process. It will then start capturing bits at the frequency of the specified timing source, such as timer 2, phase 2 of the clock, or an external clock, as specified by bits 2, 3, 4 of the ACR. Whenever 8 bits have been accumulated, the corresponding interrupt flag of IFR will be triggered. The program will deposit a value such as "0" in the SR, then test continuously the value of IFR bit 2. Whenever an interrupt is detected, the shift is complete. The shift register should then be disabled by zeroing bits 2, 3, 4 of ACR, while the program is storing data away. Naturally if data is coming in continuously, the shift register will not be disabled and the program should "come back" quickly enough not to lose data.

PROGRAMMING THE 6522

The 6522 is a combination PIO, timer, and shifter. The basic input-output operations on the PIO are performed essentially as on the 6520, except that the registers may be selected directly and that one does not need to switch bit 2 of the control register to differentiate between them. This leads to simpler and shorter programming. However, the control facilities provided by the 6522 are extensive, and quite different from those of the 6520. Let us therefore examine first some examples of basic input-output, then some examples of the control options.

Basic Input

Input is accomplished by loading all zeroes in the data direction register of the port which is to act as input, then reading the contents of the OR. In this simple program, we will, in addition, store the data, which has just been read, into memory location 20. The program appears below:

```
INPUT    LDA   #0
         STA   DDRA   PORT A IS INPUT
         LDA   ORA    READ DATA (IF VALID)
         STA   $20    SAVE THEM IN MEMORY
```

RS3	RS2	RS1	RS0	R/W	REGISTER	COMMENT
0	0	0	0	W	ORB	
0	0	0	0	R	IRB	
0	0	0	1	W	ORA	controls handshake
0	0	0	1	R	IRA	
0	0	1	0	-	DDRB	
0	0	1	1	-	DDRA	
8	1	8	8	W	T1L-L	latch
0	1	0	1	R	T1C-L	counter
0	1	0	1		T1C-H	T1L-L into T1C-L
0	1	1	0		T1L-L	
0	1	1	1		T1L-H	
1	0	0	0	W	T2L-L	latch
1	0	0	0	R	T2C-L	counter
1	0	0	1		T2C-H	triggers T2L-L into T2C-L
1	0	1	0		SR	
1	0	1	1		ACR	
1	1	0	0		PCR	
1	1	0	1		IFR	
1	1	1	0		IER	
1	1	1	1		ORA	no effect on handshakes

Fig. 2-34: 6522 Register Selection is Direct

Basic Output

Output is performed in exactly the same way as input; the data direction register for port B will be loaded for all ones, thus specifying all outputs. The data to be sent to port B is assumed to reside at memory location 20 so that it will be first loaded into the accumulator, then transferred to the ORB. The reader will remember that there is no instruction in the 6502 which allows transferring directly from memory location 20 to ORB. An extra instruction is therefore required to transfer first the data from memory into the accumulator, and then from the accumulator to ORB. The program appears below:

```
OUTPUT   LDA   #$FF
         STA   DDRB    B = OUTPUT
         LDA   $20     GET DATA FROM MEMORY
         STA   ORB     OUTPUT IT
```

Using the Control Options

We will configure here port A as all inputs. It will be assumed that the peripheral or device connected to port A will send the "data ready" strobe on line CA1. The strobe will be active during its low-to-high transition. The 6522 will have to detect this "data ready" strobe transition, and the program will poll the 6522 to determine whether any data has been received. If data has been received, it will read it and store it at location 20 in memory. The program has already been developed (see "Basic Input" page 39) and appears again below:

```
READYIN  LDA   #0      A = INPUT
         STA   DDRA
         LDA   #1      CA1 INT LO TO H'
         STA   PCR
TEST     LDA   IFR     TEST BIT 1
         AND   #$2     00000010  BINARY
         BEQ   TEST    = 1?
         LDA   ORA     READ DATA
         STA   $20     SAVE IN MEMORY
```

As usual, the data direction register is set to all zeroes to configure ORA as inputs:

```
LDA   #0
STA   DDRA
```

The control register PCR will now be conditioned so that an internal interrupt is generated whenever a low-to-high transition occurs:

```
LDA   #1
STA   PCR
```

The two instructions above load the binary value 00000001 into PCR. Referring to Fig 2-23, the reader should verify that this is indeed the correct value. Bit zero of the peripheral control register PCR specifies which active transition of the input signal will be recognized. Since we want the CA1 interrupt flag to be set by a positive transition (low-to-high), PCR0 must be set to the value 1.

Bits 6 and 7 of the ACR relate to the timer 1 operating mode. Since the timer is not being used, their contents are irrelevant here. Bits 2, 3, and 4 of ACR specify the operation of the shift register. Since the shift register is not used here, they should be zero, as specified on Fig 2-33. Bit 5 of the ACR is T2 control, and therefore unused here. Bit 1 is the PB latch enable, and is unused here. Bit zero is the port A latch enable. When specified (by writing a "1"), data present on the A input will be latched whenever the CA1 interrupt flag is set. This would be accomplished by:

```
        LDA   #1
        STA   ACR
```

Since we assume here that polling is used, instead of a hardware interrupt, the program will be responsible for reading the contents of the interrupt flag and determining whether an interrupt has occurred. The contents of the interrupt flag register are shown in Fig 2-28. Bit position 1 of the IFR needs to be tested in order to determine whether the CA1 "data ready" signal has been received. This is performed by the following three instructions:

```
TEST    LDA   IFR
        AND   #$2
        BEQ   TEST
```

The AND instruction masks out all bits except bit position 1 so that it can be tested.

As long as bit 1 is zero, this program will remain in this polling loop. Once the "data ready" signal has been recognized, data can be read from the ORA and transferred to their final memory location, which we will assume to be, as usual, memory location 20:

```
        LDA   ORA
        STA   $20
```

Reading the contents of ORA into the accumulator will also automatically clear bit 1 of IFR (the CA1 status indicator), so that the internal interrupt will be automatically reset.

It is important to remember that *interrupt flags must explicitly be cleared every time they* are used. The 6522 is organized in such a way that the "normal" operation, such as reading the contents of ORA after detecting an interrupt, will take care of it automatically. However, the reader should be alert to the fact that if he should use "non-standard programming," errors might occur as the interrupt flag might remain continuously on. A technique which may be used in such a case is to write back the contents of IFR after reading it:

```
        STA     IFR
```

This "programming trick" will reset only the bit which had been set to "1," thus effectively clearing the bit without modifying any other (unless more than one bit was "1").

A Handshake Protocol on Input

We will assume here that the complete handshake sequence is used: first the program is responsible for sending a "start" pulse (active high) to the device. Later, the device will respond with a "data ready" strobe (active high-to-low here), and the program will be responsible for determining that the signal has been received, then transferring the data into memory location 20. The program appears below:

```
NSHAKE  LDA     #0
        STA     DDRA    A IS INPUT
        STA     ACR
        LDA     #$0C    BITS 2 AND 3 ON
        STA     PCR     CLEAR START PULSE
        LDA     #$0E    BITS 1, 2, 3 ON
        STA     PCR     GENERATE START ON CA2
        LDA     #$0C
        STA     PCR     CLEAR IT
WAIT    LDA     IFR     INTERRUPT?
        AND     #$02    (START PULSE?)
        BEQ     WAIT    POLLING LOOP
        LDA     ORA     DATA READY
        STA     $20     SAVE IN MEMORY
```

Let us examine the program. As usual, port A is conditioned as input by storing zeroes in the DDRA:

```
        LDA     #0
        STA     DDRA    ZERO DDRA
        STA     ACR
```

We will assume here that no latching is necessary on input (see previous program if you wish to latch data on input). The PCR register must now be conditioned so that a start pulse will be generated, active high. The level of CA2 (the line which we will use to provide the start signal CA1 can only be used as input) will first be set low, then high, to guarantee a low-to-high transition. Conditioning the CA2 output low is accomplished by loading the value "110" respectively in bits 3, 2, and 1 of PCR (see Fig 2-24). This is accomplished by the following instructions:

```
        LDA   #$0C     00001100
        STA   PCR
```

Next, the level on the CA2 output must be specified as high. This is accomplished by loading the value "111" in bits 3, 2, 1 of PCR:

```
        LDA   #$0E     00001110
        STA   PCR
```

We will assume here that a brief pulse is sufficient to provide the "start" signal. Some devices might require that this pulse be of a longer duration. In such a case, a delay would have to be added at this point to guarantee that the pulse remains high for a specific duration of time. Here, we will simply turn the signal off again:

```
        LDA   #0C      00001100
        STA   PCR
```

At this point, we proceed, as in the previous program, by polling bit one of the IFR to detect whether the CA1 has been set to one:

```
WAIT    LDA   IFR
        AND   #$02     00000010
        BEQ   WAIT
```

Then, as above, the data is read from ORA and stored in memory location 20:

```
        LDA   ORA
        STA   $20
```

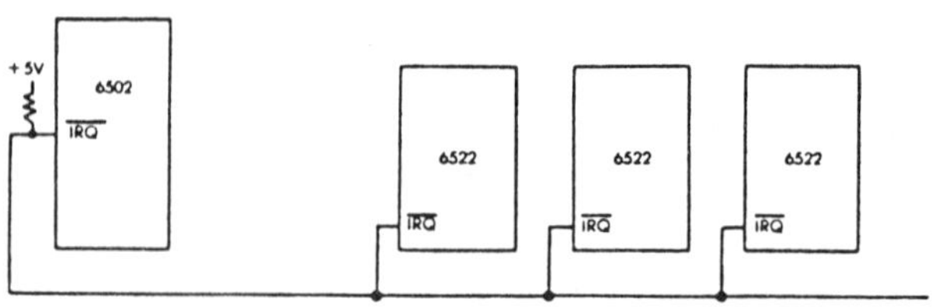

Fig. 2-35: Connecting Multiple 6522's - Generating an IRQ

Using Multiple 6522's

In the case where multiple 6522's are used, their interrupt request output IRQ is usually connected to the IRQ line as shown on Fig 2-35. However, once an IRQ is received by the 6502, the program must determine which 6522 originated it. A polling loop is generally used. This polling loop will interrogate in turn each IFR of the devices to determine which one has generated an interrupt. This information is readily available in bit 7 of the interrupt flag register as shown on Fig 2-22. The reader will recall that bit 7 is universally used as a preferred position for polling, since once the contents of the register under test are loaded into the accumulator, the contents of bit 7 will condition the sign bit of the microprocessor flags register (bit N). The next instruction in the program may readily test bit N and determine whether it was "0" or "1." This is exactly what the polling program does here. A typical polling program appears below:

```
                LDA   IFR1
                BPL   NEXT1
INTFOUND1       . . .              (IDENTIFY 1 OF 7 CAUSES)
   .
   .
   .
NEXT1           LDA   IFR2
                BPL   NEXT2
   .
   .
   .
```

The program loads the contents of the IFR of the first 6522 and tests whether it is positive. If it is positive, no interrupt has been generated by the device and the program tests the next one, and so on. However, if the device is found to have generated an interrupt, a specific routine must then determine what to do next. Let us examine it.

Identifying one out of 7 possible internal interrupts for the 6522

Referring to Fig 2-22, it can be seen that seven possible conditions may set an internal interrupt in the IFR register of the 6522: T1, T2, CB1, CB2, SR, CA1, CA2. If all of the internal resources of the 6522 are used simultaneously, as is often the case, then all possibilities should be checked. A simple program which will identify one out of 7 interrupts appears below:

```
ONEOF7  ASL   A
        BMI   TIMER1
        ASL   A
        BMI   TIMER2
        ASL   A
        . . .
```

The program checks successively bit 6, bit 5, bit 4, etc., by simply shifting the contents of the accumulator left by one bit position every time. It should be noted that the order in which the shifts occur establish a priority of the interrupts within the device. Using the program as shown above, Timer 1 will have the highest priority, then Timer 2, etc. The user might want to assign different priorities to the interrupts by testing the bits in a different order.

Generating Delays with a Timer

The reader should study the details of the timers in the manufacturer's data sheets before using them. Timer 2 is simpler than Timer 1. Both timers are not identical, and it is important to understand their specific characteristics before using them. Since a complete study of the timer operating modes is not necessary for the purposes of this book, we will show here two typical examples of the generation of delays, using respectively Timer 2 and Timer 1. Other examples will be presented in the applications chapters.

Generating a One-Shot Delay with Timer 2

The program appears below:

```
ONESHOT2  LDA   #0
          STA   ACR    SELECT MODE
          STA   T2LL   LOW-LATCH=0
          LDA   #$01   DELAY DURATION
          STA   T2CH   HIGH PART=01HEX. START
          LDA   #$20   MASK
  LOOP    BIT   IFR    TIME OUT?
          BEQ   LOOP
          LDA   T2CL   CLEAR TIMER 2 INTERRUPT
```

Bits 6 and 7 of the ACR must be set to zero to specify the one-shot mode (PB7 not used with T2). Since we assume here that none of the other resources such as the shift register are being used, we simply load all zeroes into the ACR register:

```
        LDA   #0
        STA   ACR
```

Timer 2, like Timer 1, contains a 16-bit OR so that the two halves of the register must be loaded separately. We will first load the low half, then the high half:

```
        STA   T2LL
        LDA   #$01
        STA   T2CH
```

Loading the value $01 into T2C-H also results in clearing any interrupt flag and starting the counter automatically.

Fig 2-28 shows that bit 5 of the IFR is the one indicating that Timer 2 has timed out. Bit 5 of the IFR therefore must be tested for the value "1." This is accomplished by the next three instructions:

```
        LDA   #$20     BIT 5=1
LOOP    BIT   IFR
        BEQ   LOOP
```

The value 20 hexadecimal is equal to "00100000." It is used to test whether bit 5 is indeed a "1." The BIT instruction performs a logical AND, without modifying the contents of the accumulator. As long as bit 5 remains "0," the program loops, waiting for the Timer 2 interrupt. Whenever Timer 2 generates the interrupt, it is detected, and the program exits the loop.

Finally, the program must explicitly clear the Timer 2 interrupt before branching to another task. This could be accomplished by reloading a new value into the counter register. However, since this program should be useful in any environment, we make no assumption as to what will be done after this program terminates. The interrupt flag will be cleared either by writing into T2C-H or by reading T2C-L. Since we do not want to start the counter running again, we will not write in T2C-H, but instead read T2C-L, simply to clear the interrupt:

```
        LDA   T2CL
```

Generating a One-Shot Delay with Timer 1

We will use Timer 1 here in a manner essentially analogous to Timer 2 above. However, Timer 1 is equipped with a true 16-bit latch register, unlike Timer 2. Ther program appears below:

```
ONESHOT1  LDA  #0
          STA  ACR    1-SHOT MODE - NO PB7
                      PULSES
          STA  T1LL   LOW LATCH
          LDA  #$01   DELAY
          STA  T1CH   LOADS ALSO T1CL AND
                      STARTS
          LDA  #$20
  LOOP    BIT  IFR    TIME OUT?
          BEQ  LOOP
          LDA  T1LL   CLEAR INT FLAG
```

The program is essentially analogous to the one above, and should be self explanatory. The only difference is that the low latch is loaded first, then the program writes into T1C-H, the high part of the counter proper. This instruction also results in transferring the contents of T1L-L into T1C-L (see Fig 2-34 showing the 6522 internal registers) and starts the counter. The rest of the program is identical.

Generating a Pulse

The above programs will generate a delay for a program. If an actual pulse must be generated, then the proper output pin must be specified. For Timer 1, the PB7 pin will be used to provide the output pulse PB7 will be an output if either DDRB7 or ACR7 equals "1."

Timer 2 does not send a direct pulse on a pin for *output.* The pulse must be generated by adding instructions which explicitly turn on and off one of the bits of the port. However, Timer 2 may *count* pulses easily in its pulse-counting mode. Pin PB6 is then used for this purpose. This underlines again the practical differences between these timers. In any practical application, the reader is encouraged to review the manufacturer's data sheets to take best advantage of them.

Shifting in and out

The shift register SR is connected to pin CB2 of the 6522. All pulses will be generated or sensed on this specific pin. The combination of bits 2, 3, and 4 of the ACR determines the way in which the shifter operates. The 8 combinations are shown on Fig 2-33 above.

In our examples so far, the contents of bits 2, 3, 4 of the ACR have always been zero, so that the shifter register was disabled. The shifter will shift in or shift out under control of one of three possible timing sources: Timer 2, Phase 2 of the clock, or an external clock. In addition, it provides a special mode with a free running output at the rate determined by Timer 2. The reader is again referred to the manufacturer's data sheets for the complete specifications on the shifter. We will simply present here two typical examples of shifting in and shifting out.

Shifting in With an External Clock

The program appears below:

```
SHIFTIN    LDA   #0
           STA   ACR     CLEAR SR
           LDA   #$0C    EXTERNAL CLOCK MODE
           STA   ACR     START SHIFTER
  LOOP     LDA   IFR     DONE FLAG?
           AND   #$04    TEST BIT 2
           BEQ   LOOP    WAITING LOOP
           LDA   SR      READ 8 BITS INTO ACC
           STA   $20     SAVE IN MEMORY
```

The shift register is first cleared by loading zeroes into the ACR:

```
           LDA   #0
           STA   ACR
```

Then the correct operating mode is specified by loading the value "011" in bits 4, 3, 2, respectively of the ACR:

```
           LDA   #$0C
           STA   ACR
```

This specifies a shift-in under control of an external clock (see Fig 2-33).

Once the 8 shifts have occurred, the shifting mechanism is automatically disabled, and the SR interrupt flag is set in the IFR register. After the shifting has been started, the program therefore simply checks the contents of bit position 2 of the IFR (see Fig 2-28) to verify whether it is "1." The polling loop appears below:

```
LOOP       LDA   IFR
           AND   #$04
           BEQ   LOOP
```

At this point, the contents of shift register SR simply need to be transferred into memory location 20 as usual:

```
           LDA   SR
           STA   $20
```

Shifting out Under Phase 2 Control

The program is essentially similar to the one above except that the control bits to be loaded in the ACR are different, in order to specify the proper operating mode. Assuming that we simply have to send one word of 8 bits out, no waiting loop is necessary here to determine whether the shift is finished or not. The program appears below:

```
SHIFTOUT   LDA   #0
           STA   ACR     CLEAR SR
           LDA   #$18
           STA   ACR     Φ2 OUT MODE
           LDA   $20     READ DATA FROM
                         MEMORY
           STA   SR
```

As above, the shift register is first cleared, then the ACR is loaded with the value "18" hexadecimal, which specifies the combination "110" into bit positions 4,3 and 2. This specifies the shift out at a rate controlled by phase 2 of the system clock:

```
           LDA   #0
           STA   ACR
```

```
LDA    #$18
STA    ACR
```

The data is then fetched from memory location 20, and deposited into the shift register. Depositing the data into the shift register automatically starts it.

```
LDA    $20
STA    SR
```

If we had to send a succession of 8-bit words, the program here should wait for one shift to be completed before starting the next one. This would be accomplished by a waiting loop like the one above. Once 8 bits have been shifted out, the 6522 automatically sets bit 2 of the IFR (see Fig 2-28) . The program therefore would simply test continuously bit 2 of the IFR until it takes the value "1." Once the value "1" has been detected, the shift will be resumed.

Summary of the 6522

The three functions of this component are: PIO, timer, shift. Additionally, complex control signals can be specified for the PIO and the timer. The function of the possible control signals and options has been described. This component should be viewed as a set of three separate functions. The functions of Port A and Port B are essentially similar but not symmetrical: the two timers have some common features but offer different possibilities. Finally, the shift register is essentially symmetrical on input and output and can be used to receive or transmit bits or words at any set frequency from a number of external clock sources.

Exercise 2-4: *Save in a 2-word memory table at location* BUFFER *two successive data words from* DEVICE 1. DEVICE 1 *supplies an active low-to-high* READY *strobe. It requires an acknowledge signal (high pulse).*

Exercise 2-5: *Same as 2-4, except* DEVICE 1 *requires an active-low* START *pulse, and responds with the* READY *signal.*

Exercise 2-6: *Send data to* DEVICE 2 *from memory location* BUFFER. DEVICE 2 *supplies a* BUSY *signal when not ready.*

Exercise 2-7: *Same as 2-5, but* DEVICE 2 *requires a* STATUS *strobe to supply a* READY/BUSY *answer.*

Exercise 2-8: *Turn a printer on with a "1" on the control line, wait for* READY, *send a character, turn it off.*

Exercise 2-9: *Count 10 input pulses on PB6.*

Exercise 2-10: *Generate a pulse of 1 ms on PB7.*

Exercise 2-11: *Shift out 8 bits from memory location* BUFFER *at Timer 2 rate.*

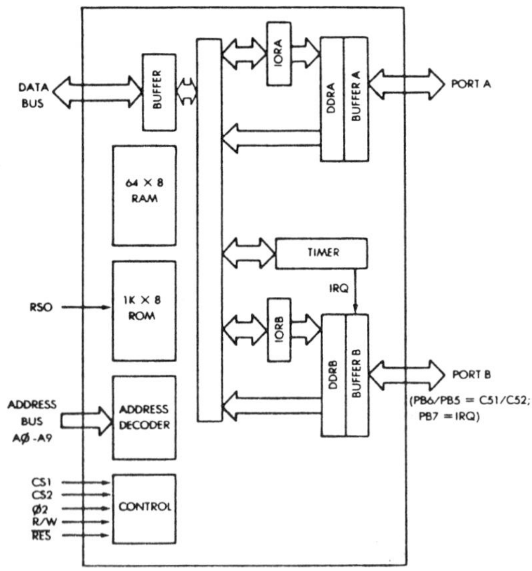

Fig. 2-36: 6530 Internal Architecture

THE 6530 ROM-RAM I/O TIMER (RRIOT)
(RRIOT stands for ROM-RAM-I/O-Timer).

The 6530 is a special combination component which combines four functions usually distinct: a PIO, a timer, a RAM and a ROM. The internal architecture of the 6530 is shown on Fig 2-36. It is equipped with the usual two PIO ports, each one of them with its own data-direction register. However, there are no control lines or interrupt logic associated with the ports. The timer is connected to port B. The RAM memory provides 64 bytes, the ROM provides 1K bytes. A ROM, once programmed, cannot be changed. Since it is uneconomical to produce ROM's in small quantities, the 6530 is only used in situations where a large number of identical components is going to be produced. As an example, the KIM board uses two 6530's which contain the internal control program or "monitor."

Three pins on this component have a dual function: CS1 and CS2 are mask options intead of PB6 and PB5. Also, PB7 may be used as an interrupt request IRQ.

The Interval Timer

The interval timer is equipped with an 8-bit register, and may be used in one of four modes. Depending on the values A0 and A1 of the

A2	A1	A0		
0	0	0	BUFFER A	
0	0	1	DDRA	
0	1	0	BUFFER B	
0	1	1	DDRB	
1	0	0	TIMER 1T	+IRQ to PB7
1	0	1	(W) TIMER 8T (R) INT FLAG	NO IRQ to PB7
1	1	0	TIMER 64T	+IRQ to PB7
1	1	1	TIMER 1024T (R) INT FLAG	NO IRQ to OB7

Note: A3 specifies whether interrupt is used.

Fig. 2-37: 6530 Memory Map

address lines, it will count in increments of 1, 8, 64, 1024 times the system clock. To the programmer, the timer appears as a set of 4 memory locations as shown on Fig 2-37.

When using the timer, pin PB7 may be used as an interrupt pin. When used as an interrupt, pin PB7 must be programmed as an input. When not used as an interrupt, it may be used for any usual purpose. For details on the utilization of PB7 as interrupt, the reader is referred to the manufacturer's data sheets.

THE 6532 RIOT

The 6532 is essentially a 6530 without the ROM. The RAM, however, is larger: it provides 128 words. In addition, the PA7 line on this device may be used an an edge-detecting input. When this mode is used, an active transition will set an internal interrupt flag (bit 6 of the interrupt flag register).

The internal architecture of the 6532 is shown on Fig 2-38. The addressing of the chip is shown on Fig 2-39. The rest of the operation of the 6532 is essentially like the 6530.

Ports A and B are not symmetrical. The main difference between the two ports is that port B is equipped with push-pull buffers which are capable of sourcing 3 mA at 1.5 volts. This allows the direct connection of this port to LED's or Darlington transistors. Further, port A reads directly from the pins. On port B, data is read from the output register instead of the peripheral pins.

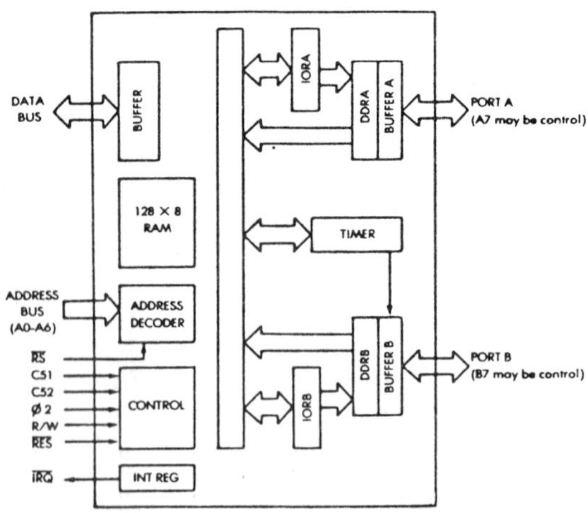

Fig. 2-38: 6532 Internal Architecture

RS	A4	A3	A2	A1	A0	R/W	SELECTION
0	-	-	-	-	-	-	RAM
1	-	-	0	0	0	-	ORA
1	-	-	0	0	1	-	DDRA
1	-	-	0	1	0	-	ORB
1	-	-	0	1	1	-	DDRB
1	1	*	1	0	0	0	WRITE TIMER ÷1T
1	1	*	1	0	1	0	÷8T
1	1	*	1	1	0	0	÷64T
1	1	*	1	1	1	0	÷1024T
1	-	*	1	-	0	1	READ TIMER
1	-	-	1	-	1	1	READ INTERRUPT FLAG
1	0	-	1	**	***	0	WRITE EDGE DETECT CONTROL

* disable (0)/enable (1) INT from timer to IRQ
** disable (0)/enable (1) INT from PA7 to IRQ
*** negative (0)/positive (1) edge detect

Fig. 2-39: 6532 Addressing

SUMMARY

Most applications will require at least the use of two or more ports on one or more PIO's, and the use of a programmable timer. Still more complex applications will require the use of control signals and the possible use of automated shifts. All the components we have reviewed - the 6520, the 6522, the 6530 and the 6532 - provide two PIO ports. Except for the 6520, they all provide at least one programmable timer. A comparison table of the four input-output devices appears on Fig 2-40.

One or more of the above PIO's will be used in all the applications in this book.

	6520	6522	6530	6532
PORT A LINES	8	8	8	8
PORT B LINES	8	8	5 to 8	8
CONTROL LINES, A	2	2	0	0
CONTROL LINES, B	2	2	0	0
DDRA	1	1	yes	yes
DDRB	1	1	yes	yes
TIMER 1	-	yes	yes	yes
TIMER 2	-	yes	-	-
ROM	-	-	1K × 8	-
RAM	-	-	64 × 8	128 × 8
OTHER	-	add 'l control registers	4 timer ratios	4 timer ratios
INTERRUPT	2	1	optional	1

Fig 2-40: Comparison Chart of the Four PIO's

CHAPTER 3

6502 SYSTEMS

INTRODUCTION

The applications presented in this volume will be connected to a "standard" 6502 system. The organization of such a "standard system" will therefore be presented first. Then, some real 6502 boards will be described and will be shown to be consistent with the standard model just introduced.

In order to present realistic applications, it is necessary to define an exact hardware configuration to which the applications are effectively connected. The majority of the examples presented in the book are directly applicable to the SYM board, and can be readily adapted to the KIM board. One section of the next chapter will specifically present KIM programs. SYBEX does not endorse any board or any manufacturer. Simply, for educational purposes, it is more practical to present applications directly applicable to existing boards, rather than invent a fictitious one. Most programs written for the SYM are compatible with the KIM, and can be readily adapted to other boards, such as the AIM65. The reader is encouraged to exercise his own judgment in determining which board will be best suited to his needs.

The architecture of the KIM, SYM, and AIM 65 are presented in this chapter. SYM is presented in more detail so that the reader who does not have a SYM can understand the interconnections used in the application programs presented in the following chapters. However, it should be stressed again that any other board can be used, and that the changes required in the programs are usually minor.

A "STANDARD" 6502 SYSTEM

Any standard microprocessor system includes at least the microprocessor unit (MPU) and its clock circuit, the ROM, the RAM, and one or more PIO's. The organization of such a standard system, using the 6502, is shown on Fig 3-1.

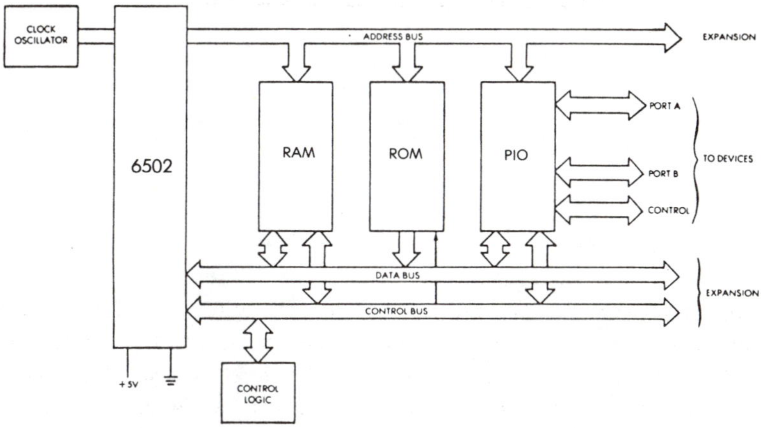

Fig. 3-1: Organization of a "Standard" 6520 System

The 6502 incorporates most of the clock's circuitry within the microprocessor chip, so that only an external crystal and an oscillating circuit are necessary. The 6502 and its clock circuit are shown on the left of the illustration. The 6502, like any "standard" microprocessor, creates three busses: the address bus (16 lines), the data bus (8 lines, bi-directional), and finally the control bus.

In the standard system, the RAM memory (read-write memory), the ROM memory (read-only memory), and the PIO are shown as separate chips connected to the 3 busses. The ROM will typically contain a *monitor* program necessary to use the microprocessor board resources, or else user programs (in industrial applications). The PIO will create two ports (8 lines each) to communicate with external devices, plus perhaps some additional control lines. In any practical application, at least two PIO's will be necessary to provide a sufficient number of I/O lines. Some additional logic is usually required for address decoding and other functions.

Because several combination-chips are available in the 6502 family, the ROM, the RAM, and the PIO may be combined on one or more chips. However, any system using the 6502 will normally incorporate all the logical elements of Fig 3-1.

Let us now examine some real boards and how they relate to our standard board.

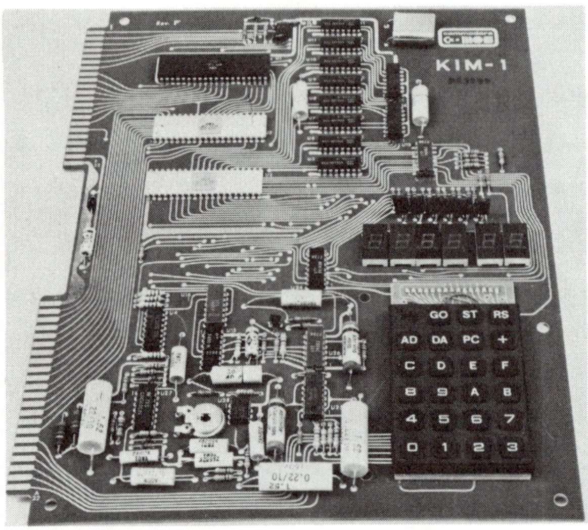

Fig. 3-2: Photo of KIM-1

THE KIM-1

The KIM-1 was an early board introduced by MOS Technology in support of their 6502 microprocessor. It incorporates a minimal number of components, is equipped with a hexadecimal keyboard and with 6 LED's, so that it can be used as a low-cost stand-alone complete microcomputer board. It is shown on Fig 3-2. Its internal organization is shown on Fig 3-3.

The KIM-1 includes a separate 1K by 8 RAM (for the user) and two 6530 combination chips. The reader will recall from the previous chapter that the 6530 is a combination chip providing a PIO, a programmable timer, a ROM, and a RAM. On this board, there is no need for an external ROM memory since the amount of ROM memory provided by the two 6530's is sufficient to contain the system monitor. Each 6530 also contains 64 bytes of RAM which are partly used by the system monitor.

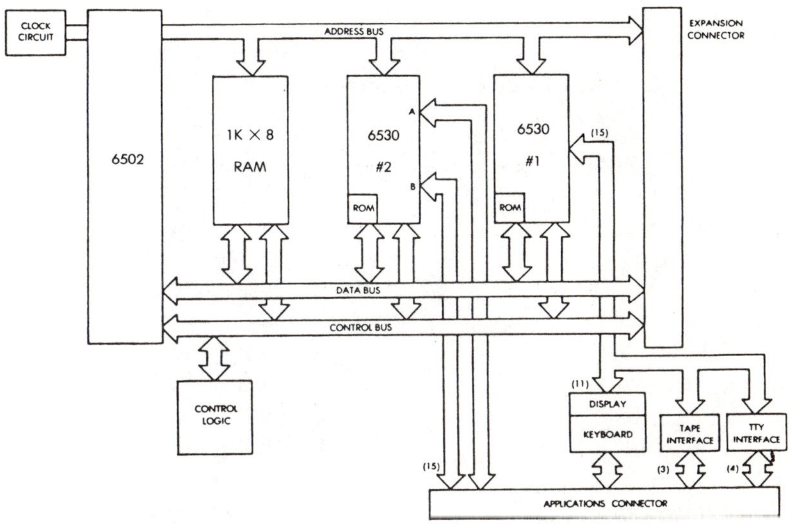

Fig. 3-3: KIM-1 Internal Organization

Additionally, the board is equipped with a keyboard, 6 LED's, a tape recorder interface, and a teletype interface. It can be expanded externally through two edge connectors, called respectively the expansion connector and applications connector, as shown on Fig. 3-3. The system memory-map is shown on Fig 3-4. The signals for the two connectors of the KIM are shown on Fig 3-5 and 3-6.

The reader should ascertain that the organization of this board does meet the description of our standard 6502 system as shown on Fig 3-1. The details of the pin interconnects are useful to those readers who will want to connect the applications presented here to this particular board.

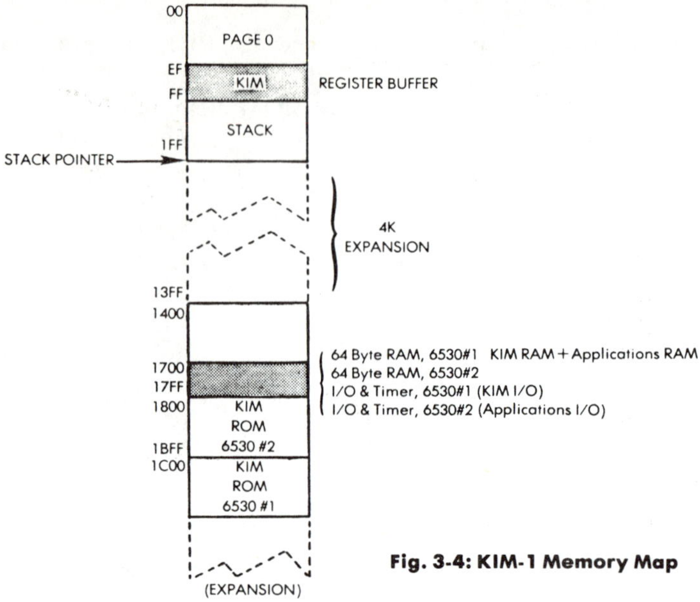

Fig. 3-4: KIM-1 Memory Map

22	KB Col D	Z	KB Row 1
21	KB Col A	Y	KB Col C
20	KB Col E	X	KB Row 2
19	KB Col B	W	KB Col G
18	KB Col F	V	KB Row 3
17	KB Row 0	U	TTY PTR
16	PB5	T	TTY KYBD
15	PB7	S	TTY PTR RTRN (+)
14	PA0	R	TTY KYBD RTRN (+)
13	PB4	P	AUDIO OUT HI
12	PB3	N	+12V
11	PB2	M	AUDIO OUT LO
10	PB1	L	AUDIO IN
9	PB0	K	DECODE ENAB
8	PA7	J	K7
7	PA6	H	K5
6	PA5	F	K4
5	PA4	E	K3
4	PA1	D	K2
3	PA2	C	K1
2	PA3	B	K0
1	Vss (GND)	A	Vcc (+5V)

Fig 3-5: KIM Application Connector

Fig. 3-6: KIM Expansion Connector

Pin	Signal	Pin	Signal
22	V_{SS} (GND)	Z	RAM/R/W
21	V_{CC} (+5)	Y	$\overline{\phi 2}$
20		X	PLL TEST
19		W	$\overline{R/W}$
18		V	R/W
17	SST OUT	U	$\phi 2$
16	K6	T	AB15
15	DB0	S	AB14
14	DB1	R	AB13
13	DB2	P	AB12
12	DB3	N	AB11
11	DB4	M	AB10
10	DB5	L	AB9
9	DB6	K	AB8
8	DB7	J	AB7
7	RST	H	AB6
6	NMI	F	AB5
5	RO	E	AB4
4	IRQ	D	AB3
3	$\phi 1$	C	AB2
2	RDY	B	AB1
1	SYNC	A	AB0

Fig. 3-7: SYM

THE SYM-1

The SYM-1 board was introduced by Synertek Systems as an expanded version of the previous board. A photo of the SYM appears on Fig 3-7. Its internal organization is shown on Fig 3-8.

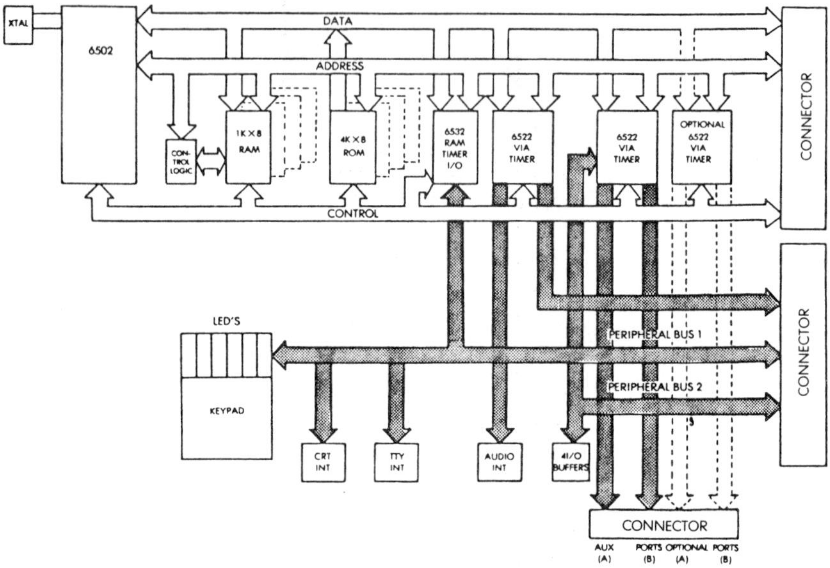

Fig. 3-8: SYM-1 Internal Organization

The essential differences from the previous board are:

- It is equipped with a separate 4K by 8 ROM. A larger ROM size allows a more complex monitor to reside on the board.
- It is equipped with more complex input-output chips and has three of them instead of two, thereby offering more IO ports and resources. Because of the extra ports, it also has one more applications connector than the previous board.
- Additional input-output facilities are available such as four input-output buffers and part of a CRT interface.

Other miscellaneous differences exist between these boards but are not relevant for the purposes of this book.

The system memory map is shown on Fig 3-9, and a more detailed RAM memory map is shown on Fig 3-10. The details of the three connectors are shown respectively on Fig 3-11, 3-12, and 3-13.

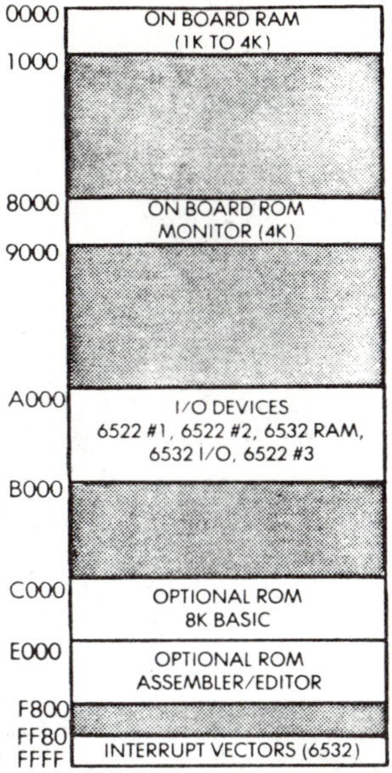

Fig. 3-9: System Memory Map

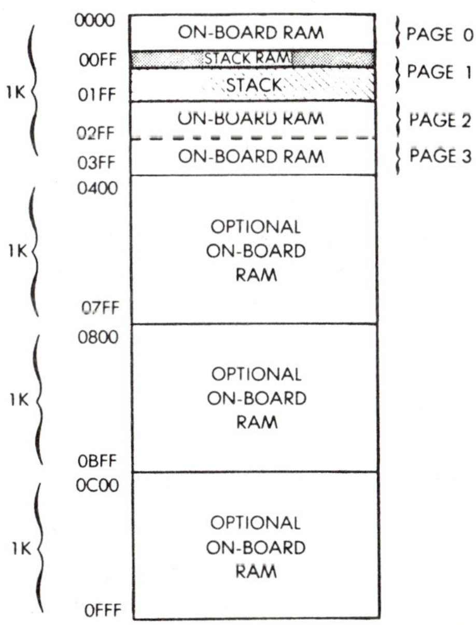

Fig. 3-10: RAM Memory Map

1	SYNC	A	AB0
2	RDY	B	AB1
3	Ø1	C	AB2
4	$\overline{\text{IRQ}}$	D	AB3
5	RO	E	AB4
6	$\overline{\text{NMI}}$	F	AB5
7	$\overline{\text{RES}}$	H	AB6
8	DB7	J	AB7
9	DB6	K	AB8
10	DB5	L	AB9
11	DB4	M	AB10
12	DB3	N	AB11
13	DB2	P	AB12
14	DB1	R	AB13
15	DB0	S	AB14
16	$\overline{18}$	T	AB15
17	DBOUT (1)	U	Ø2
18	$\overline{\text{POR}}$	V	R/W
19	Unused	W	$\overline{\text{R/W}}$
20	Unused	X	AUD TEST
21	+5V	Y	$\overline{Ø2}$
22	GND	Z	RAM - R/W

Fig. 3-11: Expansion Connector (E)

1	GND	A	+5V
2	APA3	B	$\overline{00}$
3	APA2	C	$\overline{04}$
4	APA1	D	$\overline{08}$
5	APA4	E	$\overline{0C}$
6	APA5	F	$\overline{10}$
7	APA6	H	$\overline{14}$
8	APA7	J	$\overline{1C}$
9	APB0	K	$\overline{18}$
10	APB1	L	Audio In

Fig. 3-12: Application Connector (A)

11	APB2	M	Audio Out (LO)
12	APB3	N	RCN-1 (1)
13	APB4	P	Audio Out (HI)
14	APA0	R	TTY KB RTN (+)
15	APB7	S	TTY PTR (+)
16	APB5	T	TTY KB RTN (−)
17	KB ROW 0	U	TTY PTR (−)
18	KB COL F	V	KB ROW 3
19	KB COL B	W	KB COL G
10	KB COL E	X	KB ROW 2
21	KB COL A	Y	KB COL C
22	KB COL D	Z	KB ROW 1

(1): Jumper Option

Fig. 3-12: Application Connector (A) - (continued)

1	GND	A	+5V
2	$-V_N$	B	$+V_P$
3	2 PA 1	C	2 PA 2
4	2 CA 2	D	2 PA 0
5	2 CB 2	E	2 CA 1
6	2 PB 7	F	2 CB 2
7	2 PB 5	H	2 PB 6
8	2 PB 3	J	2 PB 4
9	2 PB 1	K	2 PB 2
10	2 PA 7	L	2 PB 0
11	2 PA 5	M	2 PA 6
12	2 PA 3	N	2 PA 4
13	RES	P	3 CA 1
14	3 CB 1	R	SCOPE
15	3 PB 2	S	3 PB 3
16	3 PB 0	T	3 PB 1
17	3 PA 6	U	3 PA 7
18	3 PA 3	V	3 PA 0
19	3 PA 4	W	3 PA 1
20	3 PA 5	X	3 PA 2
21	3 PB 5 (B)	Y	3 PB 4 (B)
22	3 PB 7 (B)	Z	3 PB 6 (B)

(B): Buffered

Fig. 3-13: Auxiliary Application Connector (AA)

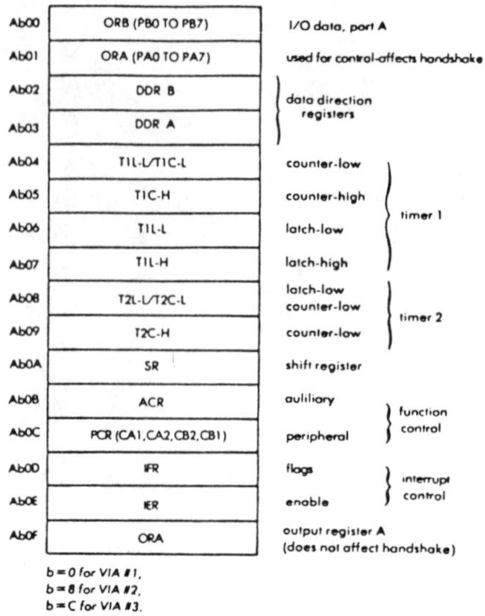

Fig. 3-14: Memory Map for the 6522's

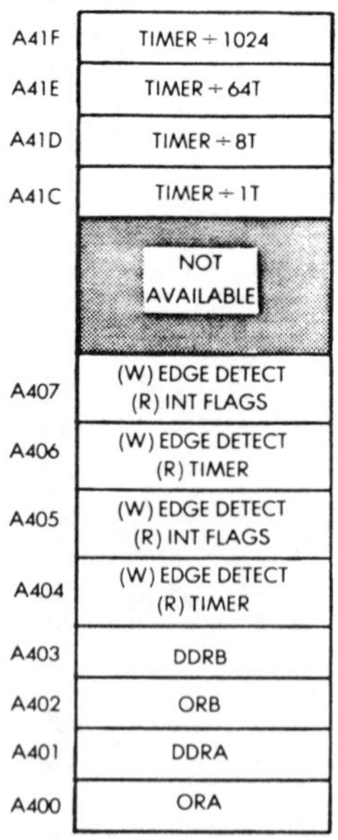

Fig. 3-15: Memory Map for the 6532

The memory map for the 6522's is shown on Fig 3-14, while the memory map for the 6532 is shown on Fig 3-15.

Since some implementation details will be used (or worked around) in some of the application programs, two relevant details are presented below.

Fig 3-16 shows the four buffered outputs available on PB4 through PB7 of 6522 #3. Fig 3-17 shows the connection to the LED's and the keyboard.

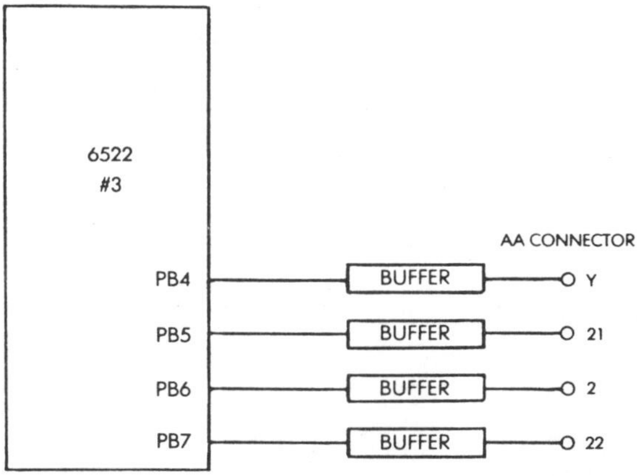

Fig. 3-16: The Four Buffered Outputs

THE AIM 65

The AIM 65 is shown on Fig 3-18. This unit, developed by Rockwell International, consists of two boards. One of them is the microcomputer board, equipped with a 20-column dot-matrix printer, and a 20-character alphanumeric display. The second board is a full ASCII keyboard, which is attached directly to the other one. The printer operates at up to 120 lines per minute, using a five-by-seven dot matrix to print the complete ASCII 64-character set (upper case only). In its minimal version, the AIM 65 is equipped with a comprehensive monitor (8K) 1K of RAM, two 6522's, one 6532, plus the usual interfaces (teletype, two audio cassette interfaces, and naturally the keyboard interface). Several additional chips can easily be placed on the board. Further, the user appli-

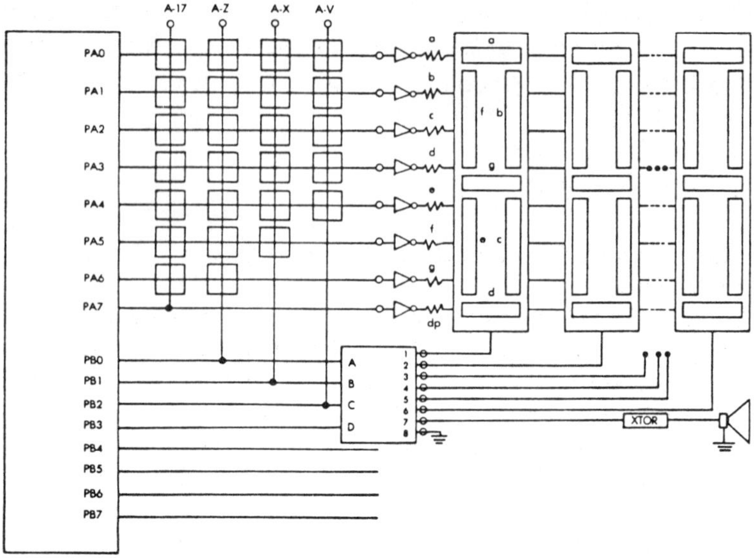

Fig. 3-17: Keyboard and LED Connection

Fig 3-18 : AIM 65 is a Board with Mini-Printer and Full Keyboard

cations connector is identical to those described for the previous boards. A user developing applications for this specific board will therefore only have to modify the programs presented here to fit the memory assignments of the AIM 65 PIO's.

OTHER BOARDS

Other boards are manufactured by various manufacturers such as Ohio Scientific.

Overall, all 6502 boards fit the description of our "standard system." As long as they use the same I/O chips (and nearly all do, as these chips offer strong advantages), there should be virtually no modification needed to the programs presented in this book, except for the PIO addresses, and the possible unavailability of specific I/O lines.

The SYM A and E connectors are equivalent to the KIM and AIM edge connectors. The vertical board, on the left of the power supply of Fig 3-19 below, is a 16K memory expansion board connected through the E connector.

At the foreground, two experiments are connected through the A connector: a hexadecimal keyboard, and a microprinter. They are described in chapter 6.

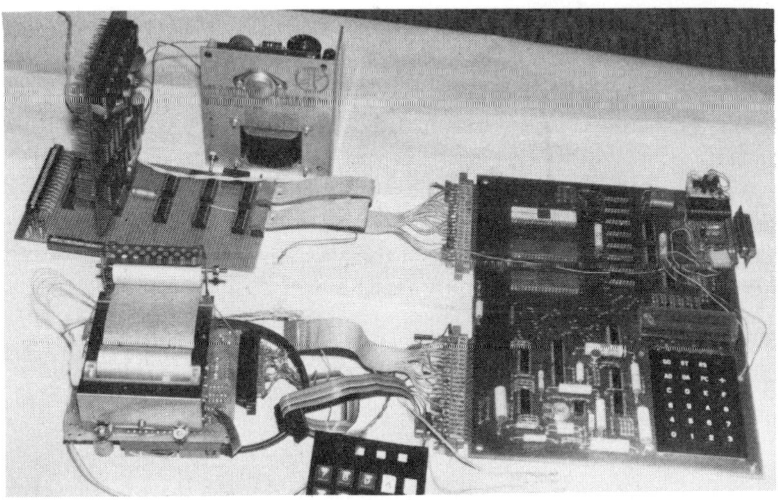

Fig 3-19: KIM/SYM/AIM Connector Compatibility

CHAPTER 4

BASIC TECHNIQUES

INTRODUCTION

In this chapter, we will connect a 6502 board to basic input-output devices. We will connect it to simple output devices such as light-emitting-diodes (LED's), relays, and a loudspeaker. On input, we will connect it to a set of switches. Then, we will use these resources to start developing simple application programs such as a Morse generator, a time-of-day clock, a simple home control program, and even an automatic telephone dialer. We will then present applications which are a direct application of these techniques: a siren, a pulse meter, a music program, a mathematical game. Then, in the following chapter we will develop more complex programs using these basic input-output devices and more complex ones.

Few components are needed to actually realize the applications board for this chapter. A picture of the actual board is shown on Fig 4-0. All the components can be purchased at low cost from any electronics store. The reader is strongly encouraged to acquire these few electronic components, and wire them as indicated in this chapter, in order to effectively apply the programs that will be described. Naturally, this will require access to a 6502-based board.

In order to present real programs, the hardware configuration of the SYM board is used in the first part, and the KIM for the second one. However, all of these programs should run with minimal modifications on any other 6502 board (see Chapter Two).

The programs to be developed in this chapter are simple, but assume a basic understanding of the 6502 instructions, as provided by the preceding book in the series, reference C202 ("Programming the 6502").

The list of components required for the applications programs in this chapter is:

perforated board	(1)	
switches	(4)	
LED driver	(1)	
LED's	(1 or more)	
12 V relays	(3)	
speaker	(1)	(high impedance preferred)
variable resistor	(1)	
resistors		
male 120 V AC plug	(1)	
female 120 AC plugs	(2)	

The hardware connection of the various components on the board will be described for each application.

It is not indispensable to assemble an applications board to read this chapter. However, many exercises will be suggested in this chapter and the following ones. Although they can be developed on paper, true programming expertise is best acquired through actual experimentation. The reader is therefore again encouraged, either before or after reading this book, to start programming on real hardware.

The goal of this chapter is to teach the basic hardware and software interfacing techniques which are required to connect any "standard" 6502 board to simple external devices. At the end of this chapter, you should know how to use the main resources of the input-output chips, and how to write programs which will sense and control input-output devices. We will build upon this knowledge in the next chapter and develop more complex industrial and home applications.

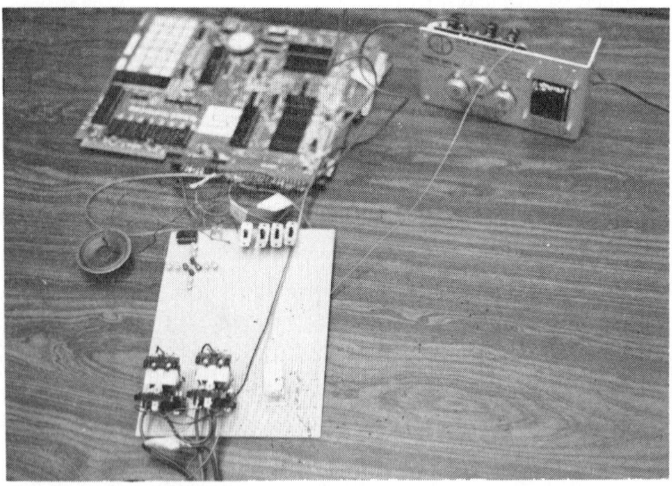

Fig. 4-0: Complete System with Power Supply, Microcomputer Board, Tape Recorder and Applications Board

SECTION 1: THE TECHNIQUES

RELAYS

A relay is used to control an external high voltage or high current circuit: the control circuit is *isolated* from the external one through the relay. A relay requires DC current. The current flows through a coil, producing a magnetic field. This field will provoke in turn the closure of a movable contact. The *external circuit* may be alternating current (AC) or direct current (DC). In order to control external devices using a significant current of voltage, such as appliances, we will use relays.

The SYM board has a special provision for high current or high voltage devices. Four buffered output ports are available on the board. They are respectively connected to bits 4, 5, 6, and 7 of the input-output register B of the PIO (6522-U29) (see Fig 4-1). We will, therfore, directly use these special outputs which can control relays. On any other board which has only PIO outputs (such as KIM) a transistor or buffer must be used. The use of a 7404 Hex Inverter is shown on Fig 4-2 to control three external relays from two output lines of a 6530.

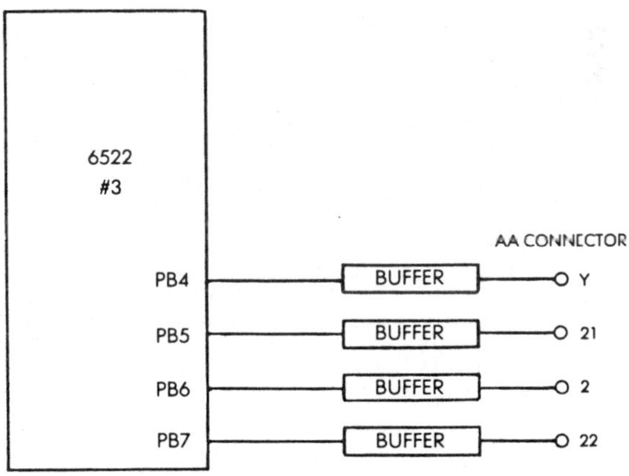

Fig. 4-1: I/O Buffers

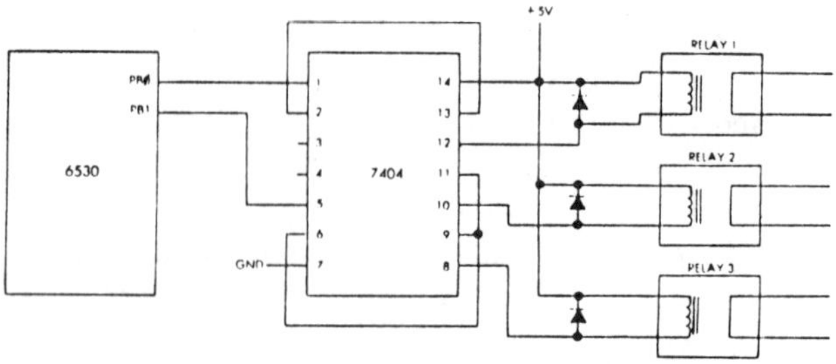

Fig. 4-2: 6530 Relay Interface

The Hardware Interface

The connection diagram for a single relay appears on Fig 4-3. This relay may be, for example, a 12 volt relay with a 50 to 500 ohms coil. The contact can be SPST (Single pole, single throw = one contact) or SPDT (Single pole, double throw = two contacts) at 10-15 amps. The current rating of the relay contacts should be sufficient to handle the external device connected to it. Most house appliances do not draw more than 10 to 15 amps so that the above specifications should be sufficient for home applications.

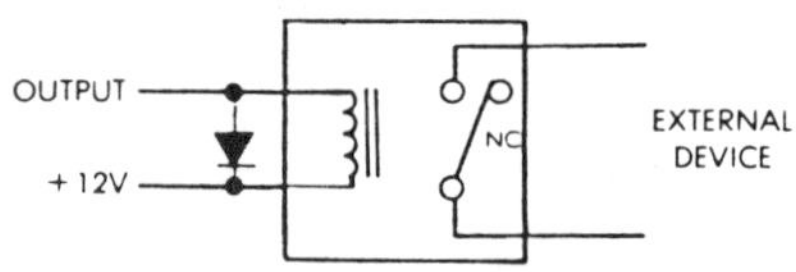

Fig. 4-3: Connecting a Simple Relay

Note on the illustration that a clipping diode is connected in parallel to the coil. This is an important precaution with any relay to avoid damage to the PIO buffer or amplifier. A reverse voltage spike occurs when the relay is turned off. Any diode which will handle the voltage may be used. For example, an IN914 should be sufficient for our purposes.

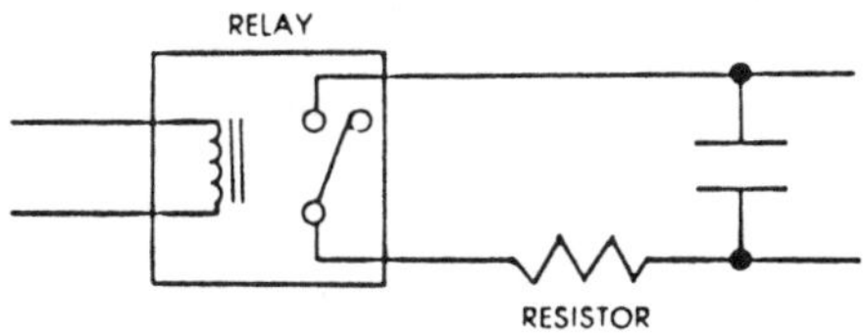

Fig. 4-4: Precautions on Device Side

On the device side of the relay, two precautions can be taken: a capacitor may be placed in parallel to the output to absorb the surge due to contact closure (this insures a longer life for the relay contacts). Also, if a significant current may be drawn, a resistor should be placed in series (see Fig 4-4).

A double-pole relay can be connected in exactly the same manner and the connection diagram appears on Fig 4-5. Such a relay is capable of switching two independent, separate circuits simultaneously.

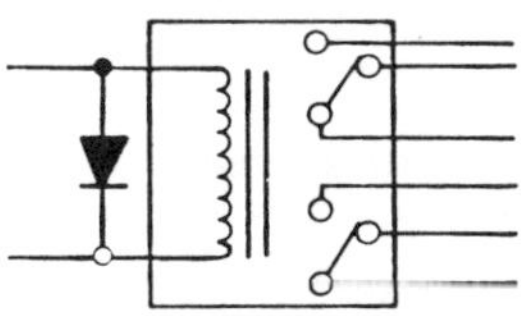

Fig. 4-5: Connecting a Double Pole Relay

Let us now consider a practical application. We will connect two relays, R1 and R2 respecitvely, to bits 6 and 7 of port B of the SYM PIO. These two relays will be used to control AC devices. In the simplest case, we will assume that these AC devices are two independent lamps. This will allow us to test the program easily, by merely verifying whether the lamps are turned on and off correctly. Naturally, instead of a lamp, the device could be any household device or appliance which does not overload the relay. The interconnect diagram appears on Figure 4-6.

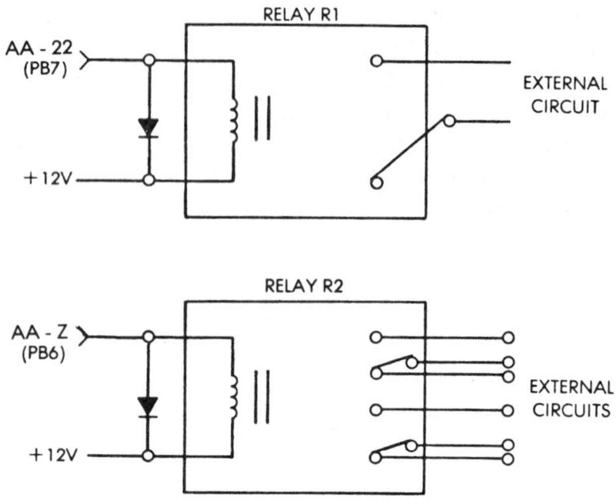

Fig. 4-6: Connecting Two Relays to the PIO

Let us inspect Figs 3-11, 3-12 and 3-13 showing the connection points for the three SYM connectors: we see that the four buffered oputputs, called PB4, PB5, PB6 and PB7, are available repectively on pins Y, 21, Z and 22. The connection points marked PB5 through PB7 on our illustration, therefore, simply need to be connected by a wire to the appropriate pin of the "auxiliary application connector."

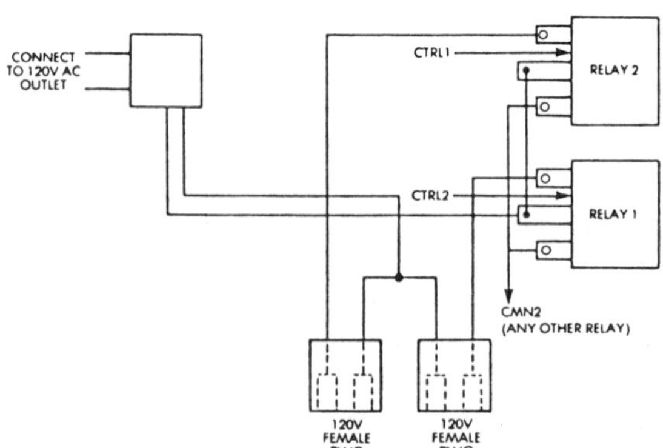

Fig. 4-7: External Circuit for the Relays

On the external circuit side of the relay, one AC plug is used which will be connected into a wall outlet and supply power to the two outlets which will be controlled by the microcomputer. These two female outlets are connected to the relays as indicated on Fig 4-7. They are powered in parallel from the AC plug. However, either one of them can be turned on independently under microcomputer control. Let us now implement the software control for these relays.

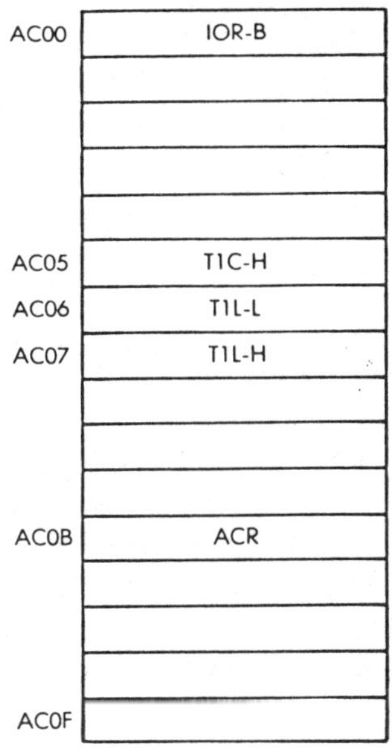

Fig 4-8: Memory Map for 6522 #3 (Third 6522 of SYM)

The Software Interface

Each of the two circuits connected to relays R1 and R2 will be turned on whenever the corresponding relay is actuated. The relay will be turned on by setting the corresponding control bit to 1. By inspecting Fig 4-8, it can be seen that Port B for the 6522 #3 is located at Memory Address AC00. The contents of memory location AC00 are illustrated on Fig 4-9. Let us now turn the relays on and off.

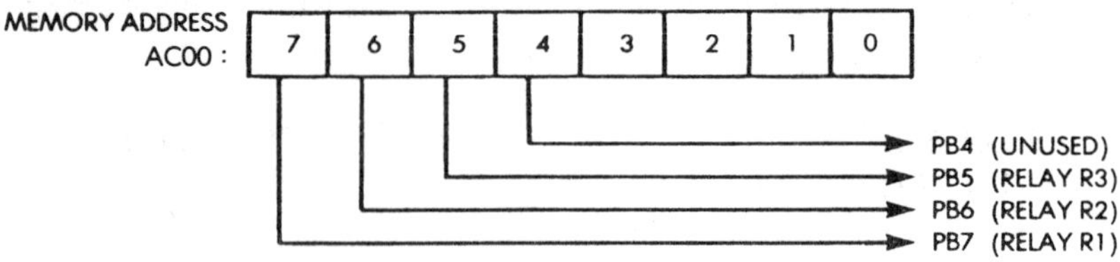

Fig. 4-9: Port B of 6522 #3

First, we must configure Port B as an output port. To simplify, we will specify that bits 0 through 7 be outputs, even though we use here only bits 5, 6, and 7. The convention could be changed in a different application. It will be remembered from Chapter 2 that, in order to specify the direction in which input-output lines will be used, the corresponding bit position of the Data Direction Register must be loaded with a zero or a one. A one in the Data Direction Register will specify an output. A zero will specify an input. Loading all ones in the Data Direction Register guarantees that all bits will be used as outputs.

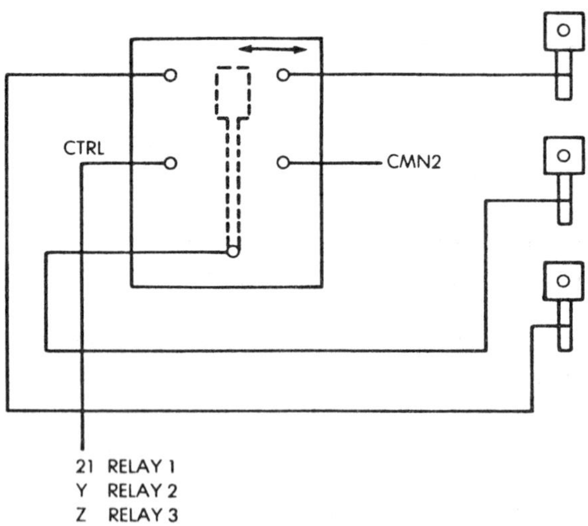

Fig. 4-10: Detail of Relay Connection on the Applications Board

As a remark, when programming, it is a good policy to always make things as simple and consistent as possible. Since we assume here that (for the time being) no other devices are connected to the other lines of Port B, it is safer to configure all lines as either inputs or outputs.

Specifying all bits as outputs will be accomplished by the following two instructions:

```
LDA #$FF      LOAD A IMMEDIATE WITH 11111111
STA $AC02     STORE A INTO ADDRESS AC02
              HEXADECIMAL
```

It can be verified on Fig 4-8 that AC02 is the address of the Data Direction Register for Port B of the 6522 device #3. "FF" hexadecimal is equivalent to "11111111" binary. Let us now turn on the relay connected to PB6.

```
LDA $AC00     READ CURRENT VALUE OF PB
ORA #$40      FORCE PB6 TO 1
STA $AC00     OUTPUT
```

The first instruction is used to read the current value of Port B. Because several devices or relays may be presently connected to Port B, we do not want to simply write a pattern such as "01000000" into Port B; this would turn on the relay connected to PB6, but would also turn off all the other relays! Therefore, we want to read the present status of PB and only change a single bit, PB6. The change is accomplished with the logical OR instruction, the second in our program (ORA). The logical OR respects the integrity of all the bits, and forces to "1" the specified bit location. If we wanted to turn on PB7 instead of PB6, the pattern "80" (hexadecimal) would be used, instead of "40." Finally, the resulting bit pattern is stored at address AC00, which corresponds to PB; the relay connected to PB6 is then turned on.

Exercise 4-1: *Write the three-instruction program which will turn on the relays connected to PB6 and PB7 simultaneously.*

Let us now turn off the relay connected to PB6:

```
LDA $AC00     READ THE CURRENT STATUS OF PB
AND #$BF      SET BIT 6 TO 0
STA $AC00     STORE RESULTING VALUE IN PB
```

The logical AND instruction is used to force a "0" at the specified bit location. All other bit locations are not affected. ("BF" hexadecimal is "10111111" in binary.)

Note: The AND instruction is traditionally used to zero a specified bit location. However, an identical result may be obtained using the EOR instruction. The program remains the same except that the AND instruction becomes:

EOR #$40

The advantage is that the pattern used to turn off is the same as the one used to turn on. This eliminates a possible mistake. The reader should naturally verify that this is a legitimate way to force a zero. This is because the exclusive OR of "1" and "1" is "0." If bit 6 was a "1," the "40" pattern will therefore force it to a zero. All other bits will be unaffected.

Verification

Let us verify now that these simple instructions are indeed sufficient to turn our relays on and off. We will connect two lamps, or two devices, to the two relays and type in these instructions at the keyboard, then verify that the lamps are turned on or off. Since the keyboard requires that input be in hexadecimal form, here is the hexadecimal equivalent of the two above programs:

To turn the relay on:
AD 00 AC
09 PATTERN (PATTERN stands for an 8 bit pattern)
8D 00 AC

The program to turn the relay off is:
AD 00 AC
49 PATTERN
8D 00 AC

If you have a board you should now key in these two programs and verify their correct operation.

SWITCHES

Two main types of switches may be connected: a push-button (SPST switch) or a two-position switch (SPDT). The connection of an SPST is illustrated in Fig 4-11. With the connection indicated, the switch is in the logical state "1" when the contact is open and in state "0" when the contact is closed. If the opposite should be desirable, the polarities would simply be reversed on the switch contact.

The connection of an SPDT switch (a two position switch) is illustrated in Fig 4-12. The connection is straightforward. One of the contact positions will be logical state "1," while the other one will be logical state "0."

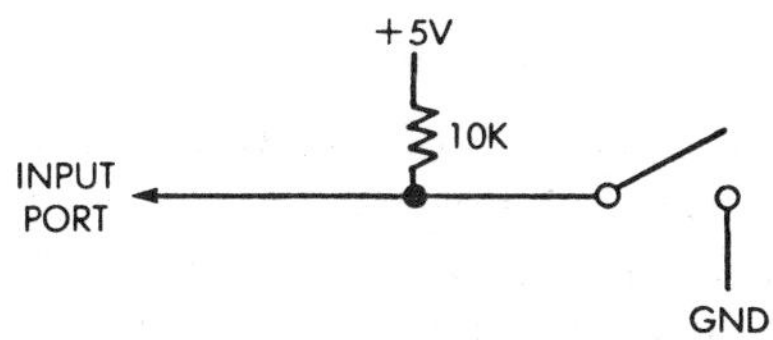

Fig. 4-11: Connecting an SPST

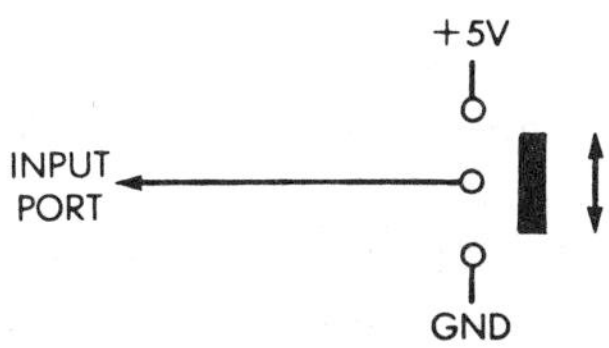

Fig. 4-12: Connecting an SPDT

Connecting Four Switches

We will use lines 1, 2, 3, and 4 of Port B of the 6522, as four input lines used to sense the status of the external switches. The actual connection appears on Fig 4-13. Let us examine the program.

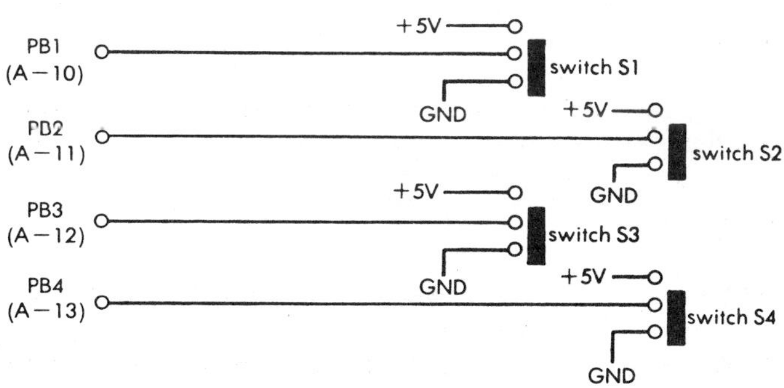

Fig. 4-13: Connecting Four SPDT Switches to the SYM

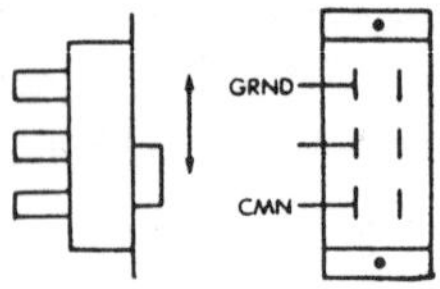

Fig. 4-14: An SPDT Switch

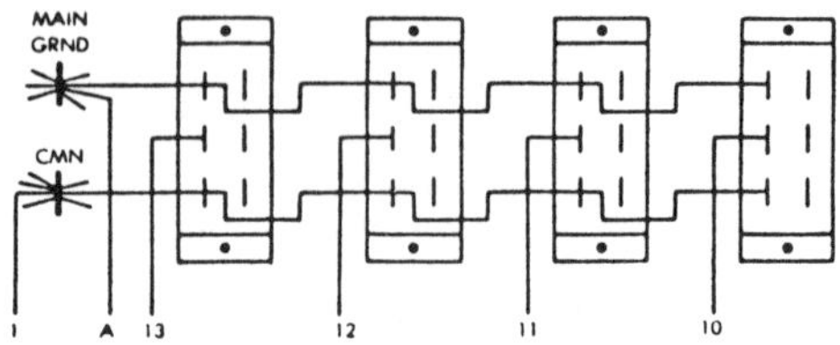

Fig. 4-15: Connection Detail for Four SPDT's

The Software Interface

We first need to configure PB1, PB2, PB3, and PB4 as input lines on Port B. This is accomplished by loading the appropriate pattern in address "A002," the data direction register for Port B.

```
LDA #$E0       SET BITS 01234 AS INPUTS
STA $A002
```

The pattern "E0" is used to configure lines 0, 1, 2, 3, 4 as inputs and lines 5, 6, 7 as outputs (they may be connected to external relays). "E0" hexadecimal is "11100000" in binary. Each "0" sets an input. Each "1" sets an output. "E1" could also be used.

Let us now read the value of the switch and branch to a specified memory location determined by this value.

```
LDA #SWITCHPTR   "02" FOR S1, "04" FOR S2, "08"
                 FOR S3, "10" FOR S4
BIT $A000        A000 IS ADDRESS
BEQ ANYADDRESS   WILL BRANCH TO SPECIFIED
                 ADDRESS IF SWITCH WAS ZERO
                 (OFF)
```

Alternatively, if we wish to branch to a specified memory location if the switch is "1" (on), we would substitute the instruction BNE instead of the BEQ in the last line of the program.

Testing the Program on the Board

The hexadecimal code for the above program is:

A9 SWITCHPTR
2C 00 A0
FO ANYADDRESS or "DO" ANYADDRESS

SPEAKER

An external speaker may be connected directly to a pin of one of the PIO devices. Pin 7 is often more powerful and is generally used. On the 6522 device, the polarity of the PB7 output signal can be controlled by one of the internal interval timers. The timer will be used to generate a tone of given frequency. The preferred position for connecting the speaker will therefore be PB7. The connection diagram appears on Fig 4-16.

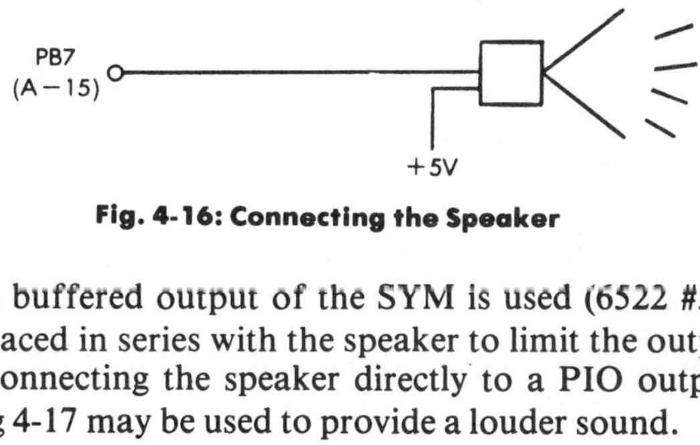

Fig. 4-16: Connecting the Speaker

When the buffered output of the SYM is used (6522 #3) a resistor should be placed in series with the speaker to limit the output current. Instead of connecting the speaker directly to a PIO output pin, the circuit of Fig 4-17 may be used to provide a louder sound.

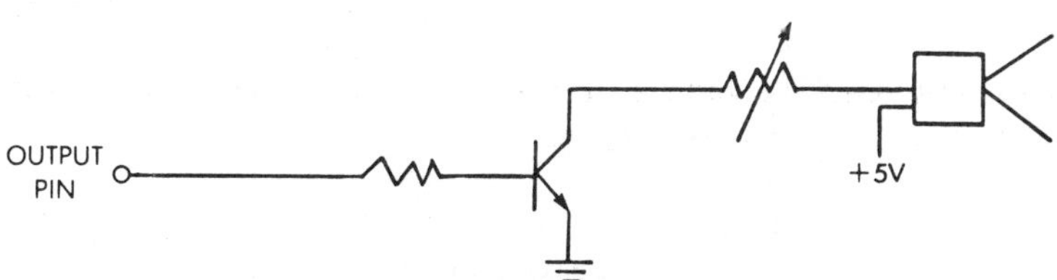

Fig. 4-17: Obtaining a Louder Output

Warning: a variable resistor is shown on Fig 4-17 for convenience. However, if it is set to zero, it will probably burn, and destroy the corresponding output transistor (this applies also to SYM).

The Software Interface

A sound can be generated by the speaker by merely turning it on and off at the desired frequency. The sound will not be as "clean sounding" as one from a musical instrument since it will have been generated by a square wave. However, it will be sufficient for our needs and can be clearly identified by its frequency. We will now build a practical application

A MORSE GENERATOR

We will develop here a program capable of generating a Morse code corresponding to any letter of the alphabet. Ths program will activate a loudspeaker, so that we can verify that the proper Morse code is being generated. In addition, it will have the capability of turning on or off an external device so that this morse code could for example be transmitted over a communications link.

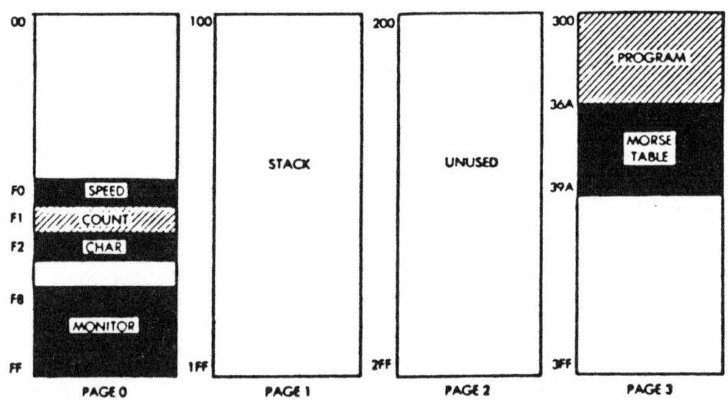

Fig. 4-18: Memory Allocation for the Morse Program

The conventions used by this program are the following:

The program itself will be stored in Page 3 of the RAM, i.e., starting at location 300. This is illustrated on Fig 4-18. This program contains a Morse equivalence table which will serve to generate the proper bit pattern for any given ASCII character. It will be shown below how this table is generated. It is assumed that the first character to be converted to Morse is contained in the accumulator at the time the program is started.

Further, the speed of the transmission will be adjustable through the variable SPEED, stored in Page 0 at memory location F0 (See Fig 4-18). Each time unit (such as the duration of a dot in Morse code) is expressed internally in milliseconds. Putting the value 100 into variable "SPEED" will result in the duration being 1/10th of a second.

Before the program is started, it is assumed that CHAR and SPEED have valid contents, and that the accumulator contains the first character to be transmitted. An external subroutine could call this subroutine repeatedly in order to transmit a string of characters. It is the responsibility of this subroutine to deposit a character in the accumulator every time it calls the Morse transmitter.

Let us now examine the algorithm used to transmit the Morse code.

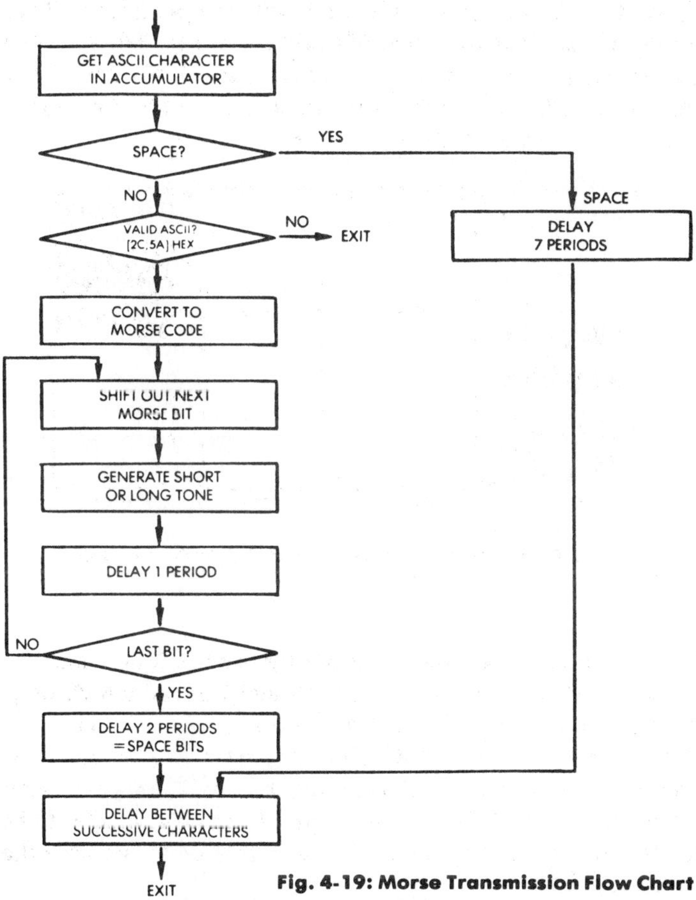

Fig. 4-19: Morse Transmission Flow Chart

This algorithm is illustrated on the flow-chart of Fig 4-19. The program first checks for a space character. If found, it will generate no signal for seven time periods, plus the delay between successive characters.

It then verifies that the ASCII character contained in the accumulator has a valid hexadecimal code. Legal codes must be between "2C" and "5A" inclusive, in hexadecimal (assuming a 7-bit ASCII code). Otherwise, an error exit occurs. After validation of character code, this ASCII code must be converted to its morse equivalent. The technique will be explained later.

The binary encoding of the morse code will consist of a "START" bit (a "1"), followed by a "0" for a ".", and a "1" for a "–". All unused bits within the 8-bit word, to the left of the start bit, will be set to "0." This conversion will be performed by the program by a table lookup described later. Let us now assume that the binary version of the morse code has been obtained. The sequence of tones must be generated. The contents of the accumulator will be shifted out left until the START is found. Following the detection of the START bit, every "0" will be interpreted as a "·" and every "1" will be interpreted as a "–", up to the eighth bit. For every "0" shifted out, a short tone will be generated. For every "1" shifted out, a long tone will be generated. The tone generation will also be described later in detail.

After generating the tone corresponding to a bit, a 1-period waiting time is inserted, and the next bit of the Morse code is checked until the last one (the eighth) has been found.

Following the transmission of the squence of tones for a Morse character, a two period delay is generated. This corresponds to "space" bits which are normally inserted at the end of every transmission for a character. A one-period delay is then generated which separates successive characters.

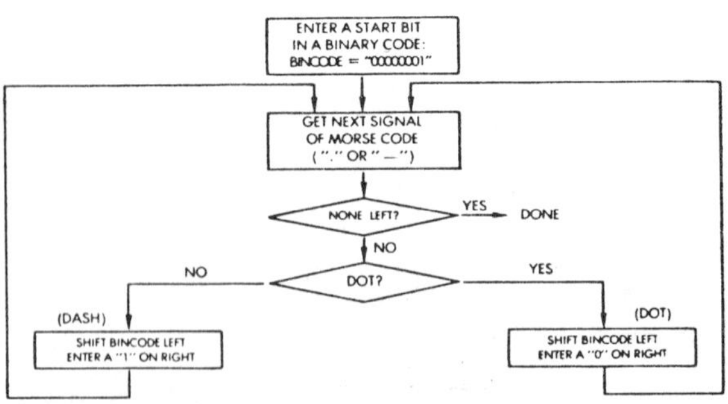

Fig. 4-20: Converting Morse to Binary

The sequence is clearly illustrated on the flow-chart of Fig 4-20 and should be verified by the reader. Let us now examine in detail the specific problems which we have not yet resolved.

Converting ASCII to Binary Morse

We want to establish here a correspondance table between the ASCII character and the binary representation of its Morse code. Let us illustrate this in an example.

The character "B" has a Morse code of "– . . . ".

Every " – " will be encoded by a "1," and every "·" by a "0". The binary equivalent of "– . . ." is, therefore, "1000".

In addition, by convention, we will add a START bit (a "1") to the left of the code we have just generated. The resulting code at this point is: "11000." Finally, every binary Morse code will be contained in an eight-bit word. The remaining bits to the left of the START bit will now be set to zero. Our resulting eight-bit code is therefore: "00011000." In hexadecimal, this is "18".

The hexadecimal representation of the binary morse encoding for B is: "18".

As an example, the table below shows the hexadecimal equivalent of A, B, C, D. A complete equivalence table for all legal morse characters appears on Fig 4-22. The algorithm corresponding to the technique just described is illustrated by the flow-chart of Fig 4-23.

Letter	ASCII	Morse	binary	hexadecimal
A	41	. —	00000101	05
B	42	— . . .	00011000	18
C	43	— . — .	00011010	1A
D	44	— . .	00001100	0C

Fig. 4-21: Converting ASCII to Morse

We now have established an equivalence table for all the ASCII characters. This table will be called the "Morse table" and will be stored at the end of the program (see Fig 4-18). Whenever we require the Morse code equivalent of a specific character, we will access the proper entry table and find there the binary code. This will be described later when we discuss the actual program.

Character	Morse Code	ASCII	Hex Table Value
,	— — . . — —	2C	73
—	— . . . . —	2D	31
.	. — . — . —	2E	55
/	— . . — .	2F	32
Ø	— — — — —	3Ø	3F
1	. — — — —	31	2F
2	. . — — —	32	27
3	. . . — —	33	23
4	. . . . —	34	21
5	. . . . .	35	2Ø
6	—	36	3Ø
7	— — . . .	37	38
8	— — — . .	38	3C
9	— — — — .	39	3E
:	User definable	3A	Ø1
;	" "	3B	Ø1
<	" "	3C	Ø1
=	" "	3D	Ø1
>	" "	3E	Ø1
?	. . — — . .	3F	4C
@	User definable	4Ø	Ø1
A	. —	41	Ø5
B	— . . .	42	18
C	— . — .	43	1A
D	— . .	44	ØC
E	.	45	Ø2
F	. . — .	46	12
G	— — .	47	ØE
H	. . . .	48	1Ø
I	. .	49	Ø4
J	. — — —	4A	17
K	— . —	4B	ØD
L	. — . .	4C	14
M	— —	4D	Ø7
N	— .	4E	Ø6
O	— — —	4F	ØF
P	. — — .	50	16
Q	— — . —	51	1D
R	. — .	52	ØA
S	. . .	53	Ø8
T	—	54	Ø3
U	. . —	55	Ø9
V	. . . —	56	11
W	. — —	57	ØB
X	— . . —	58	19
Y	— . — —	59	1B
Z	— — . .	5A	1C

Fig. 4-22: Morse Equivalence Table

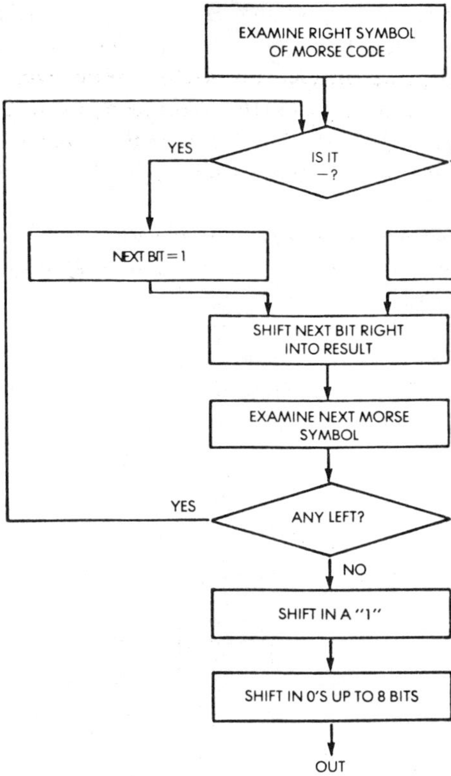

Fig. 4-23: Flow Chart for Generating Hexidecimal Morse Code

Generating a Tone with the Timer

Our next problem will be to generate a tone of set duration and frequency. We will use here a timer.

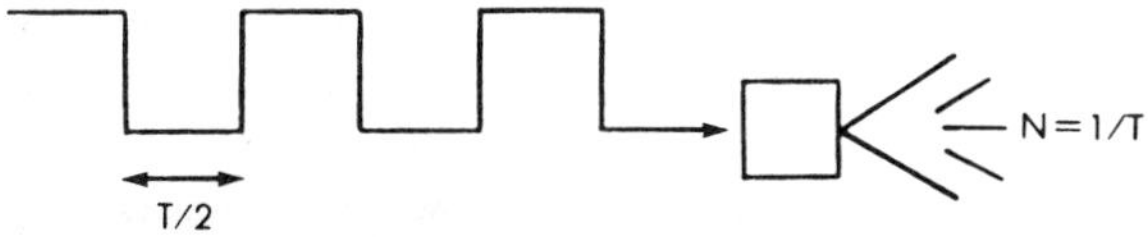

Fig. 4-24: Square Wave Generates Tone in Speaker

The tone will be generated at the speaker by sending it a square wave of the required frequency. This is illustrated by Fig 4-24. The timer can be used to generate this waveform automatically. In order to obtain this result, we will set the appropriate bits in the control register ACR (see Fig 4-25), then simply control the length of time during which this tone or wave form is generated. The actual timing diagram appears in Fig 4-26. Φ2 at the top of the illustration is Phase 2 of the system clock. In most standard 6502 systems the clock has a 1 micro-second period. The pulse generated by this timer appears on the PB7 output pin. It will last N + 1.5 subcycles, where N is the value deposited in the counter. This is because the counter of the timer decrements from N down to 0, and inverses the output port with the next high-to-low transition of the clock. This is illustrated on Fig 4-26. An interrupt (IRQ) is also generated at the same time, but will not be used here.

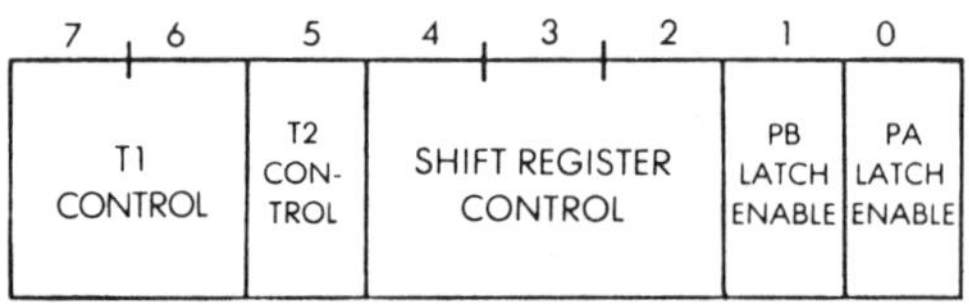

Fig. 4-25: 6522 Auxiliary Register

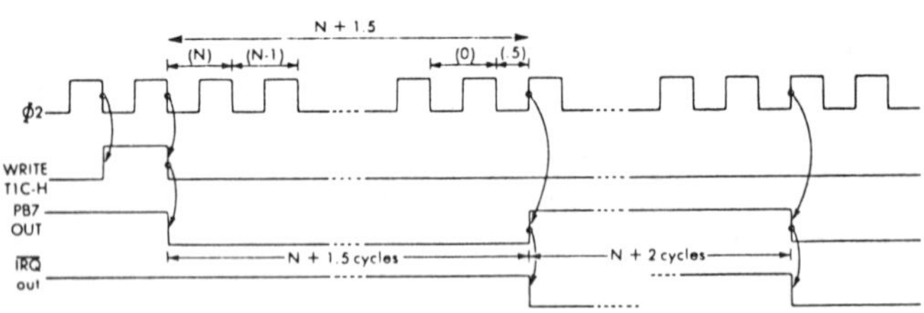

Fig. 4-26: Timing Diagram for Tone Generation

In order to use the timer, we must, therefore, deposit an appropriate value N in its counter. However, as soon as the contents of the counter are written, the counter starts running. Since the counter is a 16-bit register, we cannot load it in a single data transfer from the microprocessor. *It must be latched.* The timer is, therefore, equipped with an internal 16-bit latch called T1L. The low part of the latch is called T1L-L, while the high part of the latch is called T1L-H. The value N will be deposited in T1L-L and in T1L-H. At this point the 16-bit contents are specified but nothing happens yet. In order to start the timer, we will give a special command which will transfer the contents of the latch into the actual counter. This is the "write T1C-H" command which appears on the fourth line of Fig 4-27:

```
LDA    #VALUE LO
STA     $A006      LOAD LOW LATCH
LDA    #VALUE HI
STA     $A007      LOAD HI LATCH
STA     $A005      TRANSFER  LATCH=START
```

Fig 4-27: Program to use Timer 1

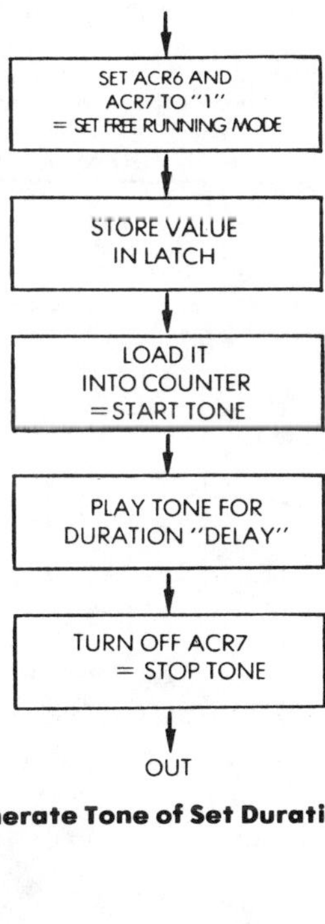

Fig 4-28: Generate Tone of Set Duration with Timer 1

The sequence of events to use the timer should now be clear. It is described on the flow chart of Fig 4-28. First, we will set the appropriate bits of the control register ACR to the required values. The timer operates in "free-running" mode where it generates a square output on PB7. This is obtained by setting bits 6 and 7 of ACR to "0" and "1" (see Fig 4-29 and 4-30). Next, the appropriate value N will be stored in the latch. Then, it will be transferred into the counter itself to start it. This will be the starting point for the tone being generated. Every time that the counter decrements to zero, it will reload the value stored in its latch register automatically. The timer will therefore from now on automatically generate a square wave with a half-period of approximately N+2. (This is approximate because the low part of the pulse has an N + 1.5 duration whereas the upper part of it has an N + 2 duration).

ACR 7 OUTPUT ENABLE	ACR 6 FREE RUN ENABLE	MODE
0	0 (ONE-SHOT)	Generate time out INT when T1 loaded PB7 disabled.
0	1 (FREE RUN)	Generate continuous INT PB7 disabled.
1	0 (ONE-SHOT)	Generate INT and output pulse on PB7 everytime T1 is loaded. =one-shot and programmable width pulse.
1	1 (FREE RUN)	Generate continuous INT and square wave output on PB7.

Fig. 4-29: 6522 ACR Selects Timer Modes

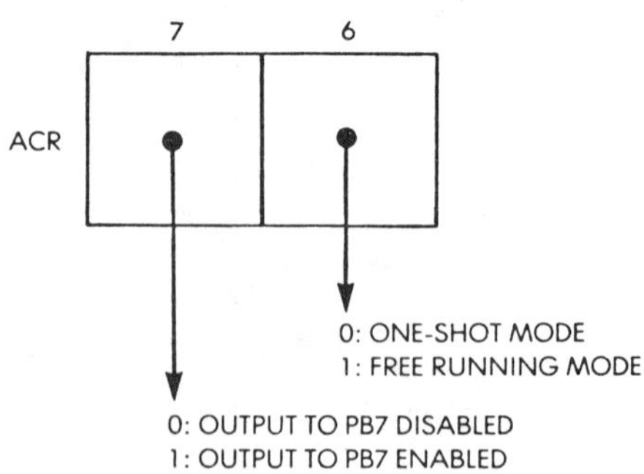

Fig. 4-30: Bits 6 and 7 of ACR

```
LOC      CODE         LINE

0000                  ;THIS IS A SUBROUTINE WHICH ACCEPTS ASCII CHARACTERS
0000                  ;IN THE RANGE 2CH TO 5AH (PLUS 20H FOR SPACE) AND PLAYS
0000                  ;THEIR MORSE CODE EQUIVILENT ON A SPEAKER HOOKED UP TO
0000                  ;PB7, 6522-U25.  IT ALSO TURNS ON AND OFF PB0, 6522-
0000                  ;U25, AND WITH A SUITABLE DRIVER, THIS BIT CAN KEY A
0000                  ;TRANSMITTER.   A MAIN PROGRAM WILL CALL THIS SUBROUTINE
0000                  ;WITH THE ASCII CHARACTER IN THE ACCUMULATOR.
0000                  ;EXAMPLES OF THE MAIN PROGRAM WOULD BE ONE THAT
0000                  ;GETS INPUT FROM A TERMINAL AND SENDS MORSE CODE OUT
0000                  ;THROUGH THIS PROGRAM, OR A PROGRAM WHICH RANDOMIZES
0000                  ; A SERIES A CHARACTERS AND SENDS THEM FOR CODE PRACTICE.
0000                  ;THE FORMAT FOR THE MORSE CODE CAHRACTERS IN THE TABLE
0000                  ;IS : MOVING FROM LEFT TO RIGHT , THE FIRST HIGH
0000                  ;BIT (A ONE) IS THE START BIT, AND AFTER THIS ,
0000                  ;EACH ONE IS A DASH, AND EACH ZERO IS A DOT.
0000                  SPEED=$F0
0000                  COUNT=$F1
0000                  CHAR=$F2
0000                          .=$300
0300: C9 20           MORSE   CMP #$20          ;IF A SPACE, DO SPACE ROUTINE
0302: F0 67                   BEQ SPACE
0304: C9 2C                   CMP #$2C          ;SEE IF ASCII CODE
0306: 90 4E                   BCC EXIT          ;    IS LESS THEN 2CH, AND RETURN IF SO.
0308: C9 5B                   CMP #$5B          ;SEE IF ASCII CODE IS OVER
030A: B0 4A                   BCS EXIT          ;     5AH, AND RETURN IF SO
030C: AA                      TAX               ;PUT CODE IN INDEX REGISTER
030D: BD 45 03                LDA TABLE-$2C,X   ;GET MORSE CHARACTER
0310: A0 08                   LDY #$8           ;NUMBER OF BITS TO BE ROTATED FROM ACCUMULATOR
0312: 84 F1                   STY COUNT
0314: 0A              STARTB  ASL A
0315: C6 F1                   DEC COUNT
0317: 90 FB                   BCC STARTB        ;SHIFT A UNTIL START BIT FOUND
0319: 85 F2                   STA CHAR
031B: A5 F2           NEXT    LDA CHAR
031D: 0A                      ASL A             ;NOW SHIFT OUT MORSE CODE (1=DASH, 0=DOT)
031E: 85 F2                   STA CHAR
0320: A0 01                   LDY #$1           ;DOT= 1 TIME PERIOD, DEFAULT TO DOT
0322: 90 02                   BCC SEND          ;IF CARRY CLEAR, DOT
0324: A0 03                   LDY #$3           ;ELSE DASH    (3 TIME PERIODS)
                      ; THIS SECTION SENDS A HIGH OUTPUT FOR (Y REGISTER ) NU
                      ;OF TIME PERIODS, AND THEN A LOW FOR 1 TIME PERIOD.
0326: A9 C0           SEND    LDA #$C0
0328: 8D 0B A0                STA $A00B         ;SET TIMER  MODE TOFREE RUNNING MODE
032B: A9 00                   LDA #$0           ; THIS VALUE,
032D: 8D 06 A0                STA $A006
0330: A9 04                   LDA #$04          ; AND THIS VALUE DETERMINE THE TONE
0332: 8D 07 A0                STA $A007         ;        OF THE OUTPUT (APPROX 1000HZ)
0335: 8D 05 A0                STA $A005         ;THIS STARTS TONE
0338: A9 01                   LDA #$1           ;TURN ON OUTPUT BIT-PB0
033A: 8D 00 A0                STA $A000
033D: 20 57 03                JSR DELAY         ;DELAYFOR ELEMENT TIME PERIOD
0340: A9 00                   LDA #$0
0342: 8D 0B A0                STA $A00B         ;TURN OFF TONE
0345: 8D 00 A0                STA $A000         ;TURN OFF OUTPUT BIT (PB0)
0348: A0 01                   LDY #$01
034A: 20 57 03                JSR DELAY         ;DELAY FOR 1 TIME PERIOD(SPACE BETWEEN ELEMENTS)
034D: C6 F1                   DEC COUNT         ;DECREMENT COUNT -SEE IF 8 BITS WERE ROTATED
034F: D0 CA                   BNE NEXT          ;  IF NOT, DO ANOTHER ELEMENT
0351: A0 02           FINISH  LDY #$2           ;DELAY FOR 3(TWO HERE PLUS PREVIOUS SPACE
0353: 20 57 03                JSR  DELAY        ;   AT END OF LAST ELEMENT) TIME PERIODS(SPACE BET
0356: 60              EXIT    RTS
                      ; THIS DELAYS FOR (Y REGISTER) *SPEED*.004 SECONDS
0357: 98              DELAY   TYA
0358: 0A                      ASL A
0359: 0A                      ASL A
035A: A8                      TAY
035B: A5 F0           D3      LDA SPEED
035D: A2 FA           D2      LDX #$FA
035F: CA              D1      DEX
0360: D0 FD                   BNE D1
0362: 38                      SEC
0363: E9 01                   SBC #$1
0365: D0 F6                   BNE D2            ;DELAY FOR 7 TIME PERIODS
0367: 88                      DEY               ;     (SPACE BETWEEN WORDS)
0368: D0 F1                   BNE D3            ;RETURN FROM MORSE PROGRAM
036A: 60                      RTS
036B: A0 07           SPACE   LDY #$7
036D: 20 57 03                JSR DELAY
0370: 60                      RTS
0371: 73              TABLE   .BYTE $73,$31,$55,$32,$3F,$2F
0372: 31
0373: 6A
0374: 32
0375: 3F
0376: 2F
0377: 27                      BYTE $27,$23,$21,$20,$30,$38
0378: 23
0379: 21
037A: 20
037B: 30
037C: 38
037D: 3C                      .BYTE $3C,$3E,$01,$01,$01,$01
037E: 3E
037F: 01
0380: 01
0381: 01
0382: 01
0383: 01                      BYTE $01,$4C,$01,$05,$10,$1A
0384: 4C
0385: 01
```

Fig. 4-31: The Morse Program
(Full-size listing in Appendix C)

```
0386: 05
0387: 1B
0388: 1A
0389: 0C                      .BYTE $0C,$02,$12,$0E,$10,$04
038A: 02
038B: 12
038C: 0E
038D: 10
038E: 04
038F: 17                      .BYTE $17,$0D,$14,$07,$06,$0F
0390: 0D
0391: 14
0392: 07
0393: 06
0394: 0F
0395: 16                      .BYTE $16,$1D,$0A,$08,$03,$09
0396: 1D
0397: 0A
0398: 08
0399: 03
039A: 09
039B: 11                      .BYTE $11,$0B,$19,$1B,$1C
039C: 0B
039D: 19
039E: 1B
039F: 1C

SYMBOL TABLE:
 SPEED      00F0        COUNT      00F1        CHAR       00F2
 MORSE      0300        STARTB     0314        NEXT       031B
 SEND       0326        FINISH     0351        EXIT       0356
 DELAY      0357        D3         035B        D2         035D
 D1         035F        SPACE      036B        TABLE      0371
```

Fig. 4-31: The Morse Program (continued)

The tone must be played during a set duration called here "DELAY." The duration of this delay can be implemented through software or hardware techniques. A software loop will be used in this program. Finally, the tone must be stopped when the specified delay has been achieved. This will be performed by turning off bit 7 of ACR.

The reader should refer to the flow-chart of Fig 4-28 and make sure that he understands the sequence of actions necessary to use the timer. The actual implementation will be presented below along with the program.

The Morse Program

We will follow here the flow-chart which has been presented on Fig 4-19 and develop the corresponding program. A number of specific techniques will be used in this program:

Indexed addressing will be used to retrieve the binary encoding of the Morse code for a given ASCII character.

The hardware timer will be used to generate a tone of fixed frequency. A software delay will be implemented to regulate the duration of the tone.

Nested loops will be used to implement a multiplication in the delay loop.

Let us now examine the program. It assumes that the accumulator has been loaded with the value of the ASCII character whose Morse code is to be transmitted. (See memory map on Fig 4-18). For flexibility, the speed of transmission is adjustable. It is expressed in units of 1 milliseconds (.001 second). The variable "SPEED" at memory location "00F0" must be set prior to entering this program. For example, if "SPEED" is set to the value 1000, the duration of a "·" will be 1000 × .001 = 1 second. The program will reside in Page 3, starting at address "0300" hexadecimal.

The beginning of the program is:

```
   SPEED  =  $00F0
   COUNT  =  $00F1
    CHAR  =  $00F2
       *  =  $0300
```

The first four lines are assembler directives. The first three directives assign respectively the memory addresses 00F0, 00F1, 00F2, to SPEED, COUNT, and CHAR respectively. The fourth directive specifies the value of the pseudo address-counter to be 0300 hexadecimal, i.e., specifies that the first executable instruction in the program will reside at memory address 0300.

We must first check that the character in the accumulator is a legal code. This is accomplished by:

```
MORSE  CMP #$20    IS IT A SPACE CODE?
       BEQ SPACE
       CMP #$2C    ERROR IF LESS THAN 2C
       BCC EXIT
       CMP #$5B    OR MORE THAN 5B
       BCS EXIT
```

The first two lines check whether the character in the accumulator is a "space" character (20 hexadecimal). If so, a delay of seven time periods is implemented followed by the normal delay between characters.

The next four instructions verify that the ASCII code is between "2C" and "5A" inclusive. This is the range of valid ASCII characters for Morse transmission. If an illegal character is found, an error is detected, and a jump occurs to location "EXIT." In order to keep the program simple and educational, no specific action is taken here at location EXIT to flag the error. The reader is strongly encouraged (as an exercise) to add specific instructions at location EXIT which will flag the erroneous character found in the accumulator. In this program, there will simply be no transmission for this erroneous character.

Once a legal ASCII character has been found in the accumulator, it must be converted into the binary code which will be used to generate the sequence of sounds. The binary Morse code corresponding to every permissible ASCII character is stored at the end of the program, from memory location 36B to memory location 399. We would like to retrieve the first entry of the table for the ASCII character 2C, the next entry of this table for the next sequential ASCII character, and so on. This is a typical case where we wish to use *indexed addressing.* However, an extra problem arises here: the ASCII characters are numbered from 2C on, rather than from "0" or from "1" on. The solution is quite simple, and appears below:

```
TAX
LDA   TABLE-$2C,X
```

The ASCII is transferred into the index register X so that it may be used as an offset. In order to take into account the fact that the characters are numbered from 2C on, the base of the table is simply specified to be not the real base at address 36B, but the address table minus 2C (hexadecimal). The binary code can then be loaded in the accumulator with a single indexed memory access (see Fig 4-32).

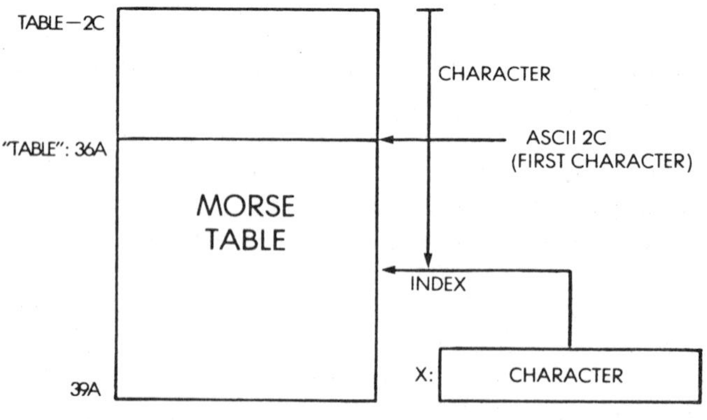

Fig 4-32: Using Indexed Addressing to Retrieve Morse Code

Our binary Morse code is now in the accumulator. Let us recall here that this code contains a leading 1, which is the START bit, followed by the 0's and the 1's representing the dashes and the periods. Any unused bits to the left of the START bit have been set to 0. The contents of the accumulator will, therefore, be shifted left until a START bit is found, then the "real" bits corresponding to the dashes and the periods will be used to generate sounds. The program is:

```
        LDY #$08    NUMBER OF BITS TO BE ROTATED
                    FROM A
        STY COUNT
STARTB  ASL A
        DEC COUNT
        BCC STARTB  SHIFT A UNTIL START BIT FOUND
        STA CHAR
NEXT    LDA CHAR
        ASL A       SHIFT OUR MORSE CODE (1=DASH,
                    0=DOT)
        STA CHAR    DOT=1 TIME PERIOD, DEFAULT
                    TO DOT
        LDY #$01
        BCC SEND    IF CARRY CLEAR, DOT
        LDY #$03    ELSE DASH (THREE TIME PERIODS)
```

The index register Y would normally be used as a counter in order to stop the successive left shifts of A, once 8 bits have been shifted out. However, the SEND routine, which will generate the sound, requires that the Y register be loaded with a duration of the sound to be generated. We can, therefore, not use index register Y for the purpose of shifting out the bits. The next idea that comes to mind is to reuse the index register X which is now available. Unfortunately, our convention in this program is that the DELAY routine uses index register X. Since neither of the two Index Registers is available as a counter, we will have to use a memory location. This is location COUNT. An important remark is that when writing the program, we might well have coded this portion of the program before coding routines SEND or DELAY. In such a case, we would probably have used index register X or Y here to store the number of bits to be shifted from the accumulator. Later on, we would have discovered the necessity of using these same registers in the routines SEND or DELAY. This is when programming discipline takes its full importance. If it is found that other routines should require the use of X and Y, one must go back in the coding and change the code in the program that precedes by using a memory location named COUNT instead of a register. Forgetting to do this is unfortunately a classical error. In that case, the other routines will accidentally destroy the contents of registers X and Y, and a severe programming error will occur. As a programming discipline, it is therefore strongly recommended *to write explicitly in the comments at the beginning of every routine which registers are changed or destroyed by this routine.* The conventions for communicating and passing information between subroutines or segments of a program should be completely clear before writing a new routine.

The left-most zeroes contained in the accumulator are ignored and its contents are shifted out until a START bit is found. Once the START bit has been found, every bit shifted out of the left of the accumulator represents either a "." or a "—" depending on whether it is "0" or "1." Once the bit shifted out of the accumulator has been identified, we will go to location SEND in order to generate the appropriate tone. Since the contents of the accumulator will be changed by the subsequent processing, they must be preserved in memory prior to going to SEND. This is the purpose of the second instruction STA CHAR.

	ADDRESS	WRITE	READ
TIMER 1	--04	T1L-L	T1C-L/ + clear T1 int flag
	--05	T1L-H + T1C-H + T1 L-L ►T1C-L + clear T1 int flag	T1C-H
	--06	T1L-L	T1L-L
	--07	T1L-H + clear T1 int flag	T1L-H
TIMER 2	--08	T2L-L	T2C-C + clear T2 int flag
	--09	T2C-H T2L-L ►T2CL + clear T2 int flag	T2C-H

Fig. 4-33: Memory Map for Timer 1

Having thus preserved the accumulator's contents at the memory location CHAR, the Index Register Y is loaded with the duration corresponding to the bit which just fell through the accumulator: a "1" if it was a dot, a "3" if it was a dash. The purpose of the STA CHAR, followed by LDA CHAR, which seems useless, is due to our desire to re-enter this program at "NEXT" with an LDA CHAR instruction.

The SEND Routine

The SEND routine uses timer 1 of the 6522 to generate the tone of set frequency. The memory map for the timer appears on Fig 4-33. The timer must first be set in the free-running mode. This is accomplished by:

```
SEND    LDA  #$C0
        STA  #A00B
```

The value C0 is deposited at address A00B which is the ACR or Control Register. It turns on bits 6 and 7 as required by the timer (see Fig 4-29 for details). The value 0400 hexadecimal is then deposited at memory addresses A006,A007:

```
LDA #$00
STA $A006
LDA #$04
STA $A007
```

These memory locations are respectively the low and the high part of the T1L or latch. It sets the frequency of the tone to be generated. 0400 hexadecimal is in binary: 00000100 00000000 or 1024. A half-period of the clock is approximately N + 2 or 1026. The period is therefore:

T = 2052 microseconds
And the frequency is N = 1 ÷ T = approximately 500 HZ

We must now start the tone and stop it after the specified duration. The tone is turned on by:

```
STA $A005
```

This instruction transfers the contents of the latch into the counter register and starts the external waveform. We have indicated that this program also turns on "manually" PB0 so that an external device such as a transmitter can be activated simultaneously with the generation of the tone in the speaker. This is accomplished by:

```
LDA #$01
STA $A000
```

It is assumed here that PB0 has been configured as an output port prior to execution of this program.

The duration of the tone is implemented by the subroutine DELAY: JSR DELAY. We will examine it below. Once the tone duration has elapsed, it must be turned off. This is accomplished by:

```
LDA #$00
STA $A00B     TURN OFF TONE
STA $A000     TURN OFF OUTPUT BIT (PB0)
```

Finally, we must leave one unit of silence between two tones. This is implemented by:

```
LDY #$01
JSR DELAY    1-PERIOD DELAY
```

Finally, we must decrement our bit counter, contained at memory location COUNT, in order to check whether any more bits need to be shifted from the accumulator. This is accomplished by:

```
DEC COUNT   8 BITS DONE?
BNE NEXT    IF NOT, GO BACK
```

Once a complete character has been transmitted, two more units of delay must be implemented to separate this character from the next one. This is accomplished by:

```
FINISH  LDY #$02
        JSR DELAY
EXIT    RTS
```

The DELAY Subroutine

This subroutine will implement a delay of: (contents of Y Register) X (SPEED) X .001 seconds. The delay will, therefore, be computed as the multiplication of three numbers. We will use here a special technique of nested loops in order to avoid performing a classical multiplication. The routine appears below:

```
DELAY      LDA SPEED
D2         LDX #$FA
D1         DEX
           BNE D1
           SEC
           SBC #$01
           BNE D2
           DEY
           BNE DELAY
           RTS
```

The corresponding flow-chart appears on Fig 4-34.

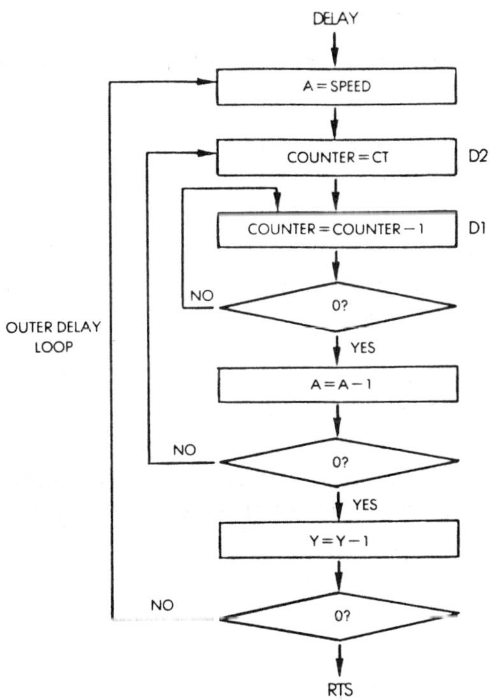

Fig. 4-34: Flow Chart for Delay

The first delay loop is the one corresponding to D1. Let us compute its duration (the time of each instruction is in parentheses):

```
(3) LDA SPEED
(2) LDX #$C6     C6 HEX = 198 DECIMAL
(2) DEX
(3) BNE D1
```

The duration of the delay introduced by these first four instructions of the program is: $3 + 2 + (2 + 3) \times 198 = 995$ microseconds.

The following two instructions are:

```
(2) SEC
(2) SBC #$01
```

Their durations are two microseconds each. These two instructions add, therefore, an additional delay of 4 microseconds. They are used to subtract 1 from the content of the accumulator. This is because both Index Registers X and Y are already used in this program as counters, so that the accumulator must be used as a third counter. Unfortunately, there is no decrement instruction which operates directly on the accumulator and a formal subtract instruction must be used. The reader will remember that the carry must be set prior to a subtract. This is the purpose of the SEC instruction prior to the SBC. The next instruction is:

```
(2/3) BNE D2
```

This is a second delay loop. Every time that the branch is successful, it requires three microseconds, and when it is not successful it requires 2 microseconds. The total delay from the entry point DELAY to this point in the subroutine is, therefore, $995 + 7 = 1002$ microseconds = 1 millisecond.

A delay of 1 millisecond will be generated every time that the loop D2 is executed. Since D2 contains the value of SPEED, these two loops are implementing a delay of SPEED × .001 second, which is what we wanted. Once this total delay of SPEED × .001 second has been achieved, one more loop is implemented using the Y Register:

```
DEY
BNE   DELAY
RTS
```

This final loop multiplies the previous delay by the value contained in Register Y. At this point, we have obtained the desired total delay Y × SPEED × .001 seconds, and we return (RTS).

Using the program. In order to use this program, it is suggested that you choose a slow transmission speed initially, unless you are familiar with Morse code, and that you generate a single character at a time. Once you see that your program works correctly, you should write a short subroutine which will feed characters to your Morse program. You can then verify that the Morse transmission proceeds correctly for any string of characters.

Exercise 4-2: *Write a subroutine which will feed your program a string of N characters contained in a table starting at address TABLE.*

Exercise 4-3: *Read the keyboard, and generate the corresponding Morse signals.*

TIME OF DAY CLOCK

We will develop here a Time of Day Clock routine which will maintain the time in hours, minutes, and seconds in three dedicated memory locations. If desired, this program could be readily extended to store fractions of a second, or any other time unit desired. The memory map for this program appears on Fig 4-35. As usual, memory locations in Page 0 (zero) are reserved for the variables. The hours, minutes, and seconds are stored respectively at memory locations 00F4 (hexadecimal), 00F5, 00F6. One more memory location is used: 00F7 contains the variable COUNT.

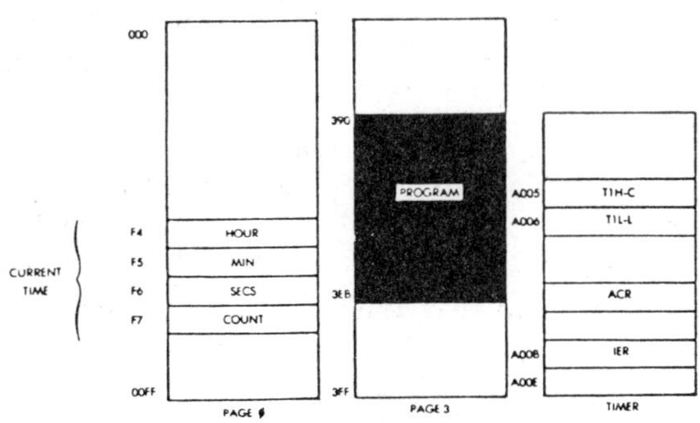

Fig. 4-35: Time-of-Day Memory Map

To start the clock, the program will be typed in, then the current 24-hour time plus one minute should be entered in locations SECS, MIN, HOUR.

Then A7 must be entered in location A67E (for SYM), and 03 in location A67F. This is an interrupt vector, and will be explained later. Finally, enter "GO 0390; then, at the exact time which has been entered in SECS, MIN, HOUR, press "CR".

The correct time will be kept from now on by the clock in SECS, MIN, HOUR.

The variable COUNT stores 20th of a second units. It is initialized with the value 20, then decremented every 20th of a second. The decrementation signal is a hardware interrupt generated by an interval timer contained in the 6522. The flow-chart for the program appears on Fig 4-36. The first phase is the initialization phase where the timer is loaded with the appropriate counter value to generate an interrupt after 50 milliseconds (1/20th of a second). Variable COUNT is initialized to the value 20, and the timer is started.

Whenever the timer times out, 1/20th of a second has elapsed and an interrupt is generated. On receiving an interrupt, the microprocessor will preserve its registers, reload the counter register of the timer with the appropriate constant for the generation of another interrupt 50 milliseconds later, and start the timer. The memory location COUNT will be decremented, since a 20th of a second has elapsed. The value of this location will be tested for the value "0." If it is not "0," exit from this routine occurs. Whenever COUNT goes through the value "0," it is reset to "20," and the memory location SECS (the number of seconds) is incremented by 1.

Every time that SECS is incremented by 1, it is checked for the value "60." If the value 60 is reached, SECS must be reset to "0" and MIN (the number of minutes) must be incremented. Similarly, MIN must be checked for the value "60." If MIN has reached "60," it is reset to "0" and the number of hours is incremented. If the number of hours reaches "24," it is reset to "0." Exit from this routine then occurs. The program will remain dormant until the next interrupt is received. In order to display the contents of this time-of-day clock, the user needs simply to examine the contents of memory locations F4, F5, and F6. A display routine could also be written to display the value of these memory locations automatically.

The program appears on Fig 4-37 and it is self-explanatory. The first segment of the program is the initialization segment INIT which sets the variable COUNT to "20" decimal = "14" hexadecimal. It

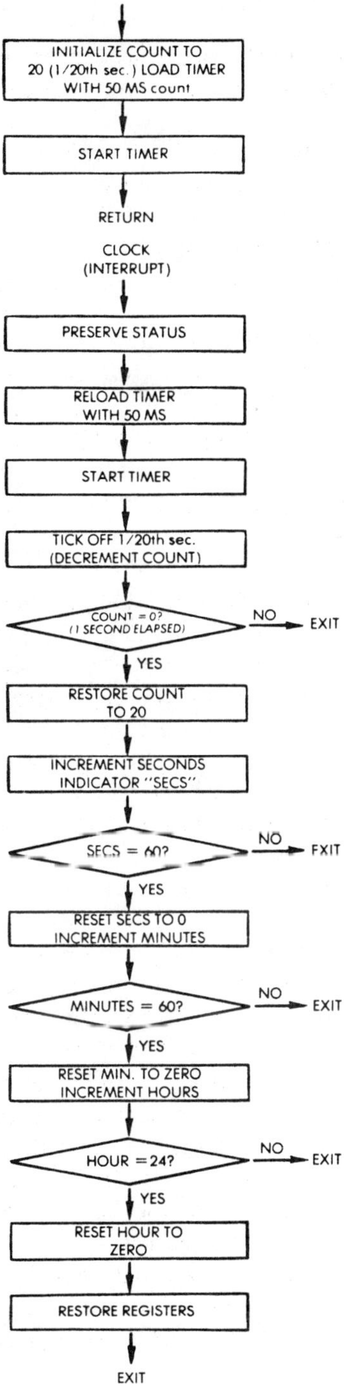

Fig. 4-36: Time-of-Day Clock

```
LOC   CODE       LINE

                 ;FIRST LOAD A7 IN LOCATION A67E, AND 03 IN A07F
0000             ;THIS IS A REAL TIME CLOCK ROUTINE WHICH MAINTAINS
0000             ;THE CURRENT TIME IN THE LOCATIONS SEC (00F6), MIN
0000             ;(00F5), AND HOUR (00F4) (24 HOUR TMEE). IT IS BRANCHED TO
0000             ;BY THE TIME OUT OF THE INTERRUPT TIMER, WHICH
0000             ;CAUSES AN INTERRUPT AND BRANCH TO THE CLOCK
0000             ;ROUTINE TWENTY TIMES PER SECOND. THE CLOCK ROUTINE
0000             ;AND INTERVAL TIMER MUST BE INITIALIZED FIRST. THE
0000             ;CODE 'INIT' DOES THIS, AND IT MUST BE BRANCHED TO TO
0000             ;START THE CLOCK. TO INITIALIZE, PUT THE CURRENT TIME
0000             ;THE CLOCK ROUTINE WILL BE STARTED IN SEC, MIN, AND
                 ;HOUR, THEN ISSUE THE COMMAND 'GO 0390 CR' AT THAT
                 ;EXACT TIME. NOTHING ELSE MUST BE DONE
0000             COUNT = $00F7          ;COUNTER FOR TWENTIETHS OF A SEC
0000             SECS = $00F6           ;CURRENT TIME
0000             MIN = $00F5
0000             HOUR = $00F4
0000             ACR = $A00B            ;TIMER MODE REGISTER
0000             TILL = $A006           ;LOW ORDER TIMER CONSTANT
0000             TIHC = $A005           ;HIGH ORDER TIMER CONSTANT
0000                     * = $0390
0390  A9 14      INIT    LDA #$14       ;SET TO FIRST TWENTY
0392  85 F7              STA COUNT      ;COUNTS
0394  8D 0B A0           STA ACR        ;SET BITS 8 AND 7 LOW
                                        ;IN ACR
0397  A9 C0              LDA #$C0       ;;SET BITS 8 AND 7 HIGH IN
0399  8D 0E A0           STA $A00E      ;THE INTERRUPT ENABLE
                                        ;REGISTER (TO ENABLE
                                        ;INTERRUPTS FROM TIMER 1)
039C  A9 50              LDA #$50       ;STORE C350 IN TIMER
039E  8D 06 A0           STA TILL       ;  (DELAY CONSTANT FOR
03A1  A9 C3              LDA #$C3       ;  50 MS)
03A3  8D 05 A0           STA TIHC       ;THIS STARTS TIMER
03A6  60                 RTS            ;RETURN TO MONITOR
03A7  08         CLOCK   PHP            ;SAVE STATUS
03A8  48                 PHA
03A9  F8                 SED
03AA  A9 50              LDA #$50       ;STORE C350 IN TIMER
03AC  8D 06 A0           STA TILL       ;  (DELAY CONSTANT FOR
03AF  A9 C3              LDA #$C3       ;  50 MS)
03B1  8D 05 A0           STA TIHC       ;THIS STARTS TIMER
03B4  C6 F7              DEC COUNT      ;DECREMENT COUNT OF
                                        ;TWENTY
03B6  D0 31              BNE EXIT       ;EXIT IF WE HAVE NOT
                                        ;COUNTED TO TWENTY YET
03B8  A9 14              LDA #$14       ;ELSE RESTORE COUNT—
03BA  85 F7              STA COUNT      ;A FULL SECOND HAS PASSED
03BC  A9 01              LDA #$01
03BE  18                 CLC
03BF  65 F6              ADC SECS       ;ADD 1 TO SEC
03C1  85 F6              STA SECS
03C3  C9 60              CMP #$60       ;SEE IF 60 SECONDS
03C5  D0 22              BNE EXIT       ;IF NOT, EXIT
03C7  A9 00              LDA #$00       ;ELSE RESET SECONDS TO 0
03C9  85 F6              STA SECS
03CB  A9 01              LDA #$01
03CD  18                 CLC
03CE  65 F5              ADC MIN        ;AND ADD 1 TO MINUTES
03D0  85 F5              STA MIN
03D2  C9 60              CMP #$60       ;SEE IF 60 MINUTES
03D4  D0 13              BNE EXIT       ;IF NOT, EXIT
03D6  A9 00              LDA #$00
03D8  85 F5              STA MIN        ;ELSE RESET MINUTES TO 0
03DA  A9 01              LDA #$01
03DC  18                 CLC
03DD  65 F4              ADC HOUR       ;AND ADD 1 TO HOUR
03DF  85 F4              STA HOUR
03E1  C9 24              CMP #$24       ;SEE IF 24 HOURS
03E3  D0 04              BNE EXIT       ;IF NOT, EXIT
03E5  A9 00              LDA #$00
03E7  85 F4              STA HOUR       ;ELSE RESET HOUR TO 0
03E9  68         EXIT    PLA            ;RESTORE STATUS
03EA  28                 PLP
03EB  40                 RTI

ERRORS = 0000 <0000>

SYMBOL TABLE

SYMBOL  VALUE

ACR     A00B    CLOCK   03A7    COUNT   00F7    EXIT    03E9
HOUR    00F4    INIT    0390    MIN     00F5    PLS     03EA
SECS    00F6    TIHC    A005    TILL    A006

END OF ASSEMBLY
```

Fig. 4-37: The Time-of-Day Program

(Full-size Listing in Appendix C)

also loads the timer with the appropriate count to generate a 50 millisecond delay. The memory map for the timer appears on Fig 4-35. Timer 1 of the 6522 is used. The table showing the bits for conditioning this device appear on Fig 4-25 and 4-29. This timer can be used in either a one-shot mode or a free-running mode. In a one-shot mode, a single interrupt (and possibly an output pulse on PB7) will be generated every time that the internal timer's counter decrements to 0 (zero). In the free-running mode, the counter will be automatically reloaded from the internal latch and continuous interrupts (and possibly a pulse on PB7) will be generated. Since the output pin PB7 is not used in this application, bit 7 of the ACR (auxiliary control register) will be set to "0". There is then a choice between a one-shot mode and a free-running mode. In the one-shot mode, the counter must be explicitly reloaded every time an interrupt is generated. In the free-running mode, the timer will automatically reload the internal counter from its latch. However, the interrupt flag must be cleared explicitly either by writing into T1C-H or by modifying the interrupt flag directly. The two options are essentially identical in terms of programming effort. The free-running mode may yield a more accurate time measurement, since the timer runs continuously and automatically going from the value "0" to the value corresponding to the 50 millisecond delay. Since a free-running mode has been used in the Morse program, we will use here a one-shot mode. The reader is encouraged to try using the alternative mode as an exercise. Using the one-shot mode is specified by setting bit ACR6 to "0". All other bits of the ACR register are not used here and will be set to "0". Bits 7 and 8 are set to "0" in ACR, specifying the one-shot mode with PB7 disabled.

Next, the interrupt flags register must be properly conditioned. When read, this register is viewed as the Interrupt Flag Register, IFR. When written into, it is called the Interrupt Enable Register, IER. In order to set specific bits of the IER, bit 7 of IER must be set to 1. For each "1" specified in register locations 0 through 6, a "1" will be written in the register, enabling the appropriate condition. A "0" in any bit position will not clear the specified bit position in the IER register, but leave the contents unchanged. Clearing is accomplished by specifying a "0" in bit position 7 and then specifying a "1" for every bit position that needs to be cleared. In this instance, we simply want to enable an interrupt from timer T1. We will therefore write at the memory location corresponding to IER the value "11000000," or "C0" hexadecimal (see Chapter 2 for detail).

Finally, we must load the appropriate constant in the timer to generate the delay which will generate and interrupt after 50 milliseconds. The value C350 hexadecimal (=50,000 decimal) is therefore loaded into the counter. It will be noted in the routine INIT that first the low part of the latch is loaded, then the high part of the counter is loaded. Loading into the high part of the counter results in transferring the lower part of the latch automatically to the lower part of the counter and starting the timer at the same time.

The INIT subroutine appears below:

```
COUNT  = $00F7      1/20 THS OF A SECOND
SECS   = $00F6
MIN    = $00F5
HOUR   = $00F4
ACR    = $A00B      TIMER MODE REGISTER
T1LL   = $A006      LOW ORDER TIMER CT
T1CH   = $A005      HIGH ORDER TIMER CT

INIT   LDA #$14     FIRST 20 COUNTS
       STA COUNT
       STA ACR      BITS 8 AND 7 LOW IN ACR
       LDA #$C0     BITS 8 AND 7 HIGH
       STA $A00E    IN INTERRUPT ENABLE  REGISTER
       LDA #$50     STORE C350 IN TIMER
       STA T1LL     (CT FOR 50 MS)
       LDA #$C3
       STA T1CH     START TIMER
       RTS
```

The initialization has now been completed, and the main program is executed from location CLOCK on. It will be noted that all additions within the routine CLOCK are performed in decimal mode. This is why the decimal flag is set with instruction SED. This way, when displaying the contents of the memory locations, they will be displayed one digit per LED in the usual decimal manner rather than in hexadecimal format.

Following execution of the INIT subroutine, a return occurs to the monitor. Provided no key is touched on the keyboard, nothing will happen until an interrupt time-out occurs. Upon detection of the interrupt, an automatic branch will occur to the clock. Whenever an interrupt occurs in the 6502, it branches automatically to memory location FFFE,FFFF where it finds the interrupt vector, i.e., the next address to be installed in the program counter register. On the SYM, the user pre-loads memory locations A67E and A67F with the desired interrupt vector. The SYM monitor, which is in execution at all times that the user program is not running, duplicates automatically the contents of memory locations A600 through A67F at addresses FF80 to FFFF. Thus, the contents of A67E and A67F are automatically copied by the SYM monitor to memory addresses FFFE, FFFF. At the time the interrupt occurs, it will branch to FFFE, FFFF, and it will find there the 16 bit contents to be installed in the program counter register.

CLOCK is the interrupt routine which is entered every time the interrupt is received. It saves the registers P (the status register) and A (the accumulator). It does not need to save the other registers as it will not be needing them.

It then reloads the timer counter with the value C350 hexadecimal = 50,000 decimal and starts the timer again. Loading the counter automatically clears the previous interrupt.

The routine then checks successively whether the variable COUNT has reached the value "20", the variable SECS has reached the value "60", the variable MIN has reached the value "60", or the variable HOUR has reached the value "24". If any one of these variables has reached its limit value, it is reset to "0", as indicated in the flow-chart of Fig 4-36, or the program of Fig 4-37.

Finally, the routine exits by restoring the two registers it had saved, A and P, and executing an RTI (Return From Interrupt).

A HOME CONTROL PROGRAM

A generalized home control program will monitor the status of a Time of Day Clock, as well as the status of an alarm system, and take various actions depending on the time of the day or on the alarm condition detected. We will use here the time of day clock program which has been developed above, display the time of the day, then depending upon the time of the day, specific actions will be taken by closing one or more relays. The program appears on Fig 4-38. The data-direction register of Port B is set to 0F hexadecimal in order to enable the four low order bits for output (for the relays). Clearly, only those bit positions actually connected to relays should be specified as outputs. The others should remain inputs. As usual, as a precaution, an explicit instruction is included in the program to turn the relays off. This is performed by depositing the value 00 hexadecimal at the memory location for IORB (Address AC00).

Two built-in routines of the SYM monitor are used by this program to facilitate the output. The accumulator is loaded from memory loca-

```
LOC    CODE       LINE

0000              ;THIS IS A SIMPLE HOME CONTROL ROUTINE WHICH RUNS
0000              ;THROUGH A LOOP. EACH TIME THROUGH IT DISPLAYS THE
0000              ;CURRENT TIME AND BRANCHES TO A NUMBER OF USER
                  SUBROUTINES
0000              ;WHICH SERVICE DEVICES.
0000              ;EXAMPLES:
0000              ;1) A SUBROUTINE COULD CHECK THE CURRENT TIME AND
0000              ;   TURN ON A LIGHT IF THE TIME WERE RIGHT.
0000              ;2) A SUBROUTINE COULD MONITOR THE STATUS OF AN
0000              ;   ALARM SYSTEM AND TAKE APPROPRIATE ACTION IF AN
0000              ;   INTRUDER WERE DETECTED.
0000              DDRB = $AC02
0000              IORB = $AC00
0000              HOUR = $00F4
0000              MIN = $00F5
0000              OUTBYT = $82FA
0000              SCAND = $8906
0000                      * = $0200
0200   D8         CONTRL  CLD                  ;
0201   A9 0F              LDA #$0F             ;SET DATA DIRECTION
0203   8D 02 AC           STA DDRB             ;REGISTER TO OUTPUT FOR
                                               RELAYS
0206   A9 00              LDA #$00
0208   8D 00 AC           STA IORB             ;TURN OFF RELAYS
020B   A5F4       LOOP    LDA HOUR             ;THIS IS THE MAIN CONTROL
                                               LOOP
020D   20 FA 82           JSR OUTBYT           ;OUTPUT CURRENT HOUR TO
                                               DISPLAY
0210   A5 F5              LDA MIN
0212   20 FA 82           JSR OUTBYT           ;OUTPUT CURRENT MINUTE
                                               TO DISPLAY
0215   20 06 89           JSR SCAND            ;REFRESH (LIGHT) DISPLAY
                                               WITH TIME
0218   EA                 .BYTE $EA,$EA,$EA
0219   EA
021A   EA
021B   EA                 .BYTE $EA,$EA,$EA  \
021C   EA                                    |
021D   EA                                    |
021E   EA                 .BYTE $EA,$EA,$EA  |
021F   EA                                    |
0220   EA                                    |
0221   EA                 .BYTE $EA,$EA,$EA  |
0222   EA                                    |
0223   EA                                    |
0224   EA                 .BYTE $EA,$EA,$EA  |
0225   EA                                    |  ;THE USER CAN PLACE
                                             |  JUMPS TO
0226   EA                                    >  ;SUBROUTINES HERE TO SER-
                                             |  VICE DEVICES
0227   EA                 .BYTE $EA,$EA,$EA  |
0228   EA                                    |
0229   EA                                    |
022A   EA                 .BYTE $EA,$EA,$EA  |
022B   EA                                    |
022C   EA                                    |
022D   EA                 .BYTE $EA,$EA,$EA  |
022E   EA                                    |
022F   EA                                    |
0230   EA                 .BYTE $EA,$EA,$EA  /
0231   EA
0232   EA
0233   EA                 .BYTE $EA,$EA,$EA
0234   EA
0235   EA
0236   4C 0B 02           JMP LOOP
0239

ERRORS = 0000<0000>
```

Fig. 4-38: Home Control Program (Full-size Listing in Appendix C)

```
SYMBOL TABLE

SYMBOL   VALUE

CONTRL   0200     DDRB   AC02     HOUR     00F4     IORB    AC00
LOOP     020B     MIN    00F5     OUTBYT   82FA     SCAND   8906

END OF ASSEMBLY
```

Fig 4-38: Home Control Program (continued)

tion HOUR which contains the time-of-day expressed in hours (see the time of day routine), then a call is made to subroutine OUTBYT which results in displaying the HOUR on the board's display. Similarly, the minutes are displayed by loading the accumulator from memory location MIN and calling OUTBYT.

The OUTBYT routine is contained at memory location 82FA of the monitor and displays the contents of A as two hex digits. Next, the routine SCAND of the monitor (at memory address 8906) is used to scan the display once. Once the time has been displayed, an appropriate jump instruction will be executed if some set condition is met. Since these conditions will vary with each application, they have been left blank in the program and should be filled in by the reader. As an exercise, it is suggested that the relays be turned on at 2 or 3 specified times a few minutes apart. The noise made by the relays when closing indicates that the program is working correctly. This should be done prior to attaching any actual device to the relays.

A TELEPHONE DIALER

We will develop here a program capable of dialing a number once it has been deposited in the memory. With a regular telephone (rotary dial), pulses are merely sent on the line. This should be simple at this point, and we are going to develop here a program capable of generat-

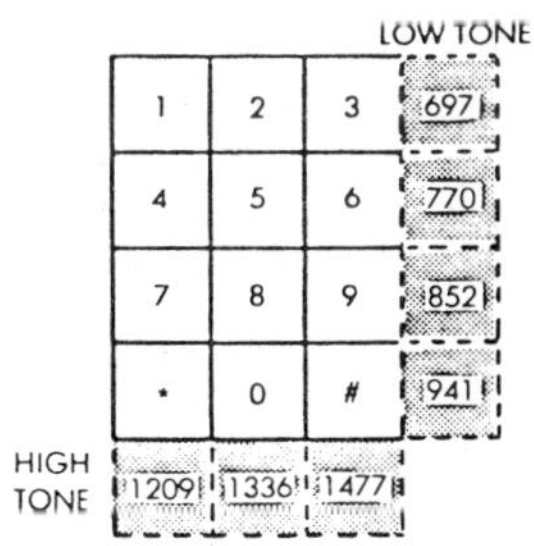

Fig. 4-39: The Telephone Frequencies

ing the tone frequencies used in the U.S. for touch phones. The table of telephone frequencies appears on Fig 4-39. Each digit will cause two tones to be generated. The various frequencies have been chosen carefully by the telephone company in order to avoid the possibility of spurious harmonics, and to use the smallest bandwidth possible. They range from 697 Hertz to 1477 Hertz as indicated on the illustration.

Our program will generate two tones simultaneously, which will be fed into the same speaker. The frequencies will have to be accurate in

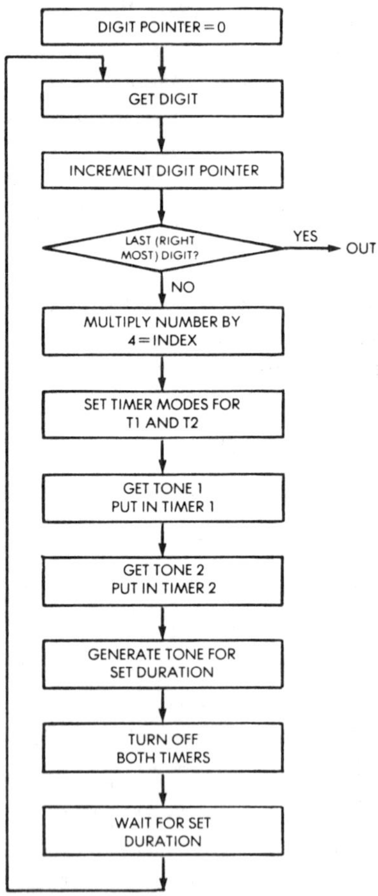

Fig. 4-40: Phone Dialer Flow Chart

order to be recognized by the telephone switching equipment. This result can be obtained by using two timers. We will use here Timer A and Timer B of our microprocessor board. Each timer will generate a frequency, and the output of both timers will be sent to the loudspeaker. For more reliable results, the use of an operational amplifier for the speaker is strongly recommended. However, the program would remain unchanged. The flow-chart for the program appears on Fig 4-40. The number of digits for the telephone number is irrelevant. This program will accommodate a telephone number of any length. The first digit to be "dialed" is obtained from the memory. An equivalence table is kept in memory, which specifies the periods for the two tones to be generated for each digit. More precisely, this table specifies the *half period,* and since two tones are associated with every digit, this table will use four bytes for every digit. The value of the digit must therefore be multiplied by four in order to be used as an index to this table.

The two table values will be obtained and loaded respectively in Timer A and Timer B which will be started. The two tones will then be generated automatically for a specified duration (say half a second or one second). Then a silence interval will be enforced, and the next digit will be fetched from memory. The process will be repeated until all digits have been dialed. The flow-chart is straightforward. Let us examine now the program. The complete program is shown on Fig 4-41.

```
LOC   CODE    LINE

0000          ;THIS IS A PROGRAM WHICH DIALS PRE STORED
0000          ;TELEPHONE NUMBERS. IT PRODUCES A TWO TONE OUTPUT
0000          ;THROUGH A SPEAKER HOOKED UP IN CONFIGURATION 2
0000          ;(TWO TONES—SEE SPEAKER). THESE TONES WILL ACTIVATE
0000          ;A STANDARD TOUCH TONE PHONE WHEN THE SPEAKER IS
0000          ;PLACED DIRECTLY OVER THE MOUTH PIECE OF THE TELE-
0000          ;PHONE. TO USE THE PROGRAM, PLACE THE PHONE
0000          ;NUMBER(S) ANYWHERE IN MEMORY, ONE DIGIT PER BYTE,
0000          ;AND ENDING WITH OF (HEX). FOR EXAMPLE, THE NUMBER
0000          ;555-1212 WOULD BE 05 05 05 01 02 01 02 0F (ALL HEX) IN
0000          ;MEMORY. THEN PLACE THE ADDRESS OF THE NUMBER,
0000          ;LOW BYTE FIRST, IN THE LOCATIONS 00C0 AND 00C1.
0000          ;THEN EITHER GO TO THIS ROUTINE FROM THE MONITOR
              ;OR JSR TO IT FROM ANOTHER PROGRAM.
0000          NUMPTR = $00C0        ;THIS POINTS TO THE ADDRESS OF
                                    ;THE TELEPHONE NUMBER
0000          ONDEL = $40           ;THIS IS THE DELAY CONSTANT FOR
                                    ;THE TIME WHEN THE
0000          OFFDEL = $20          ;DELAY CONSTANT FOR THE TIME
                                    ;WHEN THE TONES ARE 0
0000          DELCON = $FF          ;GENERAL PURPOSE DELAY
                                    ;CONSTANT
0000          ACR1 = $A00B          ;THESE ARE THE TIMER MODE
                                    ;REGISTERS (TIMER 1)
0000          ACR2 = $AC0B          ;(TIMER 2)
0000          T1CH = $A005          ;THIS IS THE TIMER 1 COUNTER
                                    ;(HIGH BYTE)
0000          T1LH = $A007          ;TIMER 1 LATCH (HIGH BYTE)
0000          T1LL = $A004          ;   (LOW BYTE)
0000          T2CH = $AC05          ;SAME AS TIMER 1 — FOR TIMER 2
0000          T2LH = $AC07
0000          T2LL = $AC04
0000                 * = $0300
0300  A0 00   PHONE  LDY #$00              ;INDEX FOR DIGITS OF
                                           ;PHONE NUMBER
0302  B1 C0   DIGIT  LDA (NUMPTR), Y       ;GET DIGIT
0304  C8             INY
0305  C9 0F          CMP #$0F              ;SEE IF END OF PHONE
                                           ;NUMBER
```

Fig 4-41: Phone Dialer Program
(Full-size Listing in Appendix C)

```
0307   D0 01                     BNE NOEND
0309   60                        RTS               ;RETURN IS SO (TO
                                                   ;MONITOR OR CALLING
                                                   ;PROGRAM)
030A   0A EA EA        NOEND     ASL A             ;MULTIPLY NUMBER BY
                                                   ;FOUR TO INDEX TABLE
030D   0A EA EA                  ASL A             ;  (EACH TABLE ENTRY IS
                                                   ;  4 BYTES)
0310   AA                        TAX               ;X = INDEX FOR TABLE
0311   A9 C0                     LDA #$C0
0313   8D 0B A0                  STA ACR1          ;SET TIMER MODE TO FREE
                                                   ;RUNNING ON BOTH TIMERS
0316   8D 0B AC                  STA ACR2
0319   BD 5D 03                  LDA TABLE,X       ;GET LOW ORDER, FIRST
                                                   ;TONE
031C   8D 04 A0                  STA T1LL          ;STORE IN TIMER 1
031F   E8                        INX
0320   BD 5D 03                  LDA TABLE,X       ;GET HIGH ORDER, FIRST
                                                   ;TONE
0323   8D 07 A0                  STA T1LH          ;STORE TIMER 1
0326   8D 05 A0                  STA T1CH          ;THIS STARTS TIMER 1
                                                   ;GOING
0329   E8                        INX
032A   BD 5D 03                  LDA TABLE,X       ;GET LOW ORDER, SECOND
                                                   ;TONE
032D   8D 04 AC                  STA T2LL          ;STORE IN TIMER 2
0330   E8                        INX
0331   BD 5D 03                  LDA TABLE,X       ;GET HIGH ORDER, SECOND
                                                   ;TONE
0334   8D 07 AC                  STA T2LH          ;STORE IN TIMER 2
0337   8D 05 AC                  STA T2CH          ;THIS STARTS TIMER 2
                                                   ;GOING
033A   A2 40                     LDX #ONDEL        ;GET TONES-ON DELAY
                                                   ;CONSTANT
033C   20 55 03        ON        JSR DELAY         ;DELAY WHILE TONE IS ON
033F   CA                        DEX
0340   DO FA                     BNE ON
0342   A9 00                     LDA #$00
0344   8D 0B A0                  STA ACR1          ;TURN BOTH TIMERS OFF
0347   8D 0B AC                  STA ACR2
034A   A2 20                     LDX #OFFDEL       ;GET TONES-OFF DELAY
                                                   ;CONSTANT
034C   20 55 03        OFF       JSR DELAY         ;DELAY WHILE TONE IS OFF
034F   CA                        DEX
0350   D0 FA                     BNE OFF
0352   4C 02 03                  JMP DIGIT         ;GO BACK FOR NEXT DIGIT
                                                   ;OF PHONE NUMBER
0355                   ;
0355                   ;THIS IS A SIMPLE DELAY ROUTINE FOR THE TONE ON AND
                       ;OFF PERI
0355                   ;
0355   A9 FF           DELAY     LDA #DELCON       ;GET DELAY CONSTANT
0357   38              WAIT      SEC               ;DELAY FOR THAT LONG
0358   E9 01                     SBC #$01
035A   D0 FB                     BNE WAIT
035C   60                        RTS
035D                   ;
035D                   ;THIS IS A TABLE OF THE CONSTANTS FOR THE TONE
035D                   ;FREQUENCIES FOR EACH TELEPHONE DIGIT. THE
035D                   ;CONSTANTS ARE TWO BYTES LONG, LOW BYTE FIRST.
035D                   ;
035D   13              TABLE     .BYTE $13,$02,$76,$01   ;TWO TONES FOR '0'
035E   02
035F   76
0360   01
0361   CD                        .BYTE $CD,$02,$9E,$01   ;TWO TONES FOR '1'
0362   02
0363   9E
0364   01
0365   CD                        .BYTE $CD,$02,$76,$01   ;    '2'
0366   02
0367   76
0368   01
0369   CD                        .BYTE $CD,$02,$53,$01   ;    '3'
036A   02
036B   53
036C   01
036D   89                        .BYTE $89,$02,$9E,$01   ;    '4'
036E   02
036F   9E
0370   01
0371   89                        .BYTE $89,$02,$76,$01   ;    '5'
0372   02
0373   76
0374   01
0375   89                        .BYTE $89,$02,$53,$01   ;    '6'
0376   02
0377   53
0378   01
0379   4B                        .BYTE $4B,$02,$9E,$01   ;    '7'
037A   02
037B   9E
037C   01
037D   4B                        .BYTE $4B,$02,$76,$01   ;    '8'
037F   02
037E   76
0380   01
0381   4B                        .BYTE $4B,$02,$53,$01   ;    '9'
```

Fig 4-41: Phone Dialer Program (continued)

```
0087    0382    02
0087    0383    53
0087    0384    01
0088    0385                    .END

ERRORS = 0000 <0000>

SYMBOL TABLE

SYMBOL    VALUE

ACR1      A00B     ACR2     AC0B     DELAY    0355     DELCON   00FF
DIGIT     0302     NOEND    030A     NUMPTR   00C0     OFF      034C
OFFDEL    0020     ON       033C     ONDEL    0040     PHONE    0300
T1CH      A005     T1LH     A007     T1LL     A004     T2CH     AC05
T2LH      AC07     T2LL     AC04     TABLE    035D     WAIT     0357

END OF ASSEMBLY
```

Fig 4-41: Phone Dialer Program (continued)

Register Y is used as a pointer to the current digit of the telephone number being dialed. It is first initialized to 0:

```
PHONE     LDY     #$00
```

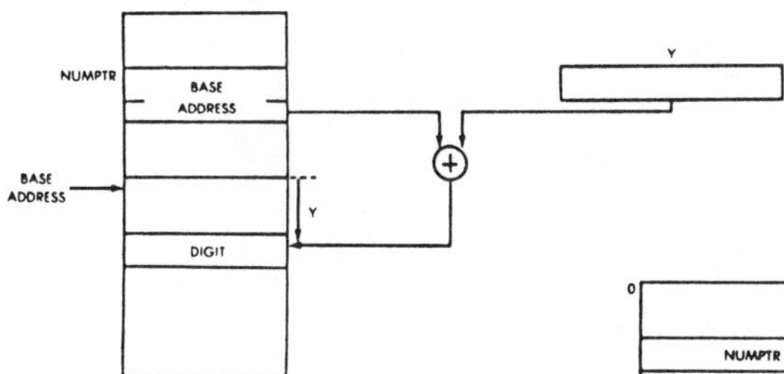

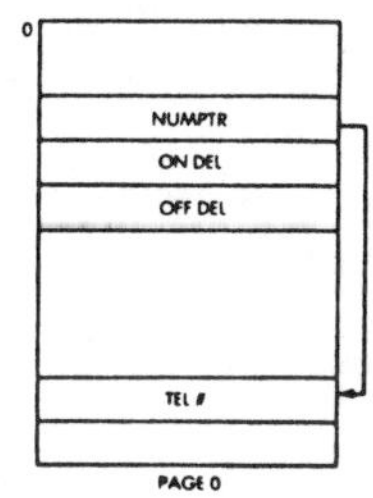

Fig 4-42: Telephone Dialer: Indirect Indexed Access (top) and Memory Map (bottom)

Next, the digit is obtained, using an indirect indexed addressing technique (see Fig 4-42). It is assumed that the complete telephone number has been stored sequentially starting at address "NUMPTR", and is terminated by the value "0F", which indicates the end of the telephone number.

```
DIGIT     LDA     (NUMPTR), Y   GET DIGIT
```

The index register Y is then incremented, so that it will point to the next digit the next time around. We check if the last digit ("0F") has been found, and, if so, the program terminates:

```
        INY
        CMP    #$0F
        BNE    NOEND
        RTS
```

We will assume that we have not yet reached the last digit of the telephone number, and we will proceed. The value of the digit itself must be multiplied by four since we have already pointed out that the equivalence table between the digits and the half periods contains four bytes per entry. The multiplication by four will be performed by two successive left shifts. The result will then be stored in register X so that it can be used as an index:

```
NOEND   ASL    A
        ASL    A
        TAX
```

Next, both Timer A and Timer B are set to the free running mode:

```
        LDA    #$C0
        STA    ACR1
        STA    ACR2
```

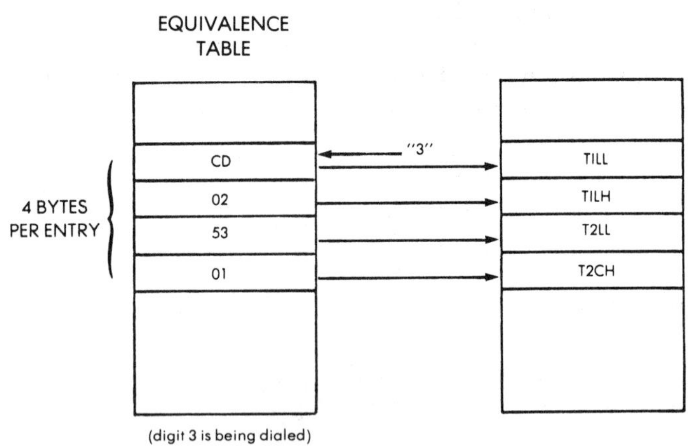

Fig. 4-43: Loading the Timer

They are then loaded each with the half-period retrieved from the equivalence table (see Fig 4-43):

```
        LDA    TABLE, X
        STA    T1LL
        INX
```

```
        LDA  TABLE, X
        STA  TILH
        STA  TICH
        INX
        LDA  TABLE, X
        STA  T2LL
        INX
        LDA  TABLE, X
        STA  T2LH
        STA  T2CH
```

Once both timers have been actuated, the tone must simply be generated for a set period of time. This duration is specified here by the value ONDEL. The required delay is obtained by the subroutine DELAY, and a secondary "ON" loop.

```
        LDX  #ONDEL
ON      JSR  DELAY
        DEX
        BNE  ON
```

Finally, once the tone has been generated for the correct duration, both timers are simply turned off:

```
        LDA  #$00
        STA  ACR1
        STA  ACR2
```

then a delay of silence is generated:

```
        LDX  #OFFDEL
OFF     JSR  DELAY
        DEX
        BNE  OFF
```

and the program returns to the beginning in order to generate the tones corresponding to the next digit:

```
        JMP  DIGIT
```

The DELAY routine is a classical one:

```
DELAY    LDA    #DELCON
WAIT     SEC
         SBC    #$01
         BNE    WAIT
         RTS
```

The equivalence table which specifies the half-period equivalence for the tones to be generated appears at the end of the program on Fig 4-41.

Let us compute here the half periods corresponding to each of the frequencies which have been generated. Seven frequencies must be generated: 697, 770, 852, 941, 1209, 1336, 1477.

As an example, for a frequency N = 697Hz, the corresponding period is 1/N = 1434.7 microseconds. The half period is therefore 717 microseconds or 02CD hexadecimal.

DESIRED FREQUENCY	HALF PERIOD	N=HALF PERIOD − 1.7	HEX for Ex. 4-4
697	717.3	716	02CC
770	649.3	648	0288
852	586.8	585	0249
941	531.3	530	0212
1209	413.5	412	019C
1336	374.2	372	0174
1477	338.5	337	0151

Fig. 4-44: Computing the Timer Constants

Similarly, the half periods for the other frequencies appear on Fig 4-44. The corresponding hexadecimal values have been used in the program of Fig 4-41.

Let us now examine some possible improvements to this basic program.

Exercise 4-4: *Some improvement is possible as to the precision with* *which the frequencies are generated. Referring to chapter 2 of this book or else to a hardware manual, you will notice that Timer 1 in free-running mode does not generate a tone of exactly the expected frequency. In fact, it adds either 1.5 microseconds or 2 microseconds to the half-period value that has been loaded in the counter register. Recompute the half frequencies that should be used assuming that both Timer 1 and Timer 2 add on the average 1.75 microseconds to every half-period.*

***Note:** Don't look yet, but the answer is on Fig. 4-44.*

***Exercise 4-5:** This program can also be improved functionally by adding a programmable "silence" symbol. This is useful in some countries for international dialing or within a company to obtain access to an outside line. One must first dial some digits to get a line then wait for a specified duration before dialing the actual number. Incorporate this change in the above program.*

A hardware improvement for cleaner frequencies is shown below.

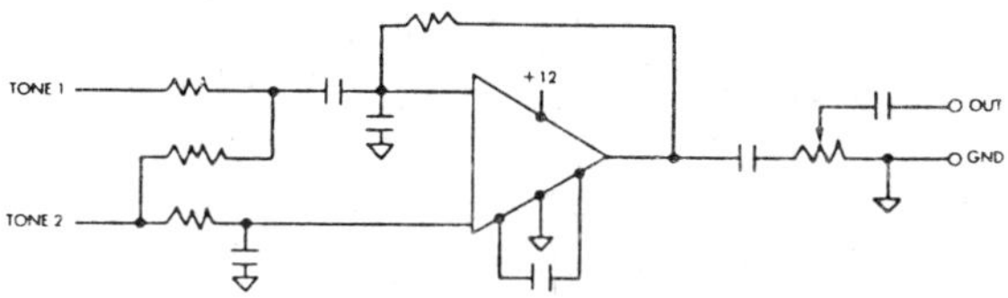

Fig 4-45: Suggested Hardware Improvement for Cleaner Frequencies

SECTION 2: COMBINATIONS OF TECHNIQUES

INTRODUCTION

The programs presented in this section will use a combination of the techniques presented in this chapter and will be developed for the KIM board. The only significant difference between KIM and SYM for the purposes of these exercises will be the location of the PIO's in the memory map. The interested reader is referred to Fig 2-4 for the actual KIM memory map. Since the programs are written in assembly-level language using symbolic labels and operands, most of them would be identical for SYM. It is only during the assembly process (either through an automatic assembler such as the one presented in Appendix A, or through manual assembly), i.e., at the time the hexadecimal representation for the instructions is generated, that differences will appear due to the differences in memory assignments.

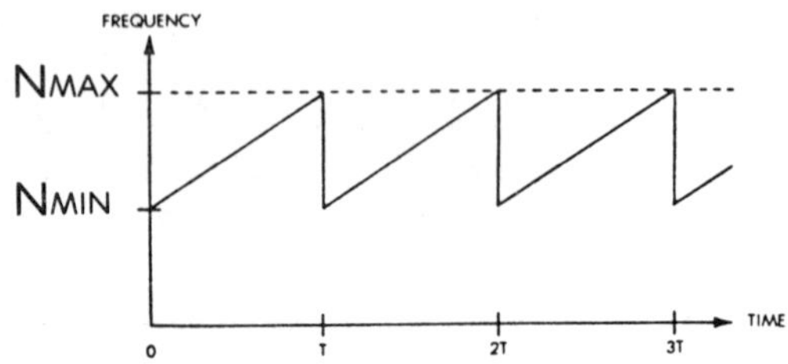

Fig. 4-46: A Siren Sound

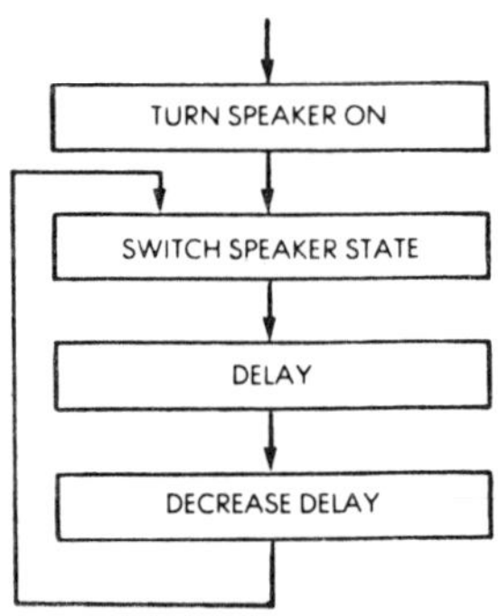

Fig. 4-47: Siren Flow Chart - Up Ramp

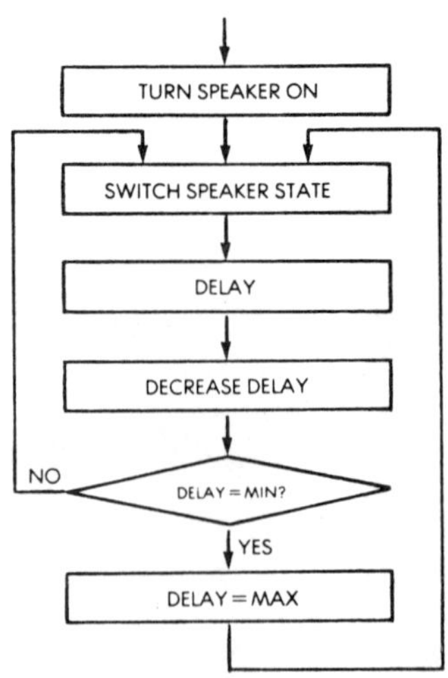

Fig. 4-48: Stopping at Nmax

GENERATING A SIREN SOUND

The graphic representation of a siren sound is shown on Fig 4-46. This sound starts at the minimum frequency N_{min}, and increases during time T up to a maximum value called N_{max}. The tone frequency drops then instantaneously to N_{min} and resumes its upward progression until time 2T, and so on. The flow-chart for generating a sound of increasing frequencies is shown on Fig 4-47. In addition, the maximum frequency should not exceed N_{max}, or else the sound will become inaudible (or else cannot be generated by the speaker any more). The flow-chart for repeatedly generating the ramp is shown on Fig 4-48.

The program is shown on Fig 4-49. It approximates the shape of Fig 4-46.

```
                        ;SIREN
                        ;
                        PA         =$1700
                        PAD        =$1701
                        ;
0000: FF                DELAY     .BYT $FF
                                  .=$40
0040: A9 01                        LDA #$01
0042: 8D 01 17                     STA PAD
0045: 8D 00 17                     STA PA
0048: EE 00 17          SWITCH     INC PA
004B: A6 00                        LDX DELAY
004D: CA                LOOP       DEX
004E: D0 FD                        BNE LOOP
0050: C6 00                        DEC DELAY
0052: 4C 48 00                     JMP SWITCH
                        ;

SYMBOL TABLE:
 PA          1700          PAD        1701          DELAY        0000
 SWITCH      0048          LOOP       004D
DONE
```

Fig 4-49: Siren program for the flow chart of Fig 4-47

The speaker is attached to the IORA register (memory address 1700), in bit position zero. It can be attached directly. For a better sound, the circuit of Fig 4-50 is recommended. The data direction register DDRA for this PIO must first be configured so that bit zero is an output:

```
LDA   #$01
STA   PAD      DDRA
```

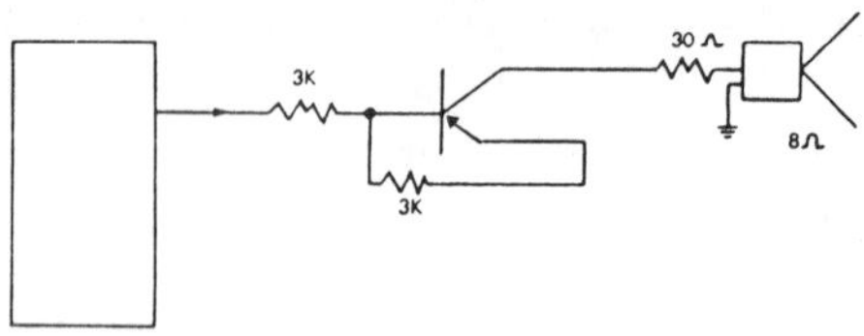

Fig. 4-50: Connecting a Speaker (Improved)

The speaker can then be turned on. Turning the speaker on and off can be easily accomplished by a programming trick. This consists of using the INC instruction. This instruction will increment the contents of the designated register and will generate successive numbers which will be alternately odd and even. This guarantees that the right-most bit (bit 0, to which the speaker is connected) will switch from the value zero to the value one. This allows turning the speaker on and off with only a single instruction, versus two if a different pattern had to be loaded in the accumulator and then transferred to the ORA. Let us turn the speaker off. The speaker will remain off for a duration specified by the constant "DELAY." The delay loop is the following:

```
         STA   PA      INITIAL VALUE IN ORA
SWITCH   INC   PA
         LDX   DELAY
LOOP     DEX
         BNE   LOOP
```

Once the value DELAY has been used, it is decremented:

```
         DEC   DELAY
```

This way, the next time around, the delay value will be smaller and the tone will be higher in pitch. The speaker must now be switched:

```
         JMP   SWITCH
```

The program above implements the upramp of the siren sound as shown on flow chart 4-47.

Exercise 4-7: Complete the program as per the flow-chart of Fig 4-48 to generate successive upramps, and generate a true siren sound.

Exercise 4-8: *Write a siren program which goes up in pitch, then down, then up again, etc.*

SENSING AN INPUT PULSE

In this program, a switch will be depressed and the program must measure the duration during which the switch is held down, then beep n times through the loudspeaker, where n is the time during which the switch was depressed, expressed in seconds. The speaker is connected to bit 0 of the IORA as in the preceding program. The switch is connected to bit 7 of the IORA, for easy detection. The connection is illustrated on Fig 4-51.

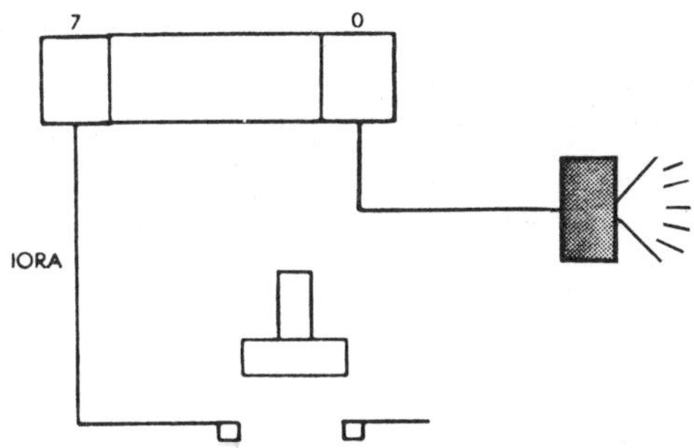

Fig. 4-51: Connecting Switch and Speaker

The flow-chart for the program is shown on Fig 4-52. The delay duration during which the key is pressed is measured in units of .25 seconds, then converted into seconds. The speaker is then activated and timed.

The program is shown on Fig 4-53. It follows the previous flow-chart and should be self-explanatory.

PULSE MEASUREMENT

In this program, the time during which the key was depressed will be measured, and a sound will be generated. The number of beeps

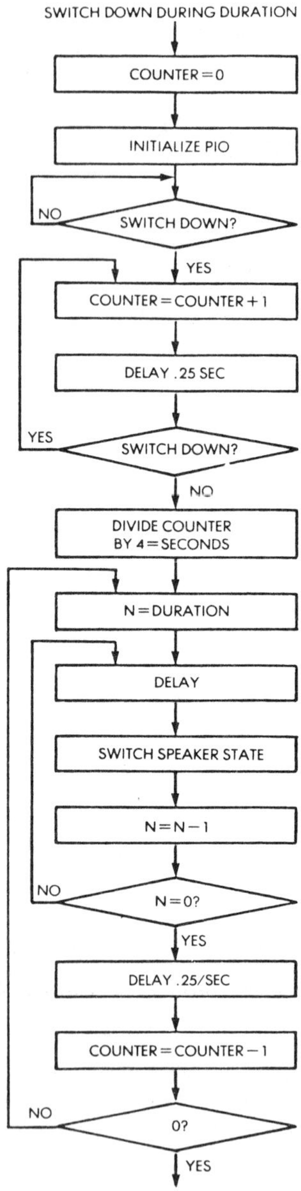

Notes
- COUNTER holds "n" (number of beeps).
- N is a duration.

Fig. 4-52: Detailed Flow Chart

```
                    T          =$00
                    PA         =$1700
                    PAD        =$1701
                    ;
                              .=$40
0040: A9 01                LDA #01
0042: 8D 01 17             STA PAD          ;PAO IS OUTPUT
0045: A9 00                LDA #0
0047: 85 00                STA T
0049: 8D 00 17             STA PA
004C: AD 00 17  POL        LDA PA
004F: 30 FB                BMI POL          ;SWITCH UP?
0051: E6 00     CPT        INC T
0053: A2 3D                LDX #$3D         ;.25 SEC DELAY
0055: A0 00     BL2        LDY #0
0057: C8        BL1        INY
0058: D0 FD                BNE BL1
005A: E8                   INX
005B: D0 F8                BNE BL2
005D: AD 00 17             LDA PA
0060: 10 EF                BPL CPT
                ;SWITCH IS UP: RING SPEAKER ONCE.
0062: 46 00                LSR T            ;DIVIDE BY FOUR
0064: 46 00                LSR T
0066: A9 00     SOUND      LDA #0
0068: A2 80                LDX #$80
006A: A0 00     CL2        LDY #00
006C: C8        CL1        INY
006D: D0 FD                BNE CL1
006F: 49 01                EOR #1
0071: 8D 00 17             STA PA
0074: E8                   INX
0075: D0 F3                BNE CL2
                ;NEW 1/4 SECOND DELAY
0077: A2 3D                LDX #$3D
0079: A0 00     DL2        LDY #00
007B: C8        DL1        INY
007C: D0 FD                BNE DL1
007E: E8                   INX
007F: D0 F8                BNE DL2
0081: C6 00                DEC T
0083: 10 F1                BPL SOUND
0085: 00                   BRK


SYMBOL TABLE:
 T            0000        PA          1700        PAD         1701
 POL          004C        CPT         0051        BL2         0055
 BL1          0057        SOUND       0066        CL2         006A
 CL1          006C        DL2         0079        DL1         007B

DONE
```

Fig 4-53: Switch Closure Measurement Program

should be proportional to the duration of the switch closure.

The flow-chart for this program is essentially analogous to the previous one and it is shown on Fig 4-54. The corresponding program is shown on Fig 4-55.

This program uses the DELAY subroutine which measures a .25 second delay. The flow-chart for this subroutine is shown on Fig 4-56. The corresponding program is shown on Fig 4-57.

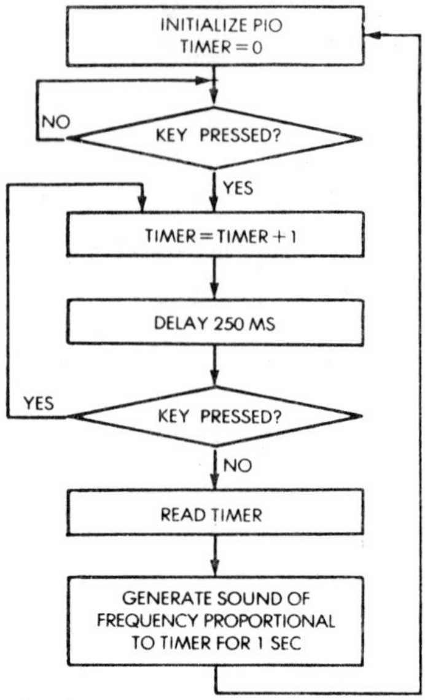

Fig. 4-54: Switch Time Measure

```
                    PA       =$1700
                    PAD      =$1701
                    DL250    =$0090
                    FREQ     =$00C0
                    ;
                             .=00
0000: 00            T        .BYT $00
                    ;
                             .=$40
0040: A9 00                  LDA #00
0042: 85 00                  STA T          ;INIT TIME
0044: 8D 00 17               STA PA
0047: A9 01                  LDA #01
0049: 8D 01 17               STA PAD        ;BIT 0 OUT
004C: AD 00 17      POL      LDA PA         ;POLLING...
004F: 30 FB                  BMI POL        ;NOT PRESSED,
0051: E6 00         CPT      INC T          ;INCREMENT TIME
0053: 20 90 00               JSR DL250      ;250 MS DELAY.
0056: AD 00 17               LDA PA
0059: 10 F6                  BPL CPT
005B: A5 00         HERE     LDA T
005D: 0A                     ASL A          ;MPY BY TWO
005E: 0A                     ASL A          ;MPY BY TWO AGAIN
005F: 20 C0 00               JSR FREQ       ;MAKE TONE.
0062: 4C 5B 00               JMP HERE

SYMBOL TABLE:
 PA          1700        PAD         1701        DL250       0090
 FREQ        00C0        T           0000        POL         004C
 CPT         0051        HERE        005B
DONE
```

Fig 4-55: The Switch Time Measurement Program: Tone Generation

```
                    ;MAKES A TONE, USES REG. A
                    ;ASSUMES PA SET FOR OUTPUT,
                    ;FREQUENCY CONSTANT IN REG. A ON ENTRY
                    ;
                    PA       =$1700
                    F        =$BF
                    ;
                            .=$C0
00C0: 85 BF         FREQ     STA F
00C2: A9 00                  LDA #0
00C4: A2 80                  LDX #$80      ;DURATION CONSTANT
00C6: A4 BF         FL2      LDY F         ;FREQUENCY CONSTANT IN Y
00C8: C8            FL1      INY
00C9: D0 FD                  BNE FL1
00CB: 49 01                  EOR #1
00CD: 8D 00 17               STA PA        ;TOGGLE PA0
00D0: E8                     INX
00D1: D0 F3                  BNE FL2
00D3: A5 BF                  LDA F
00D5: 60                     RTS


SYMBOL TABLE:
 PA          1700         F           00BF         FREQ         00C0
 FL2         00C6         FL1         00C8
DONE
```

Fig 4-55: The Switch Time Program (continued)

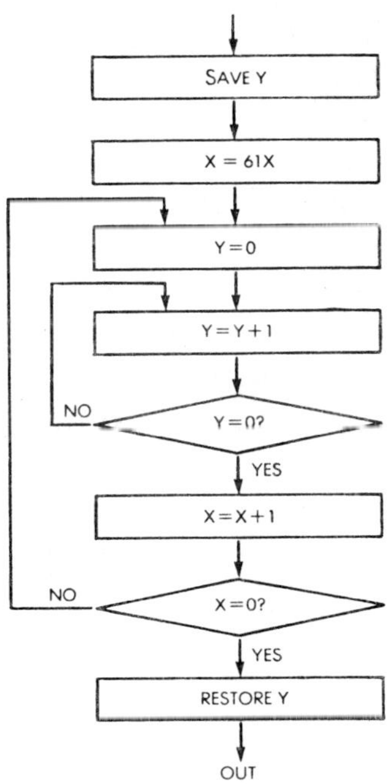

Fig. 4-56: 250ms Delay Flow Chart

```
                       ;***** DL250 *****
                       ;250 MILLISECOND DELAY
                       ;REG. Y UNAFFECTED
                       ;
                                 .=$90
0090: 98               DL250     TYA             ;SAVE Y
0091: A2 3D                      LDX #$3D
0093: A0 00            DL2       LDY #0
0095: C8               DL1       INY             ;INNER LOOP
0096: D0 FD                      BNE DL1
0098: E8                         INX
0099: D0 F8                      BNE DL2         ;OUTER LOOP
009B: A8                         TAY             ;RESTORE Y
009C: 60                         RTS

SYMBOL TABLE:
 DL250        0090        DL2        0093        DL1        0095

DONE
```

Fig.4-57: 250ms Delay

Exercise 4-9: The flow-chart of Fig 4-55 has been written so that each box in the flow-chart corresponds to one instruction in the program of Fig 4-54. Using this flow-chart, or else the program, write on the left of each box the duration of the delay it introduces. Compute the resulting internal delay duration for this subroutine. Is it exactly 250 ms?

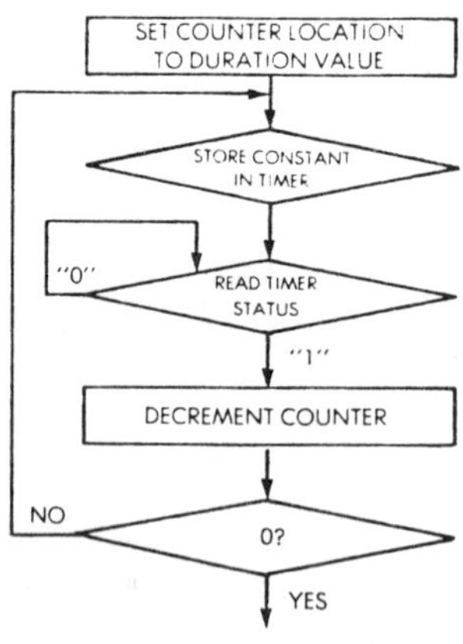

Fig. 4-58: Time 10 Flow Chart

```
                   ;***** TIME10 *****
                   ;1/10 SECOND DELAY
                   ;
                   TIMER     =$1707
                   D         =$9D
                   ;
                             .=$9E
009E: 86 9D        TIME10    STX D
00A0: A9 62        TO        LDA #$62     ;DECIMAL 98
00A2: 8D 07 17               STA TIMER
00A5: AD 07 17     T1        LDA TIMER
00A8: 10 FB                  BPL T1
00AA: C6 9D                  DEC D
00AC: D0 F2                  BNE TO
00AE: 60                     RTS

SYMBOL TABLE:
 TIMER        1707        D          009D        TIME10       009E
 TO           00A0        T1         00A5
```

Fig 4-59: Generating a 0.1 Second Delay

A SIMPLE MUSIC PROGRAM

As a preliminary step to playing music, now let us generate a sound with the speaker, using a programmed delay. The flow-chart is shown on Fig 4-58 and the delay subroutine is shown on Fig 4-59. Prior to using the subroutine, the constant F must be loaded with the appropriate delay duration which will determine the frequency of the sound.

In order to generate music which has some resemblance to actual tunes, it is necessary to generate a sound of specified frequency and also to control its duration. The musical symbols used to indicate the duration of a tone are shown below:

Musical Symbols

(. = +50%)

𝅘𝅥𝅮 = 1
𝅘𝅥 = 2
𝅘𝅥. = 3
𝅗𝅥 = 4
𝅗𝅥. = 6
𝅝 = 8
𝅝. = 12

The dot which may follow a note indicates plus 50% duration. Overall, there are seven possible durations. Additionally, it is necessary to represent a "silence". At a minimum, this information will require three bits in an *encoded* format, or else four bits in a *decoded* format. (A decoded format is one where the values 1, 2, 3, 4, 6, 8, and 12 are represented by their actual binary representation.)

To represent the notes of one octave, A, B, C, D, E, F, G must be represented, as well as the six half notes between them. This represents a total of 13 keys for one octave. If more than one octave should be used, then one full byte should be allocated to represent the tone. If the reader is limited by the amount of memory available on his board, he may wish to restrict his tunes to 16 possible keys and would then be able to use an encoding where the left half of every byte represents the duration and the right part of every byte represents the notes.

Here, we will play simple tunes and use a straightforward encoding technique, where one full byte is allocated to the duration, and one full byte is allocated to the note frequency. Three examples, a Mozart Sonatine, a Bach Chorale and a popular children's song are shown on Fig 4-60, 4-61 and 4-62.

The flow-chart for the corresponding music program is shown on Fig 4-63 and the program itself appears on Fig 4-64.

A .1 second timer is a simple preliminary subroutine which will generate a .1 second delay (see Figs 4-58, 4-59).

Address	Duration	F	Note	
00	09	20	*la*	A
2	04	4F	*do#*	C#
4	04	6B	*mi*	E
6	05	12	sol#	G#
8	01	20	*la*	A
A	01	39	*si*	B
C	0F	20	*la*	A
E	02	00		
12	09	7C	*fa#*	F#
12	04	6B	*mi*	E
14	04	91	*la*	A
16	04	6B	*mi*	E
18	04	59	*ré*	D
1A	09	4F	*do#*	C#
1C	00	00		
1E				
20				

Fig. 4-60: Mozart Sonatine

Address	Duration	F	Note
00	88	44	*do* C
02	06	59	*ré* D
04	06	6B	*mi* E
06	88	83	*sol* G
08	06	74	*fa* F
A	06	74	*fa* F
C	88	91	*la* A
E	06	83	*sol* G
10	06	83	*sol* G
12	88	A3	*do* C
14	06	9E	*si* B
16	06	A3	*do* C
18	06	83	*sol* G
1A	06	6B	*mi* E
1C	06	44	*do* C
1E	88	59	*ré* D
20	06	6B	*mi* E
22	06	20	*la* A
24	88	83	*sol* G
26	06	74	*fa* F
28	06	6B	*mi* E
2A	88	59	*ré* D
2C	06	44	*do* C
2E	06	04	*sol* G
30	06	44	*do* C
32	88	39	*si* B
34	06	44	*do* C
36	06	6B	*mi* E
38	06	83	*sol* G
3A	0E	A3	*do* C
3C	0E	44	*do* C
3E	00	00	

Fig 4-61: Bach Chorale

Address	Duration	F	Note
0	04	44	*do* ♪ C
2	04	44	*do* ♪ C
4	04	44	*do* ♪ C
6	04	59	*ré* ♪ D
8	09	6B	*mi* ♩ E
A	09	59	*ré* ♩ D
C	04	44	*do* ♪ C
E	04	6B	*mi* ♪ E
10	04	59	*ré* ♪ D
12	04	59	*ré* ♪ D
14	09	44	*do* ♩ C
16	10	00	
18	04	44	*do* ♪ C
1A	04	44	*do* ♪ C
1C	04	44	*do* ♪ C
1E	04	59	*ré* ♪ D
20	09	6B	*mi* ♩ E
22	09	59	*ré* ♩ D
24	04	44	*do* ♪ C
26	04	6B	*mi* ♪ E
28	04	59	*ré* ♪ D
2A	04	59	*ré* ♪ D
2C	09	44	*do* ♩ C
2E	00	00	

Fig. 4-62: "Au clair de la lune"

Exercise 4-10: *Verify whether the subroutine implements a .1 second delay exactly. Verify the duration of every instruction and the number of times that the loop is executed. Compute the corresponding delay.*

KIM TRAFFIC CONTROL

A possible connection for a traffic control simulation is shown on Fig 4-66. It is equipped with switches in every direction, which will be used to indicate the presence of a car or else a pedestrian call.

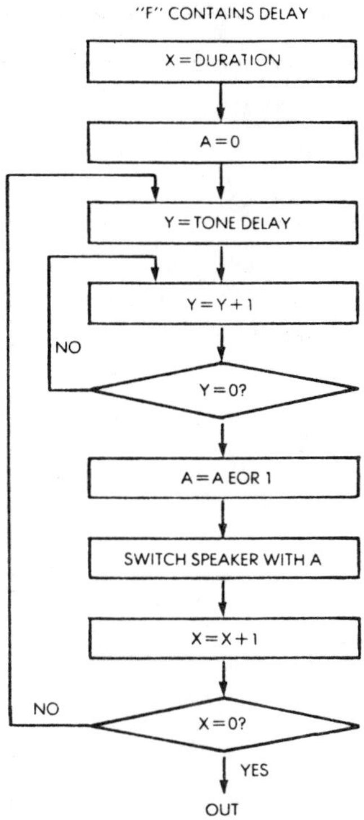

Fig. 4-63: Play Sound Flow Chart

```
                    ;***** PLAY A TUNE *****
                    PA       =$1700
                    PAD      =$1701
                    TIMER    =$1707
                             .=00
                    ADDRS    .=.+2
                    TEMP     .=.+1
                    YSAVE    .=.+1
                    F        .=.+1
                    ;
                             .=$10
0010: A9 31         TIME20   LDA #$31
0012: 8D 07 17               STA TIMER
0015: 2C 07 17      T1       BIT TIMER
0018: 10 FB                  BPL T1
001A: CA                     DEX
001B: D0 F3                  BNE TIME20
001D: 60                     RTS
```

Fig 4-64: Playing a Tune

```
                        ;
                                 .=$20
0020: 84 03             FREQT    STY YSAVE
0022: 85 04                      STA F
0024: A9 31             FT0      LDA #$31
0026: 8D 07 17                   STA TIMER      ;START TIMER (1/20 SEC.)
0029: A4 04             FT1      LDY F
002B: C8                FT2      INY
002C: D0 FD                      BNE FT2
002E: EE 00 17                   INC PA         ;SWITCH SPEAKER
0031: 2C 07 17                   BIT TIMER      ;TIME ELAPSED?
0034: 10 F3                      BPL FT1        ;NO: GO ON.
0036: CA                FT3      DEX
0037: D0 EB                      BNE FT0
0039: A4 03                      LDY YSAVE
003B: 60                         RTS
                        ;
                                 .=$40
0040: A2 0F             START    LDX #$0F
0042: 9A                         TXS
0043: A9 00                      LDA #$00
0045: 8D FA 17                   STA $17FA
0048: 8D FE 17                   STA $17FE
004B: A9 1C                      LDA #$1C
004D: 8D FB 17                   STA $17FB
0050: 8D FF 17                   STA $17FF      ;INTERRUPT VECTOR
0053: A9 01                      LDA #$01
0055: 8D 01 17                   STA PAD        ;PAD IS OUTPUT
0058: A0 00             DACAPO   LDY #$00
005A: B1 00             NEXT     LDA (ADDRS),Y
005C: 85 02                      STA TEMP
005E: 29 7F                      AND #$7F
0060: AA                         TAX            ;DURATION
0061: F0 F5                      BEQ DACAPO
0063: C8                         INY
0064: B1 00                      LDA (ADDRS),Y
0066: F0 10                      BEQ TONE
0068: 20 20 00                   JSR FREQT
006B: 24 02                      BIT TEMP
006D: 30 05                      BMI AFTER
006F: A2 02                      LDX #$02
0071: 20 10 00                   JSR TIME20
0074: C8                AFTER    INY
0075: 4C 5A 00                   JMP NEXT
0078: 20 10 00          TONE     JSR TIME20
007B: F0 F7                      BEQ AFTER

SYMBOL TABLE:
 PA          1700        PAD         1701        TIMER       1707
 ADDRS       0000        TEMP        0002        YSAVE       0003
 F           0004        TIME20      0010        T1          0015
 FREQT       0020        FT0         0024        FT1         0029
 FT2         002B        FT3         0036        START       0040
 DACAPO      0058        NEXT        005A        AFTER       0074
 TONE        0078
```

Fig 4-64: Playing a Tune (continued)

Exercise 4-11: *Write a traffic control program which meets the following specifications:*
- *Minimum yellow duration: 3 seconds*
- *Whenever a car presence is detected (by holding down one of the switches) extend the green duration for that duration by three seconds.*
- *Maximum green duration in any direction: 2 minutes, if there is a request in the opposite direction.*
- *Blink the lights at night (a night indication is provided by a separate switch).*
- *A possible flow-chart for this program is shown on Fig 4-65. Write the corresponding program.*

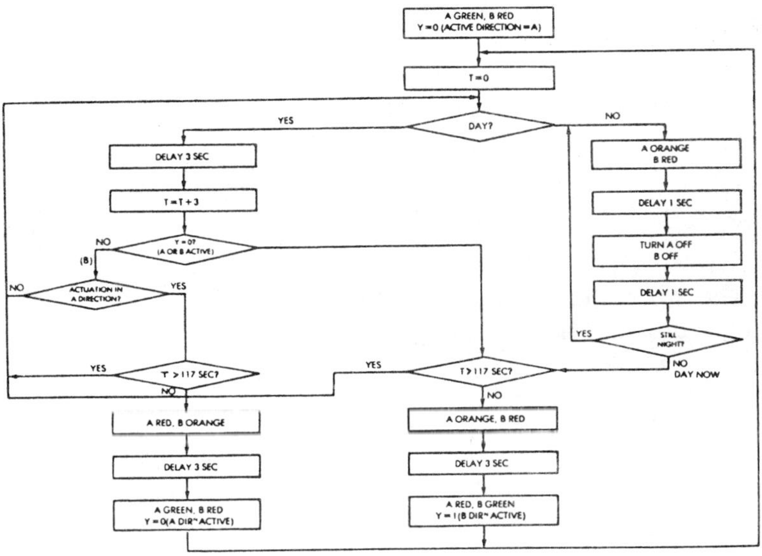

Fig. 4-65: Traffic Flow Chart

LEARN THE MULTIPLICATION TABLE

As a final exercise, this program should teach the multiplication table. The program should blink an LED or the loudspeaker n times, with n between 1 and 10, then wait 2 seconds, then blink again p times, with p between 1 and 10.

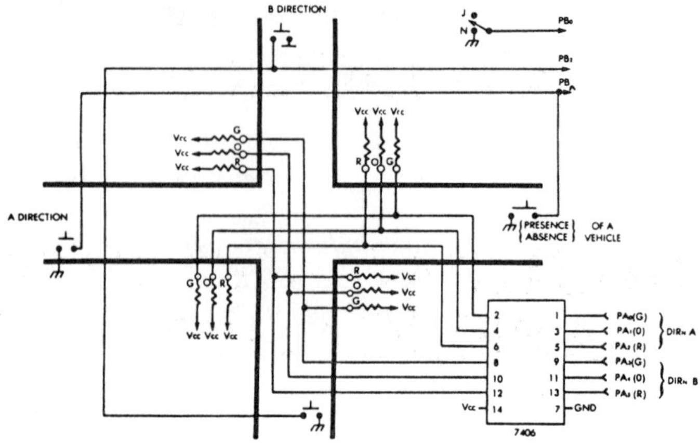

Fig. 4-66: Traffic Controller

The user must then push n times on a push-button switch to enter his answer. An audible acknowledgment should be provided by the speaker. The user terminates his answer by not pushing on the switch for 3 seconds or more. If the answer was correct, the LED should light up for five seconds. If the answer was not correct, the LED will blink.

Exercise 4-12: *Design the corresponding flow chart, and write the program. (This program is simple but somewhat longer than many of the previous ones. If you really need the answer, it is shown in Appendix B.)*

SUMMARY

Simple input-output devices have now been connected to a 6502 board. We have learned how to realize simple hardware interfaces, and how to develop simple applications software to sense and control an external environment. Although the complexity of the applications presented here has been kept low, more complex applications could be developed using the same simple hardware. We are now ready to proceed to more complex programs and interfaces in Chapter 5: Industrial and Home Applications.

CHAPTER 5

INDUSTRIAL AND HOME APPLICATIONS

INTRODUCTION

The basic skills for connecting simple devices to a 6502-based microcomputer board, and for developing the basic applications software, have been presented in Chapter 4. Here, more complex devices will be interfaced to the 6502 board, and more complex applications software will be developed. The applications presented are typical home and industrial control situations. In the next chapter, microcomputer peripherals will be interfaced to the 6502 board.

The first application presented here will be a traffic-control simulation. Traffic lights will be simulated by LED's on the board and application programs of increasing complexity will be developed. The presence of cars will even be detected by simulated loop detectors, normally embedded in the pavement, and simulated here by push-button switches. The skills required for developing these hardware and software interfaces are those required by a real industrial control environment.

Then, a 5 × 7 dot matrix LED will be interfaced to this system. This is a technique frequently used in the display of data. Dot matrices are used, not just for LED's, but to represent characters on a television screen, or on a dot matrix printer. This dot matrix will be used to display actual switch values as sensed by the 6502 board.

Tones will then be generated with the loudspeaker in order to develop simple music programs. The set of switches will be used to specify which note should be played. The skills acquired in controlling the sound of the speaker will also be used by the next program to generate sounds such as a siren.

The next application program will implement a burglar alarm system for a home or a building. A light beam will be used as one of the devices which detect a possible intrusion. Whenever the light beam is interrupted the alarm will be sounded through the speaker. Many additional improvements will also be proposed in the exercises.

The speed of an ordinary DC motor will then be controlled by the computer. It is, in fact, quite simple to control the speed of a motor using digital techniques. These techniques and the required hardware interface will be presented.

In the next application, a heat sensing device will be connected to the microprocessor board, and the temperature measurement will be output in the form of an audible sound. The higher the temperature, the higher the pitch of the tone will be. This will introduce the concept of analog to digital conversion, and the actual hardware and software techniques used to effect this conversion will be presented here.

The reader is encouraged to build the actual applications board #2 required by the programs in this chapter. All components used on this board are low in cost, and normally readily available from an electronics shop (except perhaps for the digital to analog converter which must often be ordered from a distributor). Photographs of the actual board are shown on Fig 5-1, 5-2 and 5-3.

Fig. 5-1: The Application Board #2

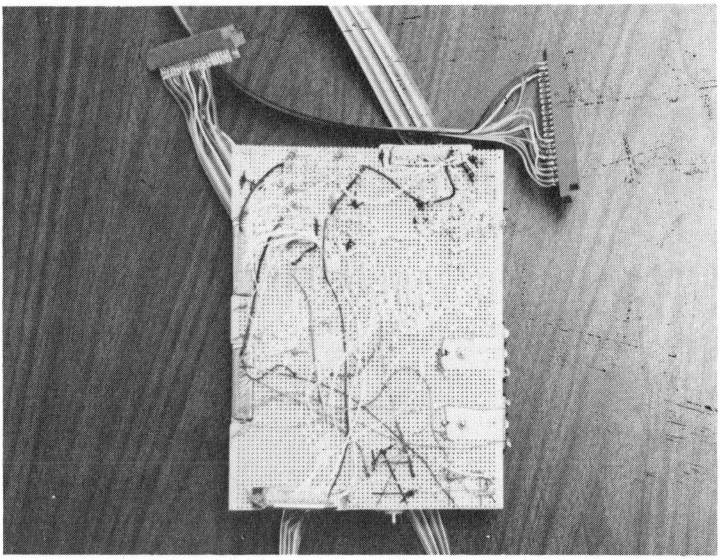

Fig. 5-2: Underside shows wire-wrap

Fig. 5-3: For convenience Application Cables connect to board

In view of the limited number of ports normally available on the output of the microcomputer board, four connectors labeled H1, H2, H3, and H4 have been installed on the board to facilitate the connections and avoid rewiring between programs. These connectors have been designed to mate directly to the SYM external connection cables but could be readily adapted to the output of other microcomputer boards. For each application, it will be necessary to plug in one or

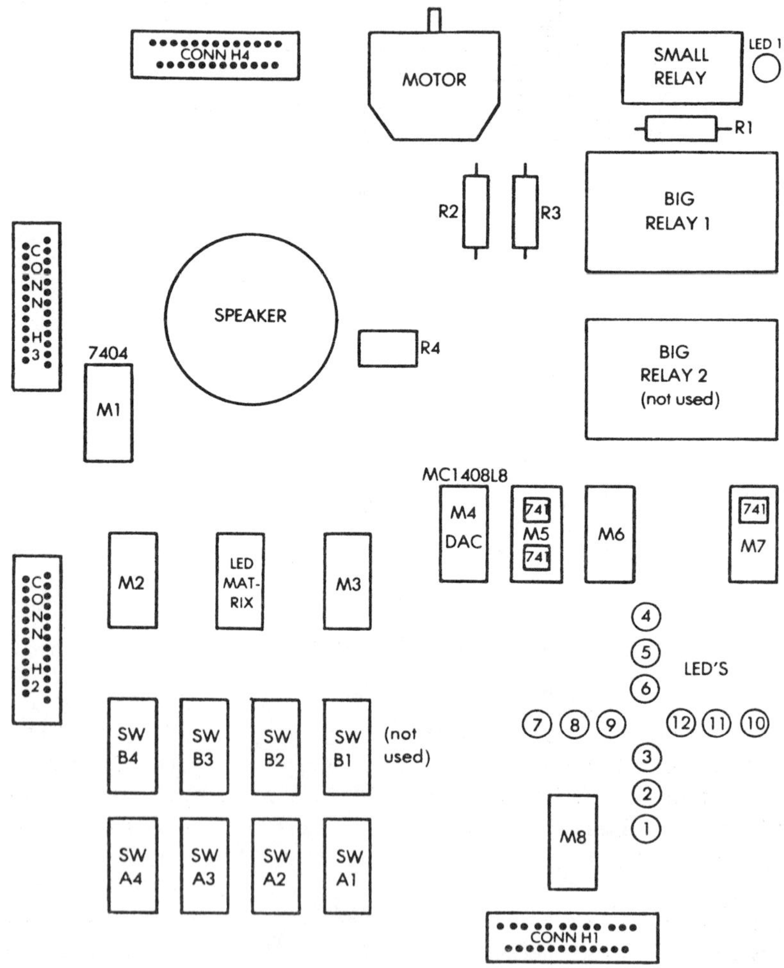

Fig. 5-4: Board Layout

two of the output cables coming from the board to the corresponding connectors shown on the applications board. The details of each connection will be indicated at the beginning of each application.

The component layout for the board is shown on Fig 5-4. The connectors detail is shown on Fig 5-5 A and B. The details of each connection is shown within the paragraph corresponding to each application.

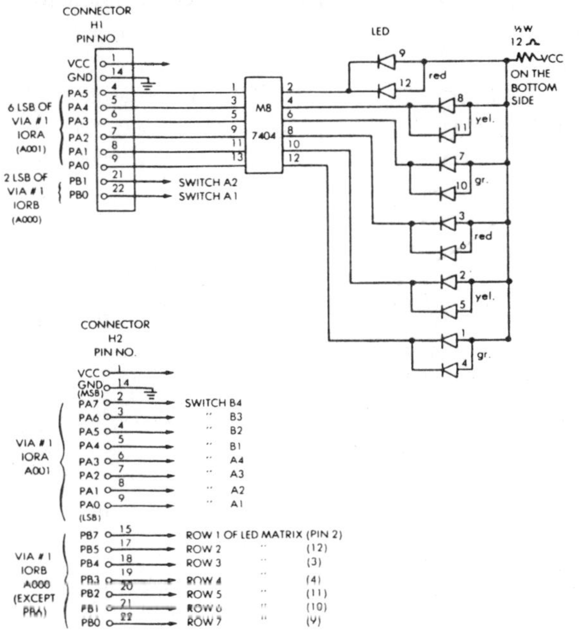

Fig. 5-5a: H1 and H2 Connectors

A wire-wrap technique has been used to connect the wires to the pins on the back of the board as shown on Fig 5-2. It is naturally possible to solder the wires. Do not forget the usual precautions in handling LSI circuits: all instruments (including yourself) should be grounded. As a final detail, the pot trimmer (variable resistor) connected in series with the loudspeaker should not be set to the value zero. If it were, the pot might burn when power is applied to the speaker, in the case of a board like the SYM where the speaker would be connected to one of the buffered outputs (in addition the output transistor is also likely to burn out). An additional resistor in series with the speaker is recommended for this reason.

The goal of this chapter is to teach you actual applications techniques which should enable you to create either home applications of significant complexity or to solve actual industrial control problems in a realistic environment. At the end of this chapter, you should have acquired all the basic skills required to start developing complex applications on your own. If specific interfacing problems should be encountered, reference C207 "Microprocessor Interfacing Techniques" is suggested.

Important note: In order to use one more input-output line, transistor 1 (centermost) of the four buffered ports of the SYM is bypassed.

The programs presented in this section have been designed to be improved. The alert reader will notice that many improvements in style are possible. Such improvements are proposed or described in the exercise section at the end of every application. When reading the programs, it is suggested that you watch for such possible improvements in the coding. However, it is only in the next chapter that we will present optimized programs, once all other problems have been solved.

Again, in this chapter, a large number of exercises will be proposed. It is strongly recommended that most of these exercises be solved either on paper or on a real microcomputer board. They have been carefully designed to insure that concepts presented in the preceding section were actually learned, and that you can use them creatively. If you can solve the exercises without looking at this book, you will have effectively learned how to resolve your own applications problems.

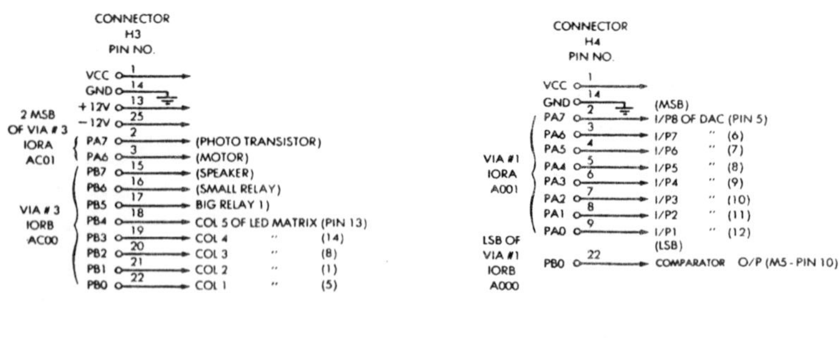

Fig. 5-5b: H3 and H-4 Connectors

A TRAFFIC CONTROL SYSTEM

We are going to develop programs to control a simulated intersection. The diagram of the intersection appears on Fig 5-6. It has two directions of traffic flow identified as A and B. In traffic control jargon they are called the "phases". The two traffic lights for both directions of a phase, such as the two traffic lights for arterial A, will display the same color (green, yellow, or red) at the same time. Similarly, the other two traffic lights for phase B will be turning on simultaneously. These four sets of traffic lights will be simulated on our board by four sets of green, yellow, and red LEDs. Additionally, we will assume that vehicle loop detectors have been imbedded in the pavement at the locations marked A-1, A-2, B-1, B-2 on the diagram of Fig 5-6.

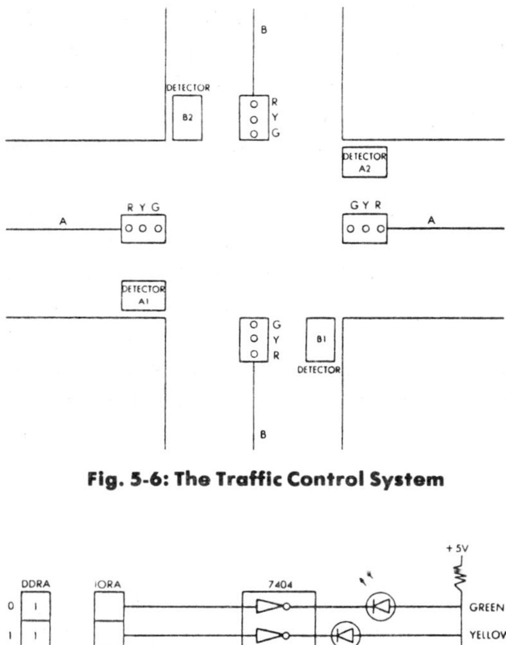

Fig. 5-6: The Traffic Control System

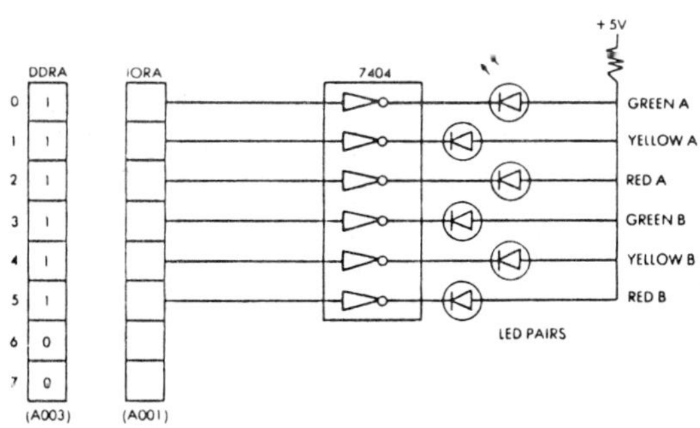

Fig. 5-7: Connecting the LED's

They are called "loop detectors," and their role will be explained later.

Let us first examine the hardware connection of our "traffic lights" (in fact, the LEDs) to the microprocessor system. Referring to Fig 5-7, we are connecting a 7404 driver to the IORA register of the 6522 #1. The LED pairs appear on the right of the illustration. For clarity, only one LED is shown on each line. In fact, two LEDs are connected in parallel on each line since there are two sets of traffic lights for every phase. The actual connection is shown on Fig 5-8. In order to configure the low order 6 bits of IORA as outputs, the direction register, DDRA, which appears to its left will have to be loaded with the proper bit pattern: "00111111." A driver (the 7404) is necessary in order to supply enough current to light up the LED's.

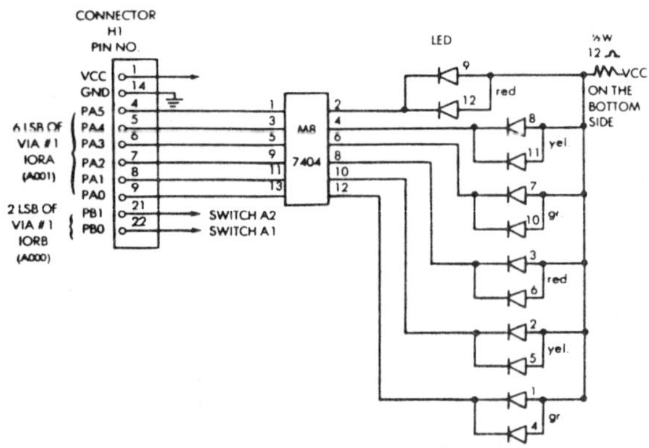

Fig. 5-8: Actual LED Connection

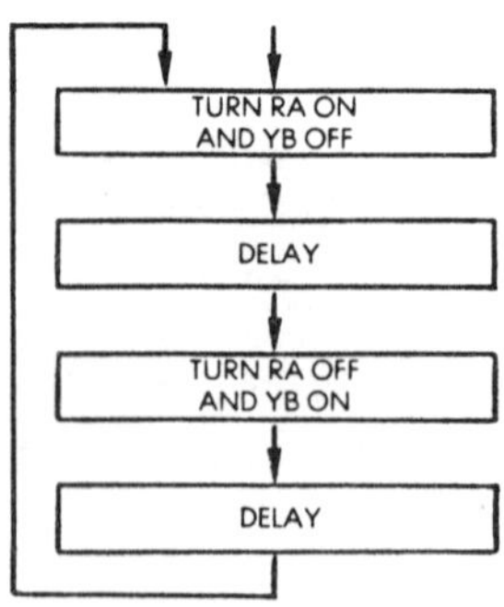

Fig. 5-9: Night Pattern

We are now going to develop programs for several traffic control algorithms. Two main cases can be distinguished: the night pattern (flashing lights), and the day pattern.

(Connection: Connector A to Connector H1)

```
0100  A9 3F      NIGHT  LDA  #$3F    *
0102  8D 03 A0          STA  $A003   Set VIA #1 DDRA = 3F for output
                                       mode
0105  A9 02      NIT2   LDA  #$02
0107  8D 01 A0          STA  $A001   Turn on yellow light in one direction
010A  A9 FC             LDA  $FC       - count.
010C  85 00             STA  $00     Set DLYA Count = $FC (i.e. -4)
                                       at location $0000
010E  20 20 01          JSR  DLYA    Call DLYA
0111  A9 20             LDA  #$20
0113  8D 01 A0          STA  $A001   Turn on red light in the other
                                       direction
0116  A9 FC             LDA  #$FC
0118  85 00             STA  $00     Set DLYA count = $FC at
                                       loc. $0000
011A  20 20 01          JSR  DLYA    Call DLYA
011D  4C 05 01          JMP  NIT2    Repeat
```

Subroutine DLYA: This subroutine takes index from location 0000, loop until this index incremented from a pre-set negative value to zero, the pre-set index is used to control the length of delay.

```
0120  A2 9D      DLYA   LDX  #$9D                          ┐
0122  A0 71      LPXA   LDY  #$71   ┐                      │
0124  C8         LPYA   INY      ┐  │ Inner     Outer      │
0125  C0 00             CPY  #$00│  │ delay     delay      │
0127  30 FB             BMI  LPYA┘  │ loop      loop       │
0129  E8                INX         │                      │
012A  E0 00             CPX  #$00   │                      │
012C  30 F4             BMI  LPXA   ┘                      │
012E  E6 00             INC  $00     Increment delay count every time an
                                       outer delay loop is completed
0130  A5 00             LDA  $00                           │
0132  C9 00             CMP  #$00                          │
0134  30 EA             BMI  DLYA    Loop till index = 0   ┘
0136  60                RTS
```

Fig. 5-10: Traffic Light Simulation: Night Mode (Program 5-1)

Night Pattern

This is the simplest pattern. The traffic lights are flashing red in one direction and amber in the other one. This traffic control strategy is used for isolated intersections with a low amount of traffic at night. The flow-chart corresponding to the algorithm appears on Fig 5-9. It states that the red for one direction and the yellow for the other one are on or off simultaneously. They are both kept on or off for a fixed duration called "DELAY". The program corresponding to this flow chart appears on Fig 5-10. It consists of a main program called "NIGHT" and a delay subroutine called "DLYA." Let us examine the program.

Referring back to Fig 5-7, the Data Direction Register for the 6522 #1 must first be properly configured so that the lower six bits of IORA will be the outputs which will drive the LEDs. This DDRA is located at memory location A003 and the IORA is located at memory location A001 (refer to Fig 3-6 for the 6522 memory map).

The first two instructions load the required contents in the Data Direction Register:

```
NIGHT    LDA  #$3F
         STA  $A003     SET DDRA
```

We then simply have to deposit the appropriate pattern in the IORA register to turn the required LEDs on or off. The pattern required for addressing each LED pair appears on Fig 5-11.

BINARY	HEX	LIGHT
00000001	01	GREEN A
00000010	02	YELLOW A
00000100	04	RED A
00001000	08	GREEN B
00010000	10	YELLOW B
00100000	20	RED B

Fig. 5-11: Pattern to Address the LED Pairs

The next two lines of the program turn on the yellow for A by depositing the hexadecimal value "02" in the IORA register.

```
NIT2    LDA  #02
        STA  $A001     SET IORA
```

A delay must then be implemented. The delay value is deposited in the accumulator and then stored at memory location "00" where it will be found by the delay routine. A subroutine jump then occurs to DLYA.

```
        LDA  #$FC
        STA  $00
        JSR  DLYA
```

Once the specified delay has elapsed, the hexadecimal value "20" is deposited into the IORA. This will turn off yellow in direction A and simultaneously turn on the red for direction B. As before, the delay duration is deposited in memory location "0", and a jump occurs again to the DLYA subroutine:

```
        LDA  #$20
        STA  $A001
        LDA  #$FC
        STA  $00
        JSR  DLYA
```

Finally, upon expiration of a specified delay, the program loops back to location NIT2 where it turns on YA and turns off RB again:

```
        JMP          NIT2
```

The operation of the program should be completely straightforward at this point. Let us examine the delay subroutine. The principle of delay loops is to load a register or a memory location with a value and then increment or decrement it until it reaches a set value. Since the reader is presumably familiar with the decrementation technique (see ref C202), we are going to use here an incrementation technique for a change. However, it requires a few more instructions. An improvement will be suggested in an exercise at the end of this section. The delay subroutine appears on Fig 5-12. Since the delay to be implemented is of the order of tens of seconds, it cannot be implemented as a single loop. A single loop delay would load a register with the value 255 (hexadecimal FF) and decrement or increment from there. The resulting delay would not be sufficient. In order to implement the longer delay, we will use nested loops: an inner delay loop, and at least one outer delay loop which will be executed every time that the inner one has counted out. Let us examine the program. Register X is used as the outer loop counter. It is loaded with the hexadecimal value 9D. This value will be justified later on:

```
DLYA      LDX  #$9D
```

The second instruction of the program loads register Y with the hexadecimal value 71. Y is the inner loop counter:

```
LPXA      LDY  #$71
```

The next three instructions implement the inner delay loop:

```
LPYA      INY
          CPY  #$00
          BMI  LPYA
```

Y is incremented until it reaches the value 0. Every time that the inner delay loop counts out (i.e., that Y reaches the value 0), the outer counter X is incremented. This is the sixth instruction in the program:

```
          INX
```

Every time that X is incremented, it is compared to the value 0, and as long as the value 0 is not reached, the branch occurs back to LPXA at the beginning of the inner delay loop:

```
          CPX  #$00
          BMI  LPXA
```

The resulting delay so far is, therefore, the inner delay value times the number of times that the outer delay loop has been executed.

Every time that this outer delay loop times out, our overall delay counter at location 00 is incremented by 1:

```
INC   $00
```

This is a third delay loop. The contents of memory location 00 are tested against the value 00 every time that they are incremented. Whenever the value 00 is reached, we exit from this routine. As long as it does not reach the value 0, we go back to location DLYA, i.e., at the beginning of the previous delay loop to execute the previous procedure again:

```
LDA   $00
CMP   #$00
BMI   DLYA
RTS
```

The overall structure of the program is shown on Fig 5-12, with its three nested delay loops, and the timing of the instructions. The overall delay will be equal to the contents of memory location 00 times the outer loop delay times the inner loop delay. Let us compute this total delay duration. The timing of the instructions appears on Fig 5-12. Let us examine the inner loop first. Every time that it is executed, three instructions are executed lasting seven microseconds. To keep things simple, we will require this inner loop to generate a delay of approximately 1 millisecond. The outer loop #1 will be responsible for implementing a 100,000 millisecond delay (0.1 second).

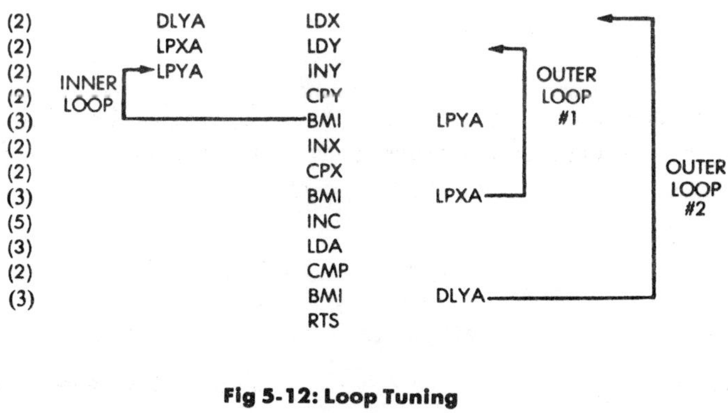

Fig 5-12: Loop Tuning

Let us start with the value "80" (hexadecimal) in register Y. This is 128 in binary, the middle of the range which can be obtained with 8 bits. Running through the inner delay loop will result in incrementing Y 128 times. The total duration of the loop will, therefore, be $7 \times 128 = 896$ microseconds. Since we want to obtain a delay of approximately 1,024 microseconds for this inner loop, we must modify the value to be loaded in register Y. Let us compute it. We want this value N to be such that $N \times 7 = 1000$. N must, therefore, be equal to $1000 \div 7 = 142.86$. The nearest integer is 143. Since, in this particular delay subroutine, we are incrementing the value contained in Y, rather than decrementing it, we want to load in Y the value $256 - 143 = 113$ decimal or 71 hexadecimal.

Let us now compute the duration of the delay introduced by the outer delay loop #1. One traversal of the outer delay loop will result in a delay equal to the duration of the first instruction of the program (at address DLYA) plus the duration of the inner delay loop, plus the following three instructions up to and including the branch BMI LPXA. The duration is:

$$2 + 7 \times 143 + 7 = 1010 \text{ microseconds.}$$

We want this outer delay loop #1 to implement a .1 second delay or 100,000 microseconds. The number of times P that it must be executed must, therefore, be such that $1010 \times P = 100000$. P must therefore be equal to $100000 \div 1010 = 99$.

Again, since we are using an incrementing technique for the delay, the number to be deposited in X must be such that it is incremented exactly 99 times before it overflows into the value "00". The number to be deposited in X must, therefore, be equal to $256 - 99 = 157$ in decimal or 9D hexadecimal. Let us now verify the total duration of the delay we have implemented. The outer loop delay is equal to $99 \times 1010 = 99990$ microseconds. The remaining four instructions to be executed at the end of the DLYA subroutine represent a duration of $5 + 3 + 2 + 3 = 13$ microseconds. 2 us must be added for the first instruction of DLYA.

The final delay for the complete traversal of DYLA is therefore $99990 + 15 = 100005$ microseconds. This represents nearly exactly a .1 second delay. In fact, it is so close to .1 second that you should be able to clock this routine with a stop watch and verify the accuracy of this method.

A word of caution: Remember that this subroutine uses an *incrementing* technique. The number to be deposited at memory location 00 will control the number of tenths of a second of delay that the subroutine will introduce. However, the number to be deposited at location 00 should be the *complement* of the actual number of tenths of a second since it will be *incremented* until it overflows through 0. In other words, to obtain a .4 second delay, you should not deposit the value 4 at location 00 but deposit the value 256 − 4 = 252 decimal = FC hexadecimal. This is what we did in the program of Fig 5-10 (night mode algorithm).

The time has come now to improve this delay routine:

Exercise 5-1: *Rewrite the delay subroutine by using a decrementation technique rather than an incrementation technique. Recompute the numbers to be loaded in X and Y so that the resulting delay introduced by the subroutine is approximately .1 second. What is the advantage of using a decrementing technique rather than an incrementing technique?*

Caution: If you decide to use the decrementing technique for the delay, do not forget to change location 09FC in the memory. A different constant must be loaded prior to calling this routine.

Exercise 5-2: *Modify the program so that the lights flash every second. Also, shorten it by using EOR to toggle the lights from one configuration to another.*

Day Mode

In this mode, each traffic light goes through a green, yellow, and red sequence in the usual manner. As long as the light in direction A is green or yellow, the light for B is red, and vice versa. The flow-chart corresponding to the control algorithm appears on Fig 5-13. The arrows on the right of the flow-chart indicate the length of time during which each of the lights is on. If we call D1 the green duration for A, D2 the yellow duration for A, D3 and D4 respectively the durations of the green and yellow for B, we can see, by inspecting the diagram, that the total duration of a cycle is D1 + D2 + D3 + D4.

At a real intersection, these delays are subject to constraints. In particular, the cycle of the intersection is normally between one minute and two minutes. The maximum is due to the fact that most drivers will not tolerate a red light duration of more than two minutes in any direction: they will simply go through once their patience is exhausted, assuming that the traffic light is malfunctioning. In addition, the

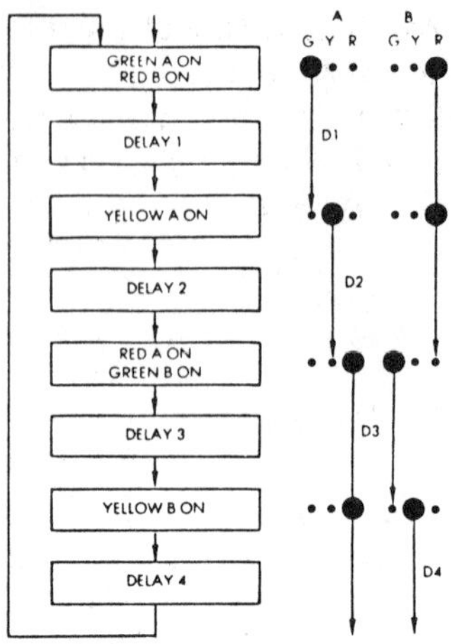

Fig. 5-13: Day Mode (Off Commands not shown)

other delays are constrained by the clearances necessary for a vehicle or a pedestrian to clear the intersection once he has entered it. The yellow time is also called the clearance time and represents the time that is necessary for a car to clear the intersection. The green may have any minimal duration as long as no pedestrians are crossing the intersection. However, if pedestrians may cross this intersection, the minimum red duration should be such that a pedestrian may safely clear the intersection. The duration of the red in direction B, for example, is equal to D1 + D2. If we assume, for example, that the minimum yellow in direction A is equal to 3 seconds and that the minimum red for direction B is equal to 10 seconds, we can see by inspecting Fig 5-13 that the minimum duration for the green in direction A is D1 = 10 − 3 = 7 seconds. Mathematically:

If we set:

GREEN A = D1
YELLOW A = D2
GREEN B = D3
YELLOW B = D4

Then:

RED A = D3 + D4
RED B = D1 + D2

In general, the cycle is fixed, and D1 + D2 + D3 + D4 = CONSTANT.

In our program, we will use faster cycles than in real life. This is simply because it is frustrating to wait for one or more minutes in order to observe the correct functioning of the traffic lights. For practical purposes, a cycle time of 10 to 20 seconds is desirable for testing purposes, and the reader should now have acquired the skills to adjust the delay easily, so that his microcomputer could be connected to a real intersection. The program appears on Fig 5-14.

```
0140  A9 3F      DAY    LDA  #$3F
0142  8D 03 A0          STA  $A003   Set VIA #1 DDRA = $3F for output
                                       mode
0145  A9 21      ONDAY  LDA  #$21
0147  8D 01 A0          STA  $A001   Turn on green and red in two
                                       directions
014A  A9 D0             LDA  #$D0
014C  85 00             STA  $00     Set DLYA count = $D0 at loc.
                                       $0000
014E  20 20 01          JSR  DLYA    Call delay
0151  A9 22             LDA  #$22    Turn on yellow and red
0153  8D 01 A0          STA  $A001
0156  A9 EA             LDA  #$EA
0158  85 00             STA  $00     Set DLYA count = $EA
015A  20 20 01          JSR  DLYA    Call delay
015D  A9 0C             LDA  #$0C    Turn on red and green
015F  8D 01 A0          STA  $A001
0162  A9 D0             LDA  #$D0
0164  85 00             STA  $00     Set DLYA index = $D0
0166  20 20 01          JSR  DLYA    Call delay
0169  A9 14             LDA  #$14    Turn on red and yellow
016B  8D 01 A0          STA  $A001
016E  A9 E8             LDA  #$E8
0170  85 00             STA  $00     Set DLYA index = $E8
0172  20 20 01          JSR  DLYA    Call delay
0175  4C 45 01          JMP  ONDAY   Repeat
```

Fig. 5-14 (Program 5-2): Traffic Light Simulation: Day Mode

(Connection: Connector A to Connector H1)

As in the previous program, the Data Direction Register DDRA must be configured in the output mode to control the 6 LEDs connected to it. This is done by the first two instructions of the program:

```
DAY        LDA  #$3F
           STA  $A003
```

Then, the green for direction A and the red for direction B are turned on by the next two instructions which load the appropriate bit pattern

(21 hexadecimal) in the I/O register:

```
ON DAY    LDA  #$21
          STA  $A001
```

A delay duration is then specified by depositing a value in memory location 00 and by calling the delay subroutine:

```
          LDA  #$D0
          STA  $00
          JSR  DLYA
```

The process is then repeated for the yellow in direction A, the red in direction A, and the green in direction B, and finally the yellow in direction B, before coming back to the starting point:

```
          LDA  #$22     YELLOW A AND RED B
          STA  $A001
          LDA  #$EA
          STA  $00
          JSR  DLYA     DELAY
          LDA  #$0C     RED A AND GREEN B
          STA  $A001
          LDA  #$D0
          STA  $00
          JSR  DLYA     DELAY
          LDA  #$14     RED B AND YELLOW B
          STA  $A001
          LDA  #$E8
          STA  $00
          JSR  DLYA     DELAY
          JMP  ONDAY    REPEAT
```

The reader should verify that the program corresponds exactly to the flow-chart of Fig 5-13. Its interpretation should be completely straight forward now. The reader is strongly encouraged to try different time constants than the ones indicated in the program and verify that the timing is what he expects. Let us now consider improvements to this traffic control algorithm.

For example, you can modify the program so that the yellow clearance, the red clearance and the cycle durations be specified by the length of time one of the switches is depressed after starting the program.

Exercise 5-3: *Implement a "dynamic response algorithm": the green time for arterial A will be extended by five seconds every time a request is sensed on the "loop detector" (a switch), up to a maximum green duration of three minutes.*

Exercise 5-4: *Implement "pedestrian calls" by using the switches. Green should be give to the pedestrian as soon as possible, while respecting the minimum clearances.*

Exercise 5-5 : *Implement a "police switch": by pushing one of the switches, the intersection will sequence manually through its sequence. If pushed quickly twice, the intersection reverts to automatic.*

DOT MATRIX LED

We will use here a 5 × 7 dot-matrix LED display (see Fig 5-15). This type of matrix is used in a number of applications. For example, dot matrix printers often use a 5 × 7 dot matrix in order to print characters on paper. TV monitors or CRT displays also use a dot matrix in order to display characters in the screen. 5 × 7 is the standard minimal dot matrix for an acceptable representation of characters but it is not the best in terms of readability. Larger dox matrices, such as 7 × 9, are used for improved readability, at increased cost. In this applica-

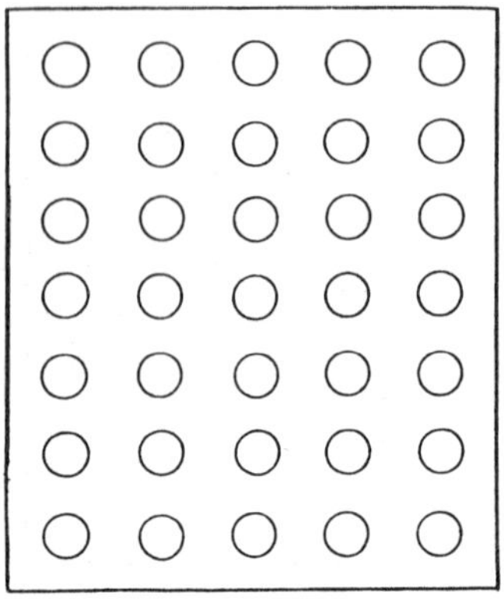

Fig. 5-15: A 5x7 Dot Matrix LED

tion we will directly conntect a 5 × 7 LED dot matrix to the I/O register B of the 6522 #1 and to the 6522 #3. Ideally, drivers should be used with LEDs in order to get sufficient light intensity. Here, to minimize the parts count, we will connect the LED directly. This means that on the actual board the LEDs will be dim and the display somewhat hard to see. For improved performance add drivers on the lines. The connection of the LED dot matrix is shown on Fig 5-16. The 7 rows numbered 1 through 7 are connected respectively to bits 7,5,4,3,2,1, and 0 of the I/O register B of the 6522 #1. Bit 6 of this IORB is not available on the SYM board because the monitor dedicates bit 6 to the cassette input function. The state of bit 6 will, therefore, be indifferent in what will follow.

The five columns of the LED display, labeled respectively 1 through 5, are connected to bits 0 through 4 of the IORB of the 6522 #3. This is illustrated on Fig 5-16. The two IORB's reside respectively at addresses A000 and AC00.

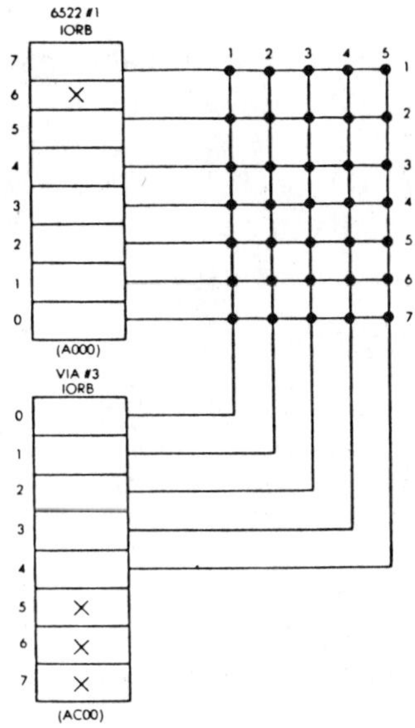

Fig. 5-16: Connecting the 5x7 LED

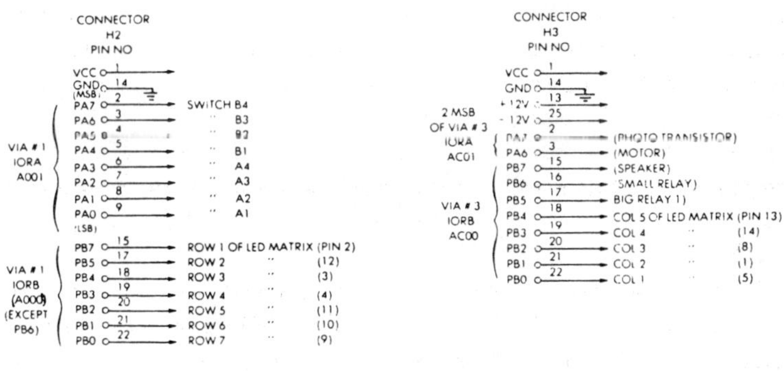

Fig. 5-17: The Connectors to the LED

The basic problem is to select the appropriate combinations of rows and columns to display the dots representing a character. Any character of the alphabet can be generated with a 5 × 7 matrix. Here we will, for example, display all the hexadecimal characters, i.e., the digits 0 through 9 and the letters A through F. Let us examine their encoding.

An LED dot "on" will be represented by a "0" bit. An LED dot "off" will be represented by a "1" bit. This is because an LED will be turned on by grounding its row connection. The pattern required to

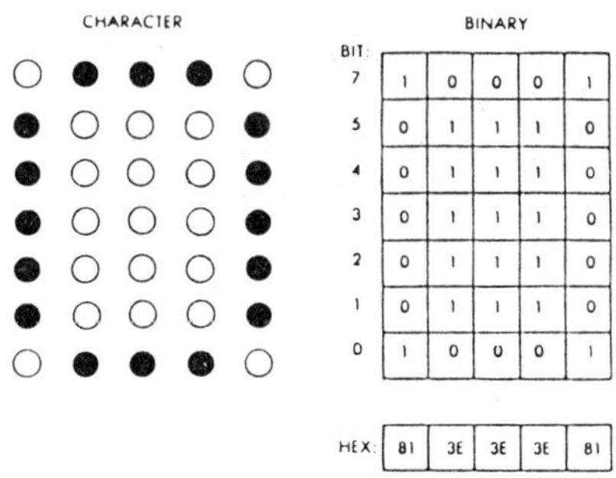

Fig. 5-18: Displaying "0"

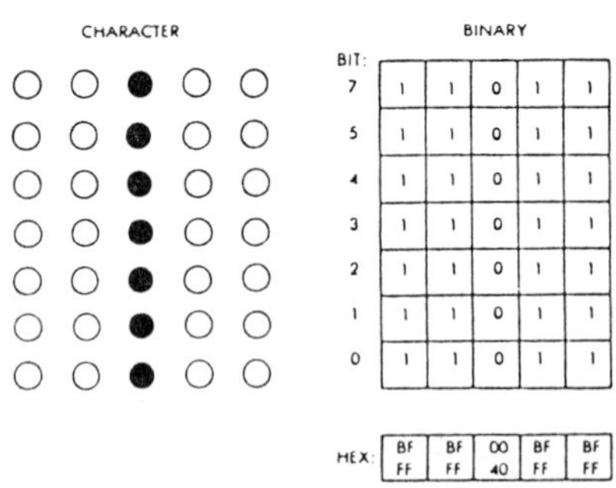

Fig. 5-19: Displaying "1"

display a "0" appears on Fig 5-18. Naturally, the user is free to choose any other pattern and other encodings may be used. For example, as an exercise, the user might want to display a "0" with square edges rather than with round edges. It should be a simple matter to modify the table accordingly.

The equivalent binary representation of the encoding appears on the right of Fig 5-18. The hexadecimal equivalent is indicated at the bottom of the binary table. The reader should remember that row 6 is not used. It is indifferent, i.e., can be assumed to be either a "0" or a "1". For example, let us look at the hexadecimal encoding for character "0" on Fig 5-18. The first column has the value "1000001", or more exactly "1-000001" where a "-" represents the value of bit 6, which is not used. Let us assume for example that bit 6 will be set at "0". Then, the value of the first column is "10000001" or "81" hexadecimal.

Similarly, the value of the second column is (adding a 0 for bit 6) "00111110" or "3E" hexadecimal.

The five columns for the digit "0" are therefore:

81, 3E, 3E, 3E, 81

Let us look now at character "1". It is shown on Fig 5-19 and the required binary encoding appears on the right of the illustration.

Assuming that bit 6 is a "0," the equivalent hexadecimal representations are:

BF, BF, 00, BF, BF

If we assume that bit 6 is set at the value 1, then the encoding would be:

FF, FF, 40, FF, FF

Any one of the values "0" or "1" for bit 6 may be used for any one of the columns as long as we do not use bit 6 for any purpose.

A complete table for encoding the characters "0" through "F" is shown on Fig 5-21.

Exercise 5-7: *Show the shape of the characters 0 through F using this table.*

Exercise 5-8: *Rewrite the table in a more consistent way assuming that bit 6 is always "0".*

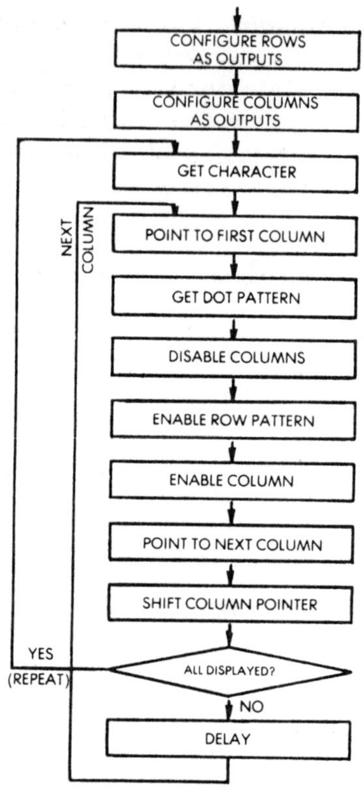

Fig. 5-20: Driving a Dot-Matrix LED

The flow chart for the LED dot matrix program appears on Fig 5-21. Both rows and columns are configured as outputs by loading the appropriate bit patterns into the corresponding data direction registers of the 6522. The dot pattern for the character must then be displayed. The dots will be displayed in succession for every column of the LED. For each character, the program must therefore access five successive entries in the dot-matrix table, corresponding to the five columns of dots required to display the character. This particular program will then cycle and display the character indefinitely. The dots are displayed by turning off the columns (erasing the previous pattern), then enabling the row pattern corresponding to the desired dot positions, and enabling the column on which they are to be illuminated. Then, the next column must be displayed. All dots should be lit up for the same period of time, if they are to appear as having a uniform intensity to the observer. Further, all columns must be scanned in a time period of less than 1/10 of a second if no visible blinking is to occur. The delay routine at the end of the program is adjucted accordingly. The program appears below and on the next page.

character	8 LSB addr	col 1	col 2	col 3	col 4	col 5
0	90	81	3E	3E	3E	81
1	95	FF	FF	00	FF	FF
2	9A	DE	7C	7A	76	CE
3	9F	DD	76	76	76	C9
4	A4	F3	EB	DB	00	FB
5	A9	05	76	76	76	79
6	AE	C1	76	76	76	D9
7	B3	7F	7F	7F	7F	00
8	B8	C9	76	76	76	C9
9	BD	CD	76	76	76	C1
A	C2	E0	DB	7B	DB	E0
B	C7	00	76	76	76	C9
C	CC	C1	7E	7E	7E	DD
D	D1	00	7E	7E	7E	C1
E	D6	00	76	76	76	76
F	DB	00	77	77	77	77

Table resides in memory locations 0090-00DF.

Fig. 5-21: A Dot Matrix Table

Connection: Connector A to Connector H2
Connector AA to Connector H3

This program gets 8 LSB character address from location 0001, then goes to table shown on Fig 5-21 to pick up the data pattern for the selected character and display it on the LED matrix.

Before executing this program, pre-load the 8 LSB of character address at loc-0001.

The character pattern should be stored on Page 0 as indicated on Fig 5-21. (The 8 MSB of character address are all 00 on Page 0)

Fig. 5-22: Basic LED Matrix Display (Program 5-3)

Note: 1) A character generator can be used to replace this table.
2) The LED matrix used is 5 × 7, i.e. 7 bits are needed to define the the pattern of each column, but the above table uses 8 bits; this is because the program uses VIA #1 I/0 register B to drive the 7 rows and only 7 bits of this register can be used. Bit 6 is indifferent because it is dedicated for ON BOARD CASSETTE IN only.

```
0180  A9 BF        BSCLED LDA  #$BF     Before execution, 0001 should be
                                          pre-set
0182  8D 02  A0           STA  $A002    To the selected character addr.
0185  A9 1F               LDA  #$1F     Set VIA #1 DDRB = BF to drive
                                          7 rows
0187  8D 02  AC           STA  $AC02    Set VIA #3 DDRB = 1F to drive
                                          5 columns
018A  A9 00               LDA  #$00
018C  85 03               STA  $03      Set 8MSB of character addr =
                                          00 at  0003
018E  A2 00               LDX  #$00
0190  A5 01        RPTCHA LDA  $01      Move the pre-set 8LSB of character
                                          addr. from  0001 to 0002
0192  85 02               STA  $02
0194  A0 10               LDY  #$10     Set (Y) = $10 for enabling last
                                          column
0196  A1 02        NXTCOL LDA  $02      (A) = current column pattern of
                                          selected character
0198  8E 00  AC           STX  $AC00    Disable all columns before enable
                                          rows
019B  8D 00  A0           STA  $A000    Enable rows
019E  8C 00  AC           STY  $AC00    Enable current column
01A1 , E6 02              INC  $02      Advance address in ($0002) for next
                                          column
01A3  98                  TYA
01A4  4A                  LSR  A        Shift (Y) right by one bit for
                                          enabling next column
01A5  A8                  TAY
01A6  C0 00               CPY  #$00     (Y) = 00 means all 5 columns
                                          displayed
01A8  D0 03               BNE  DLY3     If not, branch to DLY3 to
                                          compensate timing (1), if yes,
                                          repeat the whole character
01AA  4C 90  01           JMP  RPTCHA
01AD  A2 FF        DLY3   LDX  #$FF
01AF  E8           LP3    INX
01B0  EO 00               CPX  #$00
01B2  30 FB               BMI  LP3
01B4  4C 96  01           JMP  NXTCOL   Then go to enable next column
```

Notes: 1) This compensation is needed or else the last column will always be

Fig. 5-22: (Continued)

enabled longer making the last column brighter than the first 4 columns.

2) The compensation mentioned above only solves the problem partially. The brightness is still not even, due to a different number of LED's enabled in each column. To solve this, a more detailed program can be written to take the number of LED's enabled for each column into account for timing compensation.

Fig 5-22: (continued)

The program is shown here. The first four instructions of the program condition the data direction registers for the rows and the columns, specifying that they be outputs:

```
BSCLED   LDA #$BF
         STA  $A002     SET VIA #1 = 7 ROWS
         LDA  #$1F
         STA  $AC02     SET VIA #2 = 5 COLUMNS
```

By convention, in this program, the table location of the character to be displayed is contained at memory location "01" in page 0. The location of the character to be displayed is, for example, 90 for the character "0," 95 for character "1," and so on, as indicated in the table at the beginning of the program. (An improved program will be suggested below.) As an example, if we are to display the character "2," then the value 9A must have been deposited at memory address 01. Since we will need to point successively to 5 table entries for each of the columns corresponding to this character, we will need to generate the addresses 9A, 9B, 9C, 9D, and 9E. In order not to destroy our original character pointer "9A," we will use two extra memory locations at addresses 02 and 03 to contain the current pointer to the column dots being displayed. Since we are operating in page 0, the contents of memory location 03 will be set to "0" (high order byte of the address). This is accomplished by:

```
LDA  #$00
STA  $03
```

Whenever we enter the main display loop, register X will be assumed to have the value "00". It will be used to disable an output register:

```
LDX  #$00
```

The first column we will point to is the one at the address specified in location 01 (the character table entry pointer). We therefore transfer the contents of memory location 01 to address 02:

```
RPTCHA   LDA  $01
         STA  $02
```

Register Y is used as a shift counter and, at the same time, to enable selectively one of the columns. It is set initially to the value "10" in order to enable the first column:

```
         LDY  #$10
```

The "1" will then be shifted right by one bit position, in order to enable the next column, and so on. When the "1" finally falls off the register, all 5 columns have been displayed for the character, and the loop may be restarted. Since this register is not only used to enable one of the columns but also to count up to 5, it is labeled as a *shift-counter.* The dot pattern for the current column is obtained by accessing the table entry at address 02:

```
NXTCOL   LDA  $02
```

The dot pattern is now contained in the accumulator. Let us display it. All columns are first disabled by loading "0" in the IORB:

```
         STX  $AC00
```

The accumulator contents are then output to the IORB to enable the rows:

```
         STA  $A000
```

Finally, the appropriate column is enabled and the selected LED will light up:

```
         STY  $AC00
```

An LED will light up only when it is connected to an active column and to a grounded (0) row. Each "0" in the dot pattern will light up the corresponding dot in the selected column.

Memory location "02" is then incremented, in order to point to the next dot pattern entry for the character. We must then shift our column pointer right by one position and determine whether we have already displayed all columns or not:

```
        INC  $02
        TYA            Y CANNOT BE SHIFTED
                       DIRECTLY
        LSR  A
        TAY            STORE RESULT BACK IN A
        CPY  #$00
        BNE  DLY3
        JMP  RPTCHA
```

Since it is not possible to shift the Y register directly, it must be transferred first to the accumulator, which is then shifted, and the contents of the accumulator are copied back into register Y. The contents of the accumulator are then tested for the value "0" (a program improvement may be suggested to the present coding). If the accumulator is "0", we are done and have displayed all 5 columns. Otherwise, we must implement a delay during which the LED will light up and then display the next column:

```
DLY3    LDX  #$FF
        INX
        CPX  #$00
        BMI  LP3
        JMP  NXTCOL
```

Index register X is used as a counter, and a traditional delay is achieved by incrementing the index register a reasonable number of times, then branching back to the next column at address NXTCOL.

Program improvements: In order to improve this program by reducing the number of instructions, let us first consider some coding modifications. Then, we will examine improvements to the functions performed.

Exercise 5-9: *Rewrite the delay routine DLY3 so that it uses fewer instructions.*

Exercise 5-10: *Inspect the least three instructions of the routine NXTCOL, from address 01A6 on (see Fig 5-22). Can you suggest another way to test whether the last "1" bit in Y has been shifted out?*

Exercise 5-11: *Add a routine to this program so that, instead of depositing a pointer to the table entry at address 01, one needs to deposit only the actual character value. With this routine, the user must be able to deposit an actual value between "0" and "F," and have this program display it correctly. In order to do this, one must convert the character value to the table value. For example, "0" will correspond to "90" (see table at the beginning of program 5-3), "1" will correspond to "95", and so on. The equation is: Starting address = 90 + code × 5.*

Note: Instead of performing a formal multiplication by five, one can use a shortcut: Remember that shifting left by one bit position is equivalent to a multiplcation by 2 and that 5 = 2+ 2 +1. A multiplication by 4 can be accomplished by 2 successive left shifts.

Exercise 5-12: *Write an additional routine which will display a string of characters. It will assume that the starting address of the string of characters is contained at memory location 01. Each character will be displayed for one second. The string of characters may be terminated by any code which is not between 0 and F. The program will then pause for two seconds and display the string again.*

Let us now consider improvements to the functions of the program. We will add four switches and develop a program which displays the hexadecimal value of the switches.

DISPLAYING SWITCH VALUES

We will read here the values of four input switches in binary, and display the corresponding hexadecimal character on the LED matrix. The flow-chart for the algorithm appears on Fig 5-23. The program reads the four switches, then points to the beginning of the conversion table as defined in the previous program, then computes the table offset for the character to be displayed. The address in the table for the binary code corresponding to the dots to be illuminated is obtained by multiplying the value of the character by 5. This can be verified by in-

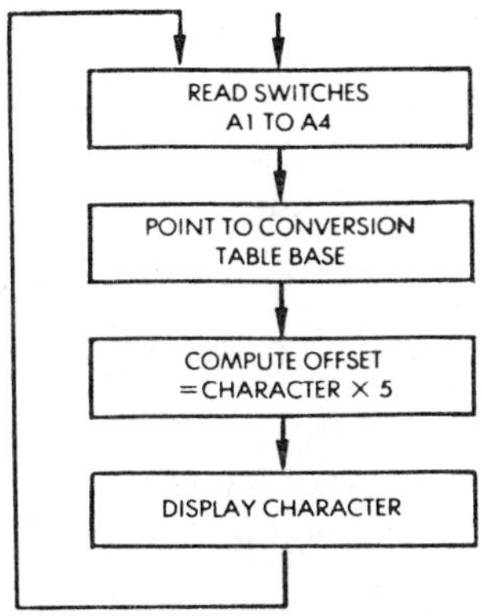

Fig. 5-23: Displaying a Switch Value

specting the table shown on Fig 5-22. The address of the first column to be displayed is then computed and deposited in address 01 in page 0. The previous program is used to display the character on the LED display. The program is:

Connection: Connector A to Connector H2
Connector AA to Connector H3

This program reads the switches A1 to A4 to compute one of 16 hexadecimal values and display it.

This program uses program 5-3 as a subroutine. Before execution, change program 5-3 as follows:

1) At loc 01A8, data 4C should be changed to 60 (60 is the machine code for RTS).
2) The timing compensation constant at loc. 1AC is FF, this should be changed to F0, because this program enables the last column longer than program 5-3.

Fig 5-24: Advanced LED Matrix Display (Program 5-4)

```
0200  A9 00        RDCHA  LDA  #$00
0202  8D 03  A0           STA  $A003    Set VIA #1 DDRA =00 for input
                                          mode
0205  AD 01  A0           LDA  $A001    Read switches B1 - B4 and A1 - A4
0208  29 0F               AND  #$0F     Ignore B1 - B4
020A  A8                  TAY           Store A1 - A4 reading in (Y)
020B  A2 90               LDX  #$90     Calculate character address and store
                                          at loc. 0001. 90 is the base address
020D  86 01               STX  $01
020F  A2 00               LDX  #$00     Addition counter
0211  18           ADD    CLC           A contains switch reading
0212  65 01               ADC  $01      Loop through the addition five times
0214  85 01               STA  $01      90 + (A)
0216  98                  TYA
0217  E8                  INX           Restore switch value in A.
0218  E0 05               CPX  #$05     (X) = 5 means calculation completed
021A  30 F5               BMI  ADD
021C  20 80  01           JSR  BSCLED   Then call BSCLED for display
021F  4C 00  02           JMP  RDCHA    Then update switch reading
```

Fig. 5-24: (Continued)

The program appears on Fig 5-24. The first two instructions configure the data direction register for port A as input, so that the switches can be read:

```
RDCHA    LDA  #$00
         STA  $A003
```

Then, the contents of switches A1 through A4 are read. This program ignores the value of switches B1 through B4.

```
         LDA  $A001
         AND  #$0F      MASK B1-B4
```

The contents indicated by the switches are saved in index register Y:

```
         TAY
```

The start address of the table (90) is then stored at memory address 01:

```
         LDX  #$90
         STX  $01
```

We will add to this start address the required offset to access the first column of dots for the character specified by the switches. The offset is computed by multiplying the value of the switches by 5. Index register X is used as a counter from 0 to 5. It is initialized to zero:

```
        LDX  #$00
```

The contents of memory location 01 are incremented by 1:

```
ADD     CLC
        ADC  $01
        STA  $01
```

The CLC instruction (clear carry) must be used prior to any addition. In addition, we assume that the binary mode has been set (the 6502 may operate either in binary mode or in decimal mode). Unless otherwise specified, the 6502 will normally operate in binary mode, since a reset operation will have cleared the flags register, thereby setting the binary mode.

The value of the switches is then restored in the accumulator from index register Y where it had been saved. The addition counter X is incremented by 1 and tested against the value 5:

```
        TYA
        INX
        CPX  #$5
        BMI  ADD
```

As long as the value of 5 has not been reached, the addition is repeated. Once the value 5 has been reached, memory location 01 has been conditioned to the proper value and the subroutine BSCLED (the previous LED display program) is called:

```
        JSR  BSCLED
```

The program then loops back in order to read the switches again and display the character they specify:

```
        JMP  RDCHA
```

TONE GENERATION

We have seen in the previous chapter how a tone may be generated by simply sending a square wave of the desired frequency to a speaker. The square wave form is generated by turning the speaker alternatively on and off. The duration during which the speaker is on or off is called the half-period. The delay measurement may be performed by software, or else by hardware, using the built-in interval timer of the 6522. This built-in interval timer has been used previously, and we will use here a *software* method to control the delay duration. We will first develop a basic program to generate a tone, then improve it to generate computer music.

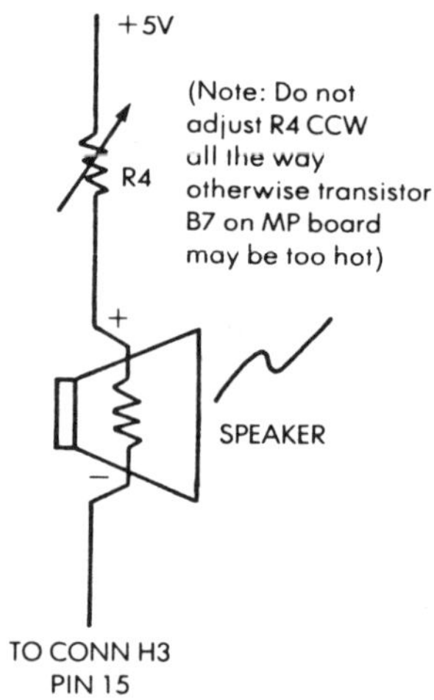

Fig. 5-25: Speaker Connection

The hardware connection is shown on Fig 5-25. An additional resistor of 50 ohms or more should be placed in series with the speaker to limit the output current. The speaker is connected to the buffered output of the SYM. Turning the variable resistor down to zero could burn out both the pot and the output transistor on the board.

The technique used to generate a tone is the usual square wave method, implemented by a delay subroutine.

Connection: Connector A to Connector H2
Connector AA to Connector H3
This program activates the speaker with a pre-set frequency which has to be loaded into loc. 0004 before execution.

```
0230  A9  80        BSCSPK  LDA  #$80
0232  8D  02  AC            STA  $AC02    Set VIA #3 DDRB = 80 for speaker
                                            output
0235  A9  80        AGAIN   LDA  #$80
0237  8D  00  AC            STA  $AC00    Set speaker driver high = activate
                                            speaker
023A  20  48  02            JSR  DLYB     Call delay
023D  A9  00                LDA  #$00
023F  8D  00  AC            STA  $AC00    Set speaker driver low = turn
                                            speaker off
0242  20  48  02            JSR  DLYB     Call delay
0245  4C  30  02            JMP  AGAIN    Repeat
```

Subroutine DLYB: This subroutine is similar to subroutine DLYA except that

1) This delay is much shorter.
2) This delay takes delay index from loc. 0004 (the index should be a negative value).

```
0248  A6  04        DLYB    LDX  $04      Load delay value into X
024A  E8            LPXB    INX           Increment X
024B  E0  00                CPX  #$00
024D  30  FB                BMI  LPXB     Loop till (X) =0
024F  60                    RTS
```

Fig. 5-26: Basic Speaker Activation (Program 5-5)

The delay parameter for this program must be loaded at memory location 0004 prior to execution. It controls the frequency of the tone which is generated. The program is shown on Fig 5-26. The data direction register B is configured for output on bit 7:

```
BSCSPK    LDA  #$80
          STA  $AC02
```

The speaker is then turned on:

```
AGAIN     LDA  #$80
          STA  $AC00
```

The speaker is left on for a duration specified by the contents of memory location 0004, by calling the delay subroutine DLYB:

```
        JSR  DLYB
```

The speaker must then be turned off. This is accomplished by resetting bit 7 of the IORB to "0":

```
        LDA  #$00
        STA  $AC00
```

The speaker must then be left off for the same duration and a call to subroutine DLYB accomplishes this:

```
        JSR  DLYB
```

The program then loops on itself:

```
        JMP  AGAIN
```

The delay subroutine DLYB is essentially like the delay subroutine DLYA of Program 5-1:

```
DYLB    LDX  $04     DELAY VALUE
LPXB    INX          COUNTER
        CPX  #$00
        BMI  LPXB
        RTS
```

Let us compute the duration of the delay introduced by this subroutine. The duration of each instruction is indicated on the right of each instruction below:

```
                                # cycles
             LDX   $04            (2)
        ┌──► INX                  (2)
Loop    │    CPX   #$00           (2)
        └─── BMI   LPXB           (3)
             RTS                  (6)
```

In addition, the JSR (Jump to Subroutine) instruction, used to call this subroutine, introduces a 6-cycle delay. The loop is executed 256 − 4 = 252 times.

The total delay duration is therefore:

$$6 + 2 + (2+2+3) \times 252 + 6 = 14 + 7 \times 252 = 1778 \text{ microseconds}$$

Exercise 5-13: *Modify the delay routine by using a decrement instruction rather than an increment instruction.*

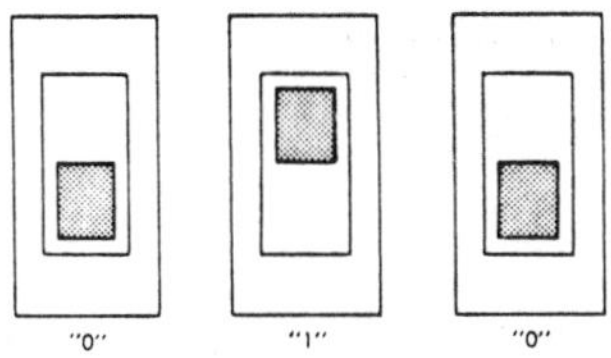

Fig. 5-27: Binary Switches Specify Tone

MUSIC

The basic method for generating a tone of set frequency has been presented. We want now to be able to play a tune. This program will read the binary value of the three switches A-1 through A-3 and generate a tone corresponding to the switch setting (see Fig 5-27). The note "C" (do) will be generated for a "0" switch setting, then a "D" (re) for "1", etc. A full octave plus one note, i.e., "C" through "C", can be played according to the setting of the three switches. This program will use the previous one as a subroutine. Before executing it, the contents of memory location 0245 should be changed from "4C" to "60". A frequency table will be constructed first, which specifies the duration of the half period of the square wave which generates the tone. It appears on Fig 5-28.

```
0050  A2 80        TUNE   LDX  #$80    Frequency for middle C
0052  4C 74  02           JMP  LD04
0055  A2 90               LDX  #$90    Frequency for D
0057  4C 74  02           JMP  LD04
005A  A2 9C               LDX  #$9C    Frequency for E
005C  4C 74  02           JMP  LD04
005F  A2 A4               LDX  #$A4    Frequency for F
0061  4C 74  02           JMP  LD04
0064  A2 B0               LDX  #$B0    Frequency for G
0066  4C 74  02           JMP  LD04
0069  A2 B8               LDX  #$B8    Frequency for A
006B  4C 74  02           JMP  LD04
006E  A2 C0               LDX  #$C0    Frequency for B
0070  4C 74  02           JMP  LD04
0073  A2 C4               LDX  #$C4    Frequency for C
0075  4C 74  02           JMP  LD04
```

Fig. 5-28: Music Frequency Table

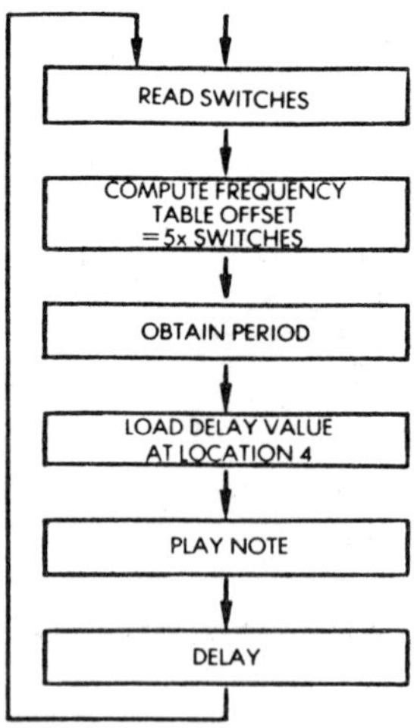

Fig. 5-29: Music Program Flow Chart

Connection: Connector A to Connector H2
Connector AA to Connector H3

This program reads switches A1 – A3 and activates the speaker at 8 different frequencies defined by the switches.

This program uses Program #5 as a subroutine, hence before execution data at loc. 0245 should be changed from 4C to 60.

This program branches to a frequency table for tuning. The frequency table has to be loaded as follows before execution:

```
0250  A9 00        MUSIC  LDA  #$00      Pre-load the 8MSB of indirect jump
                                           address
0252  85 05               STA  $05       At loc 0005 (= 00 because frequency
                                           table is on page 0 )
0254  8D 03  A0           STA  $A003     Set VIA #1 DDRA = 00 for input
                                           mode
0257  A0 C0        KEY    LDY  #$C0     (Y) = delay constant for each frequency
0259  AD 01  A0           LDA  #$A001    Read in switch setting
025C  29 07               AND  #$07      Ignore upper five bits
025E  85 04               STA  $04       Save switch setting at $04
0260  18                  CLC
0261  65 04               ADC  $04
0263  65 04               ADC  $04
0265  65 04               ADC  $04
0267  65 04               ADC  $04       Calculate relative address in
                                           frequency table
0269  85 04               STA  $04
026B  A9 50               LDA  TUNE      Add the base address of frequency
                                           table
026D  65 04               ADC  $04
026F  85 04               STA  $04       Store the calculated address (8LSB) at
                                           loc. 0004
0271  6C 04  00           JMP  ($0004)   Jump indirect into frequency table
0274  86 04        LD04   STX  $04       Get the correct frequency constant
0276  20 30  02    CBSPK  JSR  BSCSPK    Call BSCSPK to activate speaker
0279  88                  DEY
027A  C0 00               CPY  #$00      Loop till (Y) = 0 before sensing the
                                           switches
027C  D0 F8               BNE  CBSPK     Again
027E  4C 57  02           JMP  KEY       Go to sense switches again
```

Fig 5-30: The Music Program (Program 5-6)

The flow-chart for the algorithm appears on Fig 5-29. The program reads the contents of the three switches, then computes the offset required to obtain the corresponding delay from the frequency table.

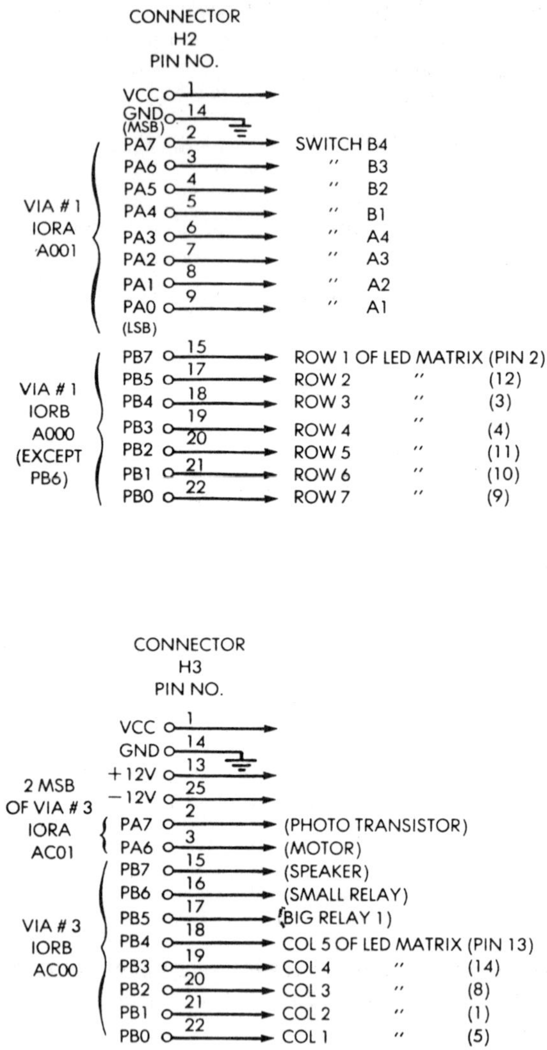

Fig. 5-31: Connections For Music Program

This offset is equal to 5 times the value specified by the switches. The period of the square wave is then obtained and the note is played for a specified duration. The program then loops on itself so that the next note (or the same) is played. The program is shown on Fig 5-30 and the connections are shown on Fig 5-31. Locations 04 and 05 will be used for an indirect jump. Since the frequency table resides in Page 0, the contents of location 05 are immediately initialized to 0:

```
MUSIC    LDA   #$00
         STA   $05
```

The data direction register, DDRA, is then configured to "00" to specify the input mode:

```
         STA   $A003
```

The duration of the tone is specified by the contents of register Y which correspond to an outer loop delay (to be explained below):

```
KEY      LDY   #$C0
```

The contents of the three switches A1, A2, and A3 are then read from the IORA at location A001, and the upper 5 bits are masked (set to 0):

```
         LDA   #$A001
         AND   #$07
```

This switch setting is then saved at memory location 04 so that the accumulator can be used for other purposes:

```
         STA   $04
```

In order to compute the offset in the frequency table, the value obtained from the switch is multiplied by 5. This is done here by adding this value to itself 4 times:

```
         ADC   $04
         ADC   $04
         ADC   $04
         ADC   $04
         STA   $04
```

The resulting offset value is then stored at memory location 04 and we are now ready to obtain the half period from the frequency table:

```
LDA    TUNE     BASE ADDRESS
ADC    $04
STA    $04      BASE & DISPLACEMENT
JMP    ($0004)  JUMP INDIRECT
STX    $04      FREQUENCY CONSTANT
```

The value is returned in register X and saved at memory location 04 then the subroutine BSCSPK is called to activate the speaker:

```
CBSPK    JSR    BSCSPK
```

This speaker will be activated as many times as specified by the contents of register Y:

```
DEY
CPY    #$00
BNE    CBSPK
```

Finally, once the tone has been generated for the specified duration, the keys are read again:

```
JMP    KEY
```

Let us improve this program:

Exercise 5-14: *We could simplify the frequency table by storing in it only the binary value for the delay, i.e.: $80, $90, etc. Modify the program above so that the switch setting is used as an index to retrieve the contents of this new table. Note the significant improvement in the length of the overall program.*

Exercise 5-15: *If you actually run this program on a microcomputer board, you will notice a minor problem: The program does indeed play the required note; however, you can hear at the same time a lower frequency note. By inspecting carefully the last 5 instructions of the music program, you should be able to determine what the problem is. Can you propose a modified program which will eliminate this? (Hint: The speaker may be turned off "too long".)*

***Exercise 5-16:** Looking at the instructions* "ADC $04" *repeated 4 times, suggest a way to achieve the same result with fewer instructions, if possible.*

***Exercise 5-17:** The third instruction from the end is* "CPY #$00". *Is it necessary?*

The table used in the music program has been designed "by ear", not by computing the correct frequencies. The values should now be checked to determine how good this table is.

In America, the Standard Pitch is A4 = 440 Hz. The frequency of notes doubles every twelve half notes. From tone T_1 to tone T_2, the frequency is $N_2 = \sqrt[12]{2} \times N_1$.

The frequencies are indicated on Fig 5-28 .

***Exercise 5-18:** Inspect the BSCSPK routine to compute its timing. Knowing the periods of the notes (Fig 5-28), compute the correct theoretical frequency constants. (Hint: Do not forget that the speaker is alternately on and off for half a period.)*

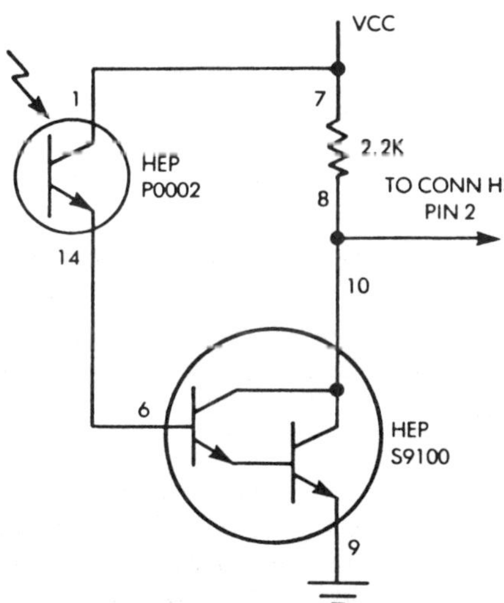

Fig. 5-32: The Photo-Transistor Circuit (on socket M3)

A BURGLAR ALARM

We are going to implement here a realistic home alarm system. Entry in the home will be detected by a phototransistor-detector set; it is assumed that the light emitter is normally on. Whenever the beam is broken, the detector will indicate it and the alarm will be triggered. This alarm will generate a siren sound in the speaker. Further improvements will be suggested at the end of the program.

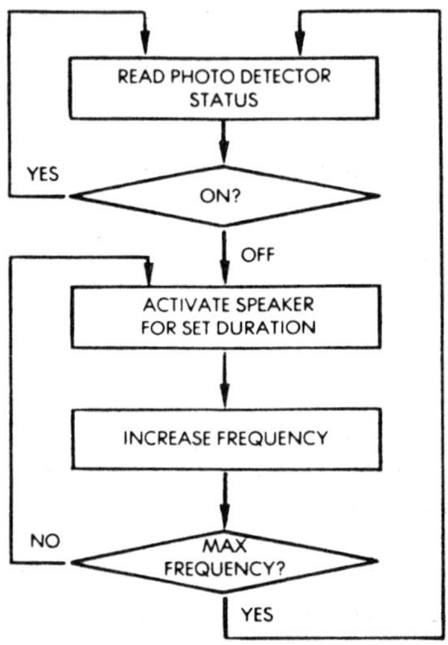

Fig. 5-33: Alarm Flow Chart

The connection of the phototransistor is shown on Fig 5-32, and the flow-chart for the algorithm appears on Fig 5-33. We will read the status of the detector. As long as it stays "on", nobody has broken the beam, and we keep reading. Whenever the beam is broken, the status of the detector will be "0" ("off"), and the speaker will be activated for a set duration. In order to generate a siren-like sound, the frequency of this sound will be progressively increased until a maximum frequency is reached (see Fig 5-35). At this point, the status of the photodetector will be probed again, and as long as it is off, the siren will keep sounding. The program appears on Fig 5-34. The phototransistor input is connected to bit 7 of the IORA of VIA #3 (see Fig 5-32).

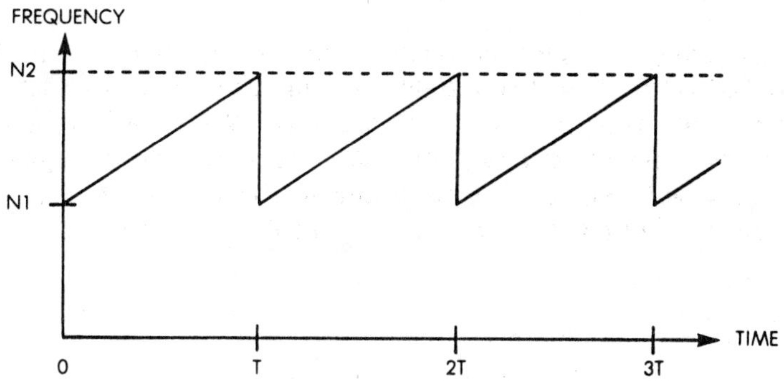

Fig. 5-34: A Siren Sound

Connection: Connector A to connector H2
Connector AA to connector H3

This program senses the phototransistor output, if the output is high, which means the phototransistor is in the dark and is in the off-state, nothing will happen, but if the output is low, which means the phototransistor gets light and is in the on-state, then sound the alarm immediately.

This program also uses BSCSPK as a subroutine, hence loc. 0245 should be changed to 60.

```
0281  A9 00        ALARM  LDA  #$00
0283  8D 03  AC           STA  $AC03   Set VIA #3 DDRA = 00 for input
                                          mode
0286  AD 01  AC  DETECT   LDA  $AC01   Read photo-transistor output
0289  29 80               AND  #$80
028B  C9 80               CMP  #$80
028D  F0 F7               BEQ  DETECT  If output = high, keep polling
028F  A9 80               LDA  #$80    Else sound the alarm by setting the
                                          initial
0291  85 04               STA  $04     Frequency constant = 80 at loc. 0004
0293  A0 F0        LP7    LDY  #$F0    Set delay constant = F0 at (Y)
0295  20 30  02  SOUND    JSR  BSCSPK  Call BSCSPK to activate speaker
0298  C8                  INY
0299  C0 00               CPY  #$00
029B  30 F8               BMI  SOUND   Loop till (Y) = 0 before changing
                                          frequency constant
```

Fig. 5-35: Burglar Alarm (Program 5-7)

```
029D  A9  01          LDA  #$01      Increment frequency constant by 1
029F  18              CLC
02A0  65  04          ADC  $04
02A2  85  04          STA  $04
02A4  C9  A8          CMP  #$A8      Loop till highest frequency constant
                                       = A8
02A6  30  EB          BMI  LP7
02A8  4C  86  02      JMP  DETECT    Then sense phototransistor o/p again
```

Fig. 5-35 (continued): Burglar Alarm

The first instructions of the program implement a polling loop which tests the status of the phototransistor:

```
ALARM    LDA   #$00
         STA   $AC03
DETECT   LDA   $AC01
         CMP   #$80
         BEQ   DETECT
```

As soon as the photodetector is off (on an experiment board, this will be achieved by covering the LED detector with a finger or a piece of cloth), the alarm will be sounded. The specified initial frequency constant is loaded at memory address 04, and the tone duration for this frequency is loaded in register Y. The previous subroutine BSCSPK is then called to sound the speaker:

```
         LDA   #$80
         STA   $04
LP7      LDY   #$F0
SOUND    JSR   BSCSPK
         INY
         CPY   #$00
         BMI   SOUND
```

The subroutine is called as many times as necessary to implement the secondary delay specified by register Y. The frequency constant is then incremented by 1, stored back at memory location 04, and compared against the maximum frequency. As long as the maximum frequency has not been reached, the program keeps generating a sound of increasing frequency.

```
LDA   #$01
CLC
ADC   $04
STA   $04
CMP   #$A8
BMI   LP7
JMP   DETECT
```

Whenever the maximum frequency has been reached, the program loops back to its starting point. Several improvements are possible.

In a realistic home use, this alarm system will be placed somewhere inside a house and the photoelectric pair including a light-emitter and a receiver will be placed somewhere in the house. (In practice, an infra-red beam is often used as it is not visible to the eye.) It may be positioned to protect a room or to protect the entrance to the house. The program should be improved so that, once the alarm has been turned on, it is possible to leave the house without triggering it. The first exercise will bring this improvement:

Exercise 5-19: *Modify the program so that the user may exit from the house within two minutes after the system has been armed (turned on). In other words, no alarm should be triggered for two minutes after the program is turned on, regardless of the status of the photodetector. After that, the alarm should operate normally.*

Another problem must be solved: Upon re-entering the house, we really do not want the alarm to sound immediately. We want to have the time to walk to the microcomputer board and turn it off. The next exercise will take care of that:

Exercise 5-20: *Once the alarm has been armed (after two minutes), it should not sound until 30 seconds after detection of an entry.*

Let us improve further: There might be some minor variations in the light beam which may cause noise on the line. We do not want this to trigger the alarm.

Exercise 5-21: *Modify the program so that the alarm is triggered only if the beam is interrupted for more than .05 second.*

Let us keep improving: In case an animal should trigger the alarm, we want to provide an automatic shut-off system. We want the alarm to sound for two minutes after detection has occurred and then turn itself off.

Exercise 5-22: *Modify the program so that the alarm will sound for two minutes after detection has occurred and then turn itself off.*

In addition, at the time that detection occurs we may want to take additional action such as turning on the lights or else dialing the police. This can be easily accomplished by merely turning on an external relay.

Exercise 5-23: *Modify the above program so that an external relay is turned on every time that entry is detected.*

Note that this feature can be used advantageously even if you cannot dial the police automatically: You could connect a lamp to the relay output so that even if an intruder came in and left quickly when the alarm sounded, his intrusion would be revealed by the fact that the lamp would be left turned on at the time you returned.

Exercise 5-24: *Could we delete the instruction* CPY #$00 *at address* 0299*?*

Exercise 5-25: *Add a "panic button" which you can press to activate the alarm at any time. Modify the sound of the alarm so that neighbors can differentiate between a "panic call" and an "alarm."*

DC MOTOR CONTROL

The goal of this program is to control the speed of an ordinary DC motor. A regular low-cost 12 volt hobby DC motor will be connected to the microcomputer board, and the rotational speed will be specified by switches. Three switches will be used, so that 8 different combinations may be specified, corresponding to 8 rotational speeds. The motor circuit is shown on Fig 5-36. The switches connection is shown on Fig 5-27.

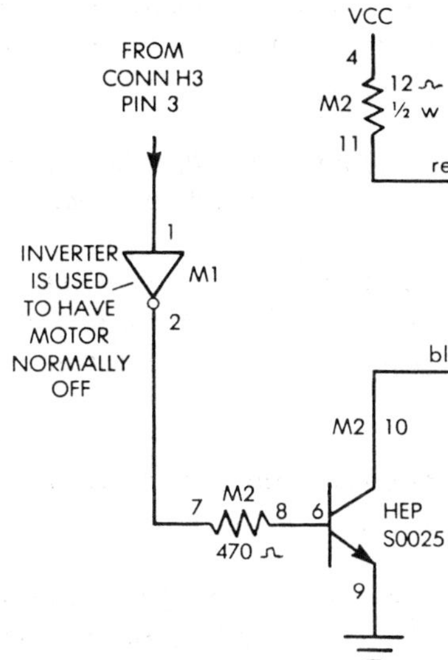

Fig. 5-36: Motor Circuit

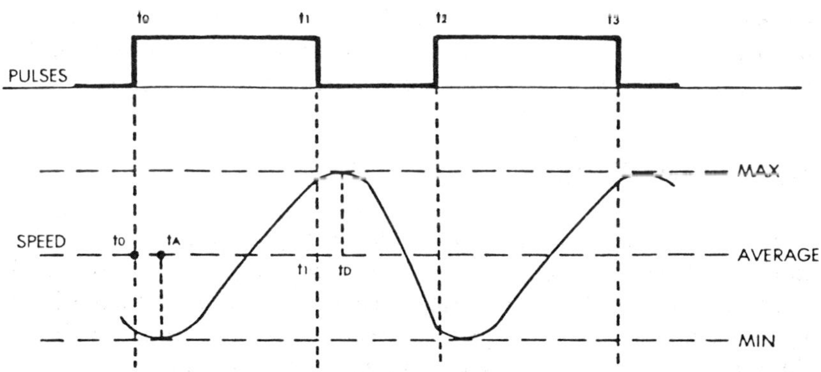

fig. 5-37: Digital Speed Control

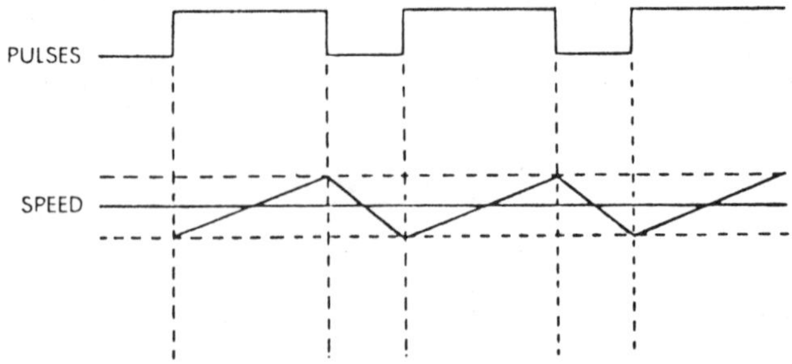

Fig. 5-38: Simplified Speed Diagram

The principle used to control the speed of the motor is to turn it on for a set duration, then turn it off. Because of its rotational inertia, the motor will keep turning for a while. A new pulse will then be generated and the motor will be turned on again. It will accelerate again. This pattern will be repeated. The resulting speed of the motor is shown on Fig 5-37. A simplified diagram showing the same curve appears on Fig 5-38. It is essentially a saw-tooth curve where the motor accelerates as long as power is applied, then decelerates until it receives the next pulse. The average speed is indicated by the horizontal line between the minimum and the maximum speeds on Fig 5-37. It can be seen from the illustration that the speed will constantly oscillate between its minimum and its maximum values. If the speed must be defined with good accuracy, then the minimum and the maximum speeds will have to be close. This will be achieved by using shorter pulses. However, as in any phenomenon that involves inertia and oscillations, instabilities will occur. In particular, it should be noted on the illustration that, if the "on" pulse is given before time "t_D", then the speed will not decrease and will keep increasing instead. This is because the inertia of the motor has not had the time to slow it down to where the speed would decrease. More complex phenomena may still occur. This topic will not be discussed in detail here. Simply, we will design a program with adjustable delays and later adjust these delays by trial and error so that they work with the type of motor we are using. The reader should simply be aware that these delays can be adjusted in various ways to improve the accuracy of the speed obtained and/or to eliminate oscillation problems.

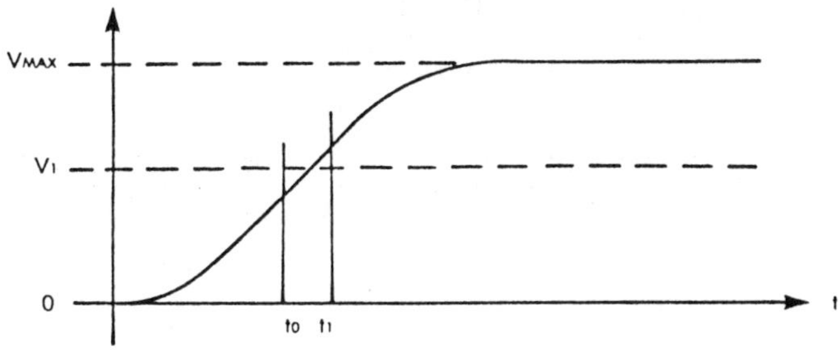

Fig. 5-39: DC Motor Speed Curve

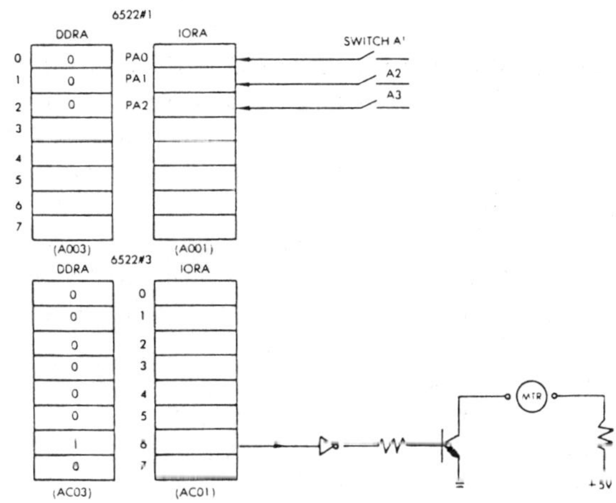

Fig. 5-40: The Connections

The Hardware Connections

Two ports are used: on the 6522 #1 and on the 6522 #3. They are shown on Fig 5-40. The IORA register is used as an input port for the three switches. The switch setting will determine the speed of the motor. The corresponding value of the DDRA is shown on the left of the illustration. The IORA of 6522 #3 is used as an output port to control the motor itself. The motor is connected to bit 6 of the IORA. The detail of the interface appears on Fig 5-36. The driver is required to invert the signal and the transistor is used to provide sufficient current.

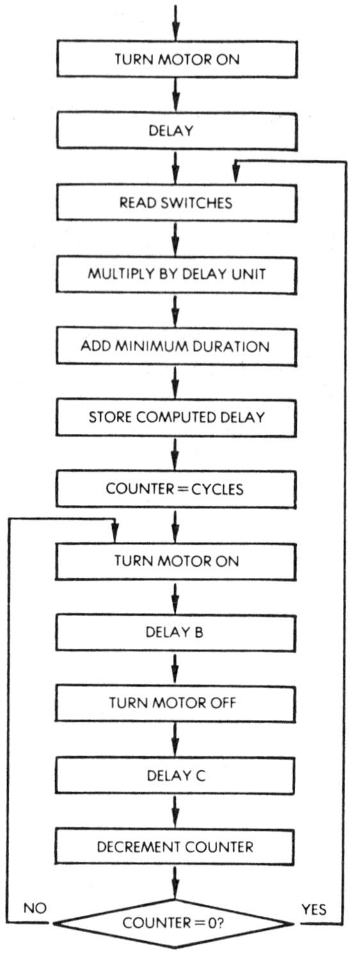

Fig. 5-41: DC Motor Flow Chart

The Program

The flow-chart for the program is shown on Fig 5-41. The motor will be turned on for a duration T_{on}, and turned off for a duration T_{off}. In this algorithm, the duration $_{off}$ is fixed, and the duration T_{on} is increased for every switch setting from "000" to "111." The minimum T_{on} duration here corresponds to the switch setting "000".

The delay corresponding to a switch setting can be computed with the formula:

$$T_{on} = \text{MIN} + \text{Unit} \times \text{switches.}$$

Numerically, the constants used for the delays are:

$$DELAY_{OFF} = C0_H = 192 \text{ decimal}$$
$$DELAY_{ON} = 80_H + \text{switches} \times 0B_H = 128 + \text{switches} \times 11 \text{ (decimal)}$$

SWITCHES	000	001	010	011	100	101	110	111
DELAYON	128	139	150	161	172	183	197	205

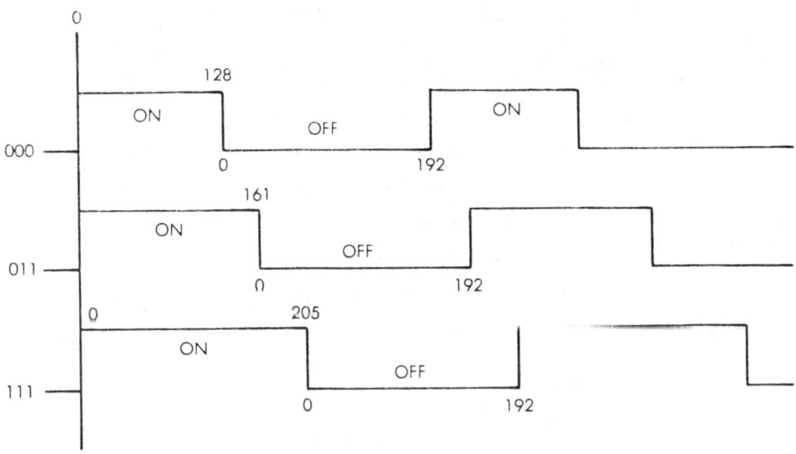

Fig. 5-42: The Waveforms

The waveforms generated by the various settings appear on Fig 5-42. Let us now turn to the flow-chart of Fig 5-41. The motor is first turned on for an initial duration to achieve initial rotational speed (otherwise, a train of short pulses might not be able to get it started). The value of the switches is then read and the resulting delay must be computed. The value of the switches multiplied by the delay unit is added to the minimum pulse duration. The resulting computed delay is stored. The motor is then turned on for the computed delay duration. This is Delay B. Then the motor is turned off for a duration called Delay C. This process is then repeated for several cycles in order for the speed to stabilize. Then, the switches can be read again and, if the setting has been changed, the new speed will be generated. Note that the built-in delay implemented by repeating the cycle several times also takes care of the switch bounce problem. If no delay was allowed for the speed to stabilize, the switches should be debounced by hardware or by software (see reference C207 for details on debouncing).

```
     Connection: Connector A to connector H2
                 Connector AA to connector H3
     This program reads switches A1 – A3 to define motor speed desired and rotates
        the motor accordingly.
     This program uses two subroutines: DLYA and DLYB.

02B0  A9 40        MOTOR  LDA  #$40
02B2  8D 03  AC           STA  $AC03    Set VIA #3 DDRA = 40 for motor
                                          driver output
02B5  A9 00               LDA  #$00     Turn on motor for one DLYA
                                          duration to obtain initial speed.
02B7  8D 01  AC           STA  $AC01
02BA  A9 FF               LDA  #$FF
02BC  85 00               STA  $00
02BE  20 20  01           JSR  DLYA
02C1  A9 00               LDA  #$00     Set VIA #1 DDRA = 00 for input
                                          mode
02C3  8D 03  A0           STA  $A003
02C6  AD 01  A0    MTRSP  LDA  $A001    Read switches
02C9  29 07               AND  #$07     Ignore upper 5 bits
02CB  A8                  TAY           (Y) = switch reading
02CC  A9 0B               LDA  #$0B     Set on-delay difference = 0B
                                          between switch settings
02CE  85 06               STA  $06
02D0  C0 00        LP8    CPY  #$00
92D2  F0 07               BEQ  ONDLY
02D4  18                  CLC
02D5  65 06               ADC  $06
02D7  88                  DEY           Loop till ($0006) = (switch reading
                                          x $0B)
02D8  4C D0  02           JMP  LP8
02DB  85 06        ONDLY  STA  $06
02DD  A9 80               LDA  #$80     Calculate the on-delay constant = 80
                                          +(switch reading × 0B)
```

Fig. 5-43: Motor Control (Program 5-8)

```
02DF  18                 CLC
02E0  65  06             ADC  $06
02E2  85  06             STA  $06      Store this constant at loc. 0006
02E4  A0  C0             LDY  #$C0
02E6  A5  06      MTRON  LDA  $06      Move (0006) to loc. 0004 before call
                                         DLYB
02E8  85  04             STA  $04
02EA  A9  00             LDA  #$00     Turn motor on
02EC  8D  01  AC         STA  $AC01
02EF  20  48  02         JSR  DLYB     Then call DLYB
02F2  A9  C0             LDA  #$C0     Set off-delay constant = C0,
                                         independent of switch reading,
                                         load this into loc. 0004
02F4  85  04             STA  $04
02F6  A9  40      MTROFF LDA  #$40     Turn motor off
02F8  8D  01  AC         STA  $AC01
02FB  20  48  02         JSR  DLYB     Then call DLYB
02FE  88                 DEY
02FF  C0  00             CPY  #$00     Repeat this on-off sequence till (Y)
                                         = 00
0301  30  E3             BMI  MTRON
0303  4C  C6  02         JMP  MTRSP    Then read switch setting & repeat
                                         over
```

Fig. 5-43: (Continued)

The program appears on Fig 5-43. The first four instructions turn the motor on by conditioning the data direction register and placing "0" in the data register:

```
MOTOR    LDA   #$40
         STA   $AC03
         LDA   #$00
AC       STA   $AC01
```

A delay value "FF" is then deposited at memory location "00", which is the agreed convention for passing a parameter to the subroutine DLYA (see Program 5-1). The subroutine DLYA is then called. It implements the initial delay required for the motor to achieve its initial speed.

```
         LDA   #$FF
         STA   $00
         JSR   DLYA
```

The value of the switches is then read:

```
        LDA   #$00
        STA   $A003
MTRSP   LDA   $A001
```

And the value of the lower three bits is extracted from the reading:

```
        AND   #$07    MASK
        TAY
```

For each switch position except "000", an additional duration unit will be added to the minimum duration of "0B" hexadecimal. The value of the switch reading is, therefore, saved in index register Y, and the initial duration delay is loaded into memory location "06".

```
        LDA   #$0B
        STA   $06
```

LP8 is an addition loop which will add the delay unit as many times as specified by the switch setting:

```
LP8     CPY   #$00
        BEQ   ONDLY
        CLC
        ADC   $06
        DEY
        JMP   LP8
```

Exercise 5-26: Can you modify the code above so that CPY #$00 is unnecessary? Why?

Once ONDLY has been reached, memory location "06" contains the additional duration for the pulse, as specified by the switches. It is then added to the minimal duration of "80" hexadecimal:

```
ONDLY   STA   $06
        LDA   #$80
        CLC
        ADC   $06
        STA   $06
```

The Y register is then loaded with the value "C0" hexadecimal which specifies the number of times that we will turn the motor on and off:

```
        LDY   #$C0
```

Once location MTRON has been reached, memory location "06" contains the constant necessary to implement the "on" delay. It is transferred to memory location "04" so that the subroutine DLYB may be used. The motor is turned on and the delay is implemented:

```
MTRON   LDA   $06
        STA   $04
        LDA   #00      TURN MOTOR ON
        STA   $AC01
        JSR   DLYB
```

The off delay must then be implemented, and the value "C0" hexadecimal is stored at memory location "04". The motor is explicitly turned off and the delay is implemented by the subroutine DLYB:

```
        LDA   #$C0
        STA   $04
MTROFF  LDA   #$40     MOTOR OFF
        STA   $AC01
        JSR   DLYB
```

After the motor has been turned off, the loop counter Y is decremented. Index register Y is used here to count the number of times that the on/off cycle will be executed. It has been loaded with the initial value "C0" hexadecimal, and is decremented every time that the motor is turned off. If the value "0" has been reached, the program goes back to the beginning and reads the next switch setting. If Y has not decremented to "0", then the program loops back to MTRON in order to go again through an on/off cycle:

```
        DEY
        CPY   #$00
        BMI   MTRON
        JMP   MTRSP
```

Let us now consider improvements to the program.

Exercise 5-26: *Let us first perform some improvements in style: Examine the program corresponding to memory addresses* 2D0 *to* 2D8. *Can you suggest any improvement to the way the code has been written?. (Hint: One instruction can be saved.)*

Exercise 5-27: *Same question for lines* 02FF *to* 0303.

Exercise 5-28: *This exercise is valuable if you are indeed performing an experiment on a real motor: increase progressively the "off" delay by changing the appropriate constant in the program. What happens?*

Exercise 5-29: *Same question by reducing the off delay. What is the problem?*

Exercise 5-30: *Another algorithm which could be used would be to send a variable number of "on" pulses of constant duration, i.e., to adjust the duration of the "off" delay rather than the "on" delay. Can you modify the program accordingly?*

Important note. Because every motor has different characteristics, the timings in the program are best determined by a trial and error process. You are strongly encouraged to modify the various constants which have been used, such as the minimum "on" delay, the minimum "off" delay, and the timing increments until you obtain by experience the settings which give the best results. In addition, if you intend to load the motor by connecting it to a real device, you will introduce additional inertia and friction parameters. Additionally, low-cost hobby motors may be poorly lubricated and after a period of a few weeks or a few months may have much higher friction. They will then require a much longer warm-up period and may also require longer pulses. As long as you are aware of the mechanical mood of your motor, you should be able to adjust the parameters accordingly.

Exercise 5-31: *Can you determine what happens if you send very short "on" pulses?*

The above program is an open control loop where we are controlling the speed of the motor but not measuring it. Let us suggest possible improvements to this technique.

Exercise 5-32: *Display the speed setting of the motor. The speed setting of the motor could be identical to the switch setting, i.e., you could just display a number between* 0 *and* 7.

In the next exercise, we are going to implement a real closed control loop. This exercise is of special interest if you want to understand the concept used to regulate a disk, for example. A simple and effective way to measure the speed of the motor is to attach a cardboard disk to the shaft. A hole, called the index hole, should be perforated in the disk. Arrange the disk so that a light emiter is on one side of the disk while a light receiver is on the other side. They sould be arranged in such a way that when the hole passes in front of the light-emitting diode, the light illuminates the receiver. (This is exactly what is done on a computer floppy disk to detect the index hole.) Every time that the receiver is illuminated, a pulse will be detected. By counting the number of pulses per second, one obtains the exact rotational speed of the motor in rotations per second. Using this information, it is possible to adjust the duration, or the frequency, of the "on" and the "off" pulses to regulate the speed with great precision. The comparison between this technique and a floppy disk stops here, as, in a floppy disk, the speed must be regulated with great precision and must be regulated even during a partial rotation of the disk, not just on the average. On a disk, additional information is therefore used: Information is recorded on a track and the pulses are used to adjust the rotational speed during part of a single revolution. In the case of our motor, it is important to measure the actual speed, since any friction or any load on the motor will modify its rotational speed. All the hardware and software techniques necessary to implement this have been already introduced.

Exercise 5-33: *Write the program that will accomplish it.*

ANALOG TO DIGITAL CONVERSION (A HEAT SENSOR)

A thermistor will be used here to measure temperature. Any other heat sensing device could be used. The resistance of a thermistor changes with the temperature. We will use this feature to detect temperature changes in the environment and take action depending on the temperature measured. The main problem is, given an analog value (one which changes value continuously, here the resistance of the thermistor), the main problem is to measure it with a binary number. This is called the analog to digital conversion problem. Components exist today which will perform this conversion essentially with a single component. Here, we are going to use a less costly (and more educational) solution which uses a digital-to-analog converter plus some opamps. The analog-to-digital conversion will be performed by program. (For details on analog to digital conversion techniques, the reader is referred to Chapter 5 of our reference book C207 Microprocessor Interfacing Techniques.)

We will use here a *successive approximations technique.* An initial binary value will be generated, then converted to analog form. This analog approximation will then be compared with a comparator to the value generated by the thermistor. The result of the comparison, "0" or "1" depending on whether it is smaller or greater, will be used to generate the next successive approximation.

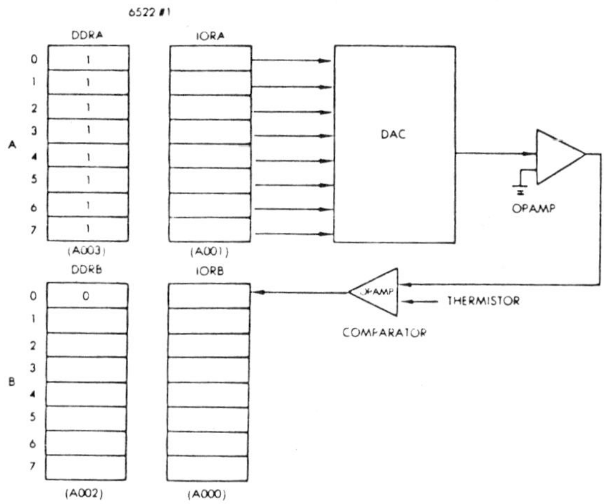

Fig. 5-44: Connection for ADC

The hardware connection used in this experiment is shown on Fig 5-44. The 8-bit output of IORA is connected to an 8-bit DAC, a digital-to-analog converter. This digital-to-analog converter transforms the 8-bit binary number into an analog signal whose value is then compared to the one of the thermistor. The comparator output is connected back to bit 0 of IORB, where it can be sensed.

The algorithm will turn on in succession every bit of IORA from the most significant bit (bit 7), down to bit 0.

The initial value tried will be "10000000". If it is found to be too small, then bit 7 will be left unchanged, and bit 6 will be turned on. In this example, the next approximation will be "11000000". If at this point the approximation is too high (as decided by reading the output of the comparator), then bit 6 will be turned off. The next approximation will be "10100000". Bit 5 has been automatically turned on. And so on.

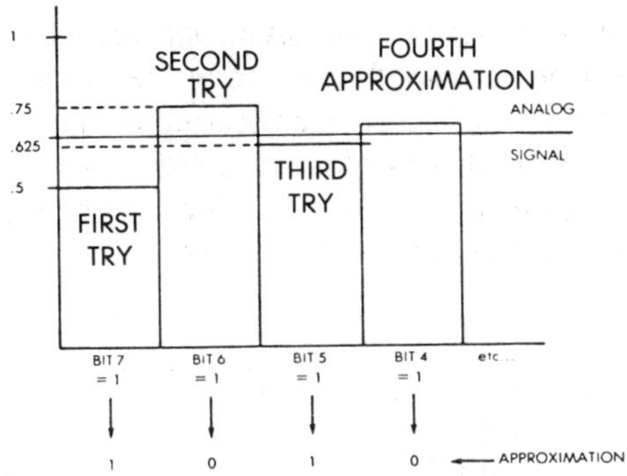

Fig. 5-45: Successive Approximations

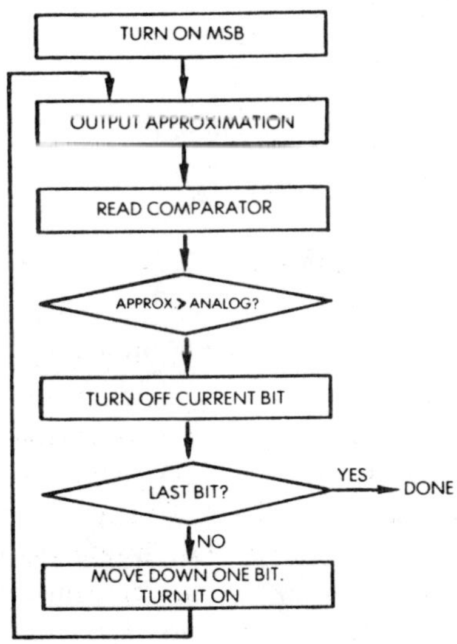

Fig. 5-46: Successive Approximation Flow Chart

The formal algorithm is illustrated on Fig 5-45, and on the flow chart of Fig 5-46. The process continues until all 8 bits have been used. The resulting binary value is the best possible approximation of the analog value, with the precision afforded by an 8-bit representation. Naturally, the process assumes that the algorithm is executed fast enough, so that the analog value does not change faster than it can be measured. Otherwise, *a sample-and-hold* circuit should be used. The illustration of Fig 5-45 shows the successive-approximations closing in on the exact value of the analog signal. Every time that a new bit is used, the interval is divided by two.

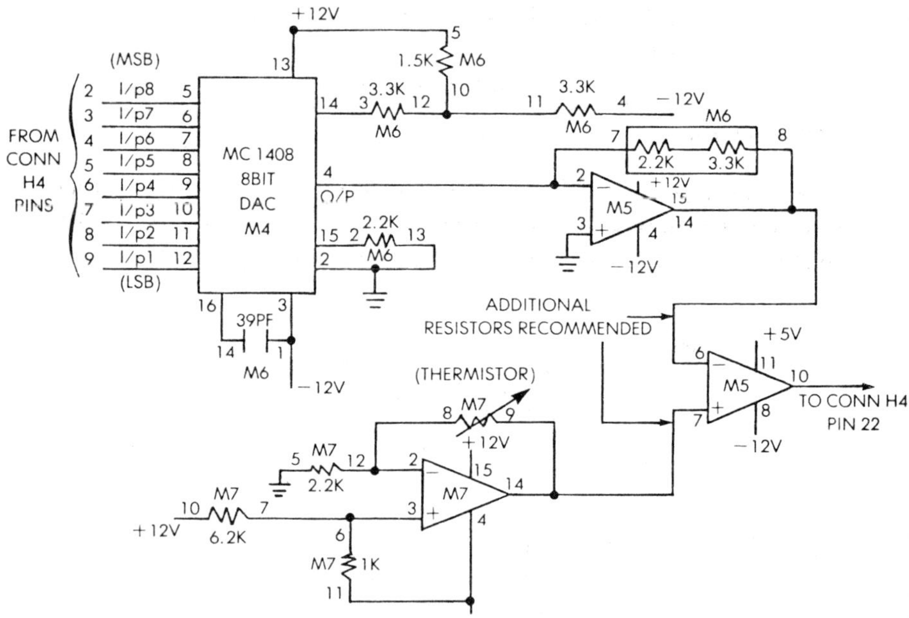

Fig. 5-47: ADC Interface

The Hardware Connection

The hardware connection is shown in Fig 5-47 and 5-48. The DAC used here is an MC1408, which requires a 12-volt power supply. Its output drives the M5 opamp which feeds into the comparator input. The thermistor appears at the bottom of the illustration, and feeds into the other input of the comparator. The comparator output connects to pin 22 of connector H4 and feeds into bit 0 of IORB for the 6522 #1.

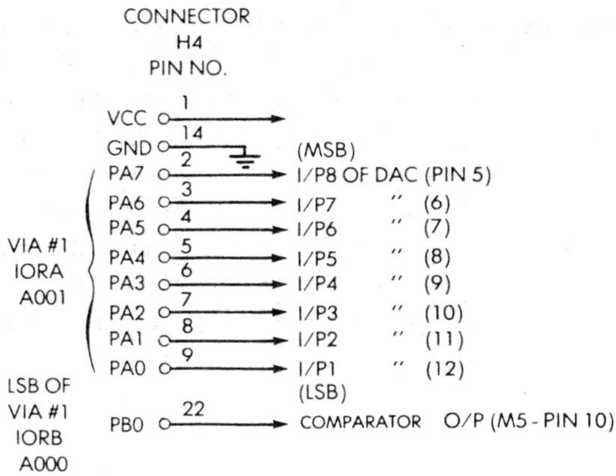

Fig. 5-48: Connection to H4

The Program

In this program, the value of the temperature measured on the thermistor will be indicated by the frequency of a tone on the speaker. The tone's pitch will become higher as the temperature increases.

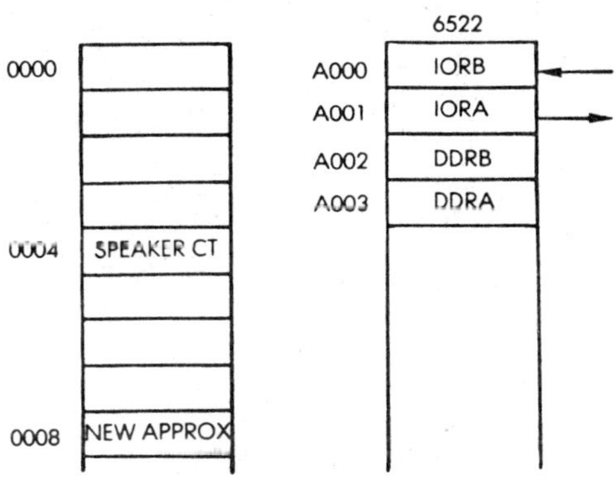

Fig. 5-49: ADC Memory Map

The memory map for the analog-to-digital conversion program is shown on Fig 5-49. Memory location 4 is used to store the constant used by the DLYB program, which generates a delay specified by the value of the constant. Location 8 is used to store the new approximation being computed by the program. The 6522 #1 is shown at memory locations A000 and following.

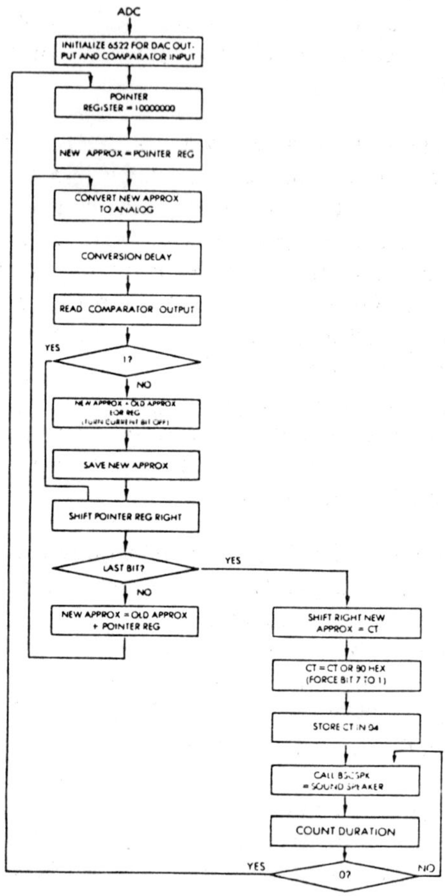

Fig. 5-50: ADC Flow Chart

The flow-chart appears on Fig 5-50. The 6522 is first initialized to configure IORA as output for the DAC, and IORB bit 0 is used as comparator input. The pointer register is set to its initial value of "10000000" which is the initial approximation value. This pointer register will point to the bit being turned on in the approximation sequence loop. The bit will be shifted right every time that a loop has been completed.

The initial value of the approximation is set equal to the pointer register. It is then converted to analog. A delay is implemented in order to give enough time to the DAC to perform the conversion, then its output is examined. If the comparator output is "1", then the new approximation is too small and its value does not need to be changed. If the comparator output is "0", then the approximation value is too high and the current bit must be turned off. Next, the pointer register is shifted right by one bit position, in order to point to the next bit to be used in this technique. If the last bit has been reached, the final approximation has been computed. If not, a new approximation is obtained by adding the value of the pointer register to the old approximation and a new iteration is started.

Once an approximation value has been obtained, a tone must be generated whose pitch depends on the value of the measurement. A minimum tone frequency is used and the pitch constant is obtained by adding the value of the approximation to this minimum frequency. The speaker routine is then called to sound the speaker (BSCSPK). After the speaker has sounded for a minimum period of time, the program reads the value of the thermistor again.

On the board, the fastest way to obtain an audible response is to use a soldering iron (or a cigarette) and put its tip close to the thermistor. The sound coming from the speaker should increase quickly in pitch. When the soldering iron is removed, the speaker will go through a reverse sequence. Naturally the thermistor could be located away from the board. Properly isolated, it could be placed on a wall, in a cup, or in any other device whose temperature should be measured. A thermocouple could also be used or be immersed in liquid so that the liquid's temperature could be measured. The temperature of the environment could be controlled, for example, by using a heating coil connected to one of the relays. One remaining problem would be to calibrate the thermistor so that precise temperature measurements can be made.

Connection: Connector A to connector H4
Connector AA to connector H3

This program uses successive approximations with a DAC so that the analog value of a thermistor can be sensed continuously. Then the approximated digital value is used as a parameter to control the frequency of the speaker. From the frequency change, one can tell whether the temperature is increasing or decreasing.

Speaker frequency is proportional to temperature (or resistance of the thermistor)

This program uses BSCSPK and DLYB subroutines.

```
0360  A9 FF        ADC     LDA  #$FF
0362  8D 03  A0            STA  $A003     Set VIA #1 DDRA = FF for output
                                            to drive DAC
0365  A9 00                LDA  #$00
0367  8D 02  A0            STA  $A002     Set VIA #1 DDRB = 00 for input to
                                            read comparator
036A  A9 80        FSTBIT  LDA  #$80      Set MSB for approximation
036C  A8                   TAY            (Y) stores current bit under test
036D  85 08                STA  $08       Loc. 0008 stores current value under
                                            test
036F  A5 08        NXTBIT  LDA  $08
0371  8D 01  A0            STA  $A001     Output current value to DAC
0374  A2 20                LDX  #$20      Delay for comparator to settle
0376  CA           LP9     DEX
0377  E0 00                CPX  #$00
0379  10 FB                BPL  LP9
037B  AD 00  A0            LDA  #$A000    Read comparator output
037E  29 01                AND  #$01      Get bit 0
0380  C9 01                CMP  #$01
0382  F0 05                BEQ  SHFBIT    Comparator output = 1 means DAC
                                            output is still too low, keep
                                            current value and go to shift bit
                                            else, DAC output is too high
                                            deduct current bit from current value,
0384  98                   TYA              then shift bit
0385  45 08                EOR  $08
0387  85 08                STA  $08
0389  98           SHFBIT  TYA
038A  4A                   LSR  A         Right shift (Y) by 1 bit for next
                                            approximation
038B  A8                   TAY
038C  C9 00                CMP  #$00
038E  F0 08                BEQ  ECHO      (Y) = 0 means approximation
                                            completed, go to turn on speaker
0390  18                   CLC
```

Fig. 5-51: Analog-Digital Converter (Program 5-9)

```
0391  65  08                ADC  $08     (Y) = 0, current value plus next bit
                                           as the output to DAC for next
                                           approximation
0393  85  08                STA  $08
0395  4C  6F  03            JMP  NXTBIT
0398  A0  F0       ECHO     LDY  #$F0    Delay constant for each frequency
039A  A5  08                LDA  $08
039C  4A                    LSR  A
039D  85  04                STA  $04
039F  A9  80                LDA  #$80
03A1  05  04                ORA  $04     Calculate corresponding frequency
                                           constant and store it at loc. 0004
03A3  85  04                STA  $04
03A5  20  30  02   SPKR     JSR  BSCSPK  Call BSCSPK to activate speaker
03A8  88                    DEY
03A9  C0  00                CPY  #$00
03AB  30  F8                BMI  SPKR
03AD  4C  6A  03            JMP  FSTBIT  Repeat for next approximation
                                           sequence
```

Fig. 5-51: (Continued)

Let us now examine the program, then suggest improvements. The program is shown on Fig 5-51. The first four instructions condition the data direction registers for Ports A and B of the 6522 #1, respectively as output (with a DAC), and as input (for the comparator):

```
ADC     LDA   #$FF
        STA   $A003   DDRA 1 = FF = OUTPUT
        LDA   #$00
        STA   $A002   DDRB1 = 00 = INPUT
```

The next two instructions store the literal value "80" hexadecimal into register Y. This is the pointer register which is set to the initial value "10000000" binary.

```
FSTBIT  LDA   #$80
        TAY
```

The memory location "08" has been reserved to store the current approximation. It is initialized to 10000000:

```
        STA   $08
```

The main iteration loop is then entered. The binary approximation is obtained from memory location "08" and sent to the DAC:

```
NXTBIT    LDA   $08
          STA   $A001
```

A delay is then implemented to allow the comparator to settle:

```
          LDX   #$20
LP9       DEX
          CPX   #$00
          BPL   LP9
```

The output of the comparator is read:

```
          LDA   #A000   COMPARATOR OUTPUT
```

Bit 0 of IORB is then extracted and tested:

```
          AND   #$01    BIT 0
          CMP   #$01
          BEQ   SHFBIT
```

If its output is "1", the approximation is still too low, and the next bit must simply be turned on. If it is "0," the value is too high and the current bit must be turned off:

```
          TYA
          EOR   $08
          STA   $08
```

Having adjusted the value of the current approximation if necessary, the pointer register is now shifted right for the next bit of the iteration:

```
SHFBIT    TYA
          LSR   A
```

If the last bit has been reached, we have obtained the best possible approximation and we branch to location ECHO to sound the speaker:

```
          TAY
          CMP   #$00
          BEQ   ECHO
```

Otherwise, we turn on the next bit of the approximation and we go back to the beginning of the loop:

```
        CLC
        ADC   $08
        STA   $08
        JMP   NXTBIT
```

The ECHO routine will sound the speaker in function of the value measured. In this routine, register Y is used to implement the delay during which the speaker will be sounding. It is loaded here with the initial value "F0" hexadecimal. The value of the approximation is read from memory location "08", and shifted right by one bit position. This means that the value of the last bit of the approximation will not be reflected by a variation in the pitch of the note in this technique.

Bit 7 is forced to the value "1", so that the speaker oscillates at a minimum guaranteed frequency to be audible.

The resulting value is stored at memory location "04" which used to pass a parameter to the BSCSPK routine which has already been presented:

```
ECHO    LDY   #$F0
        LDA   $08
        LSR   A
        STA   $04
        LDA   #$80
        ORA   $04
        STA   $04
SPK     JSR   BSCSPK   ACTIVATE SPEAKER
```

Next, the routine is called and sounds the speaker at the specified frequency. Register Y is then decremented and tested, and, as long as it does not reach the value "0", the speaker will sound:

```
        DEY
        CPY   #$00
        BMI   SPKR
        JMP   FSTBIT
```

Once the speaker has sounded for the set duration, the program returns to the beginning of the approximation to sense again the status of the thermistor.

Exercise 5-34: *Display in hexadecimal the value of the approximation you have obtained.*

Exercise 5-35: *Is it possible to eliminate all "CPY #$00" from the program?*

Exercise 5-36: *Calibrate your thermistor by determining the computed measurement which corresponds to given temperatures measured with a thermometer. Store these values in a table so that you can display the actual temperature and not the approximation register value.*

Exercise 5-37: *Modify the program so that the speaker will sound 1 to 10 times, depending on the temperature it is measuring. At room temperature, it will sound once. At high temperature, it will sound 10 times. This is an audible way to communicate the results of the measurement (with a poor precision).*

Exercise 5-38: *Having calibrated your thermistor, add a heating coil (which can be obtained from a hardware store at low cost) and regulate the temperature of a glass of water so that the water remains at precisely temperature T. Caution: Most thermistors are not waterproof, so that they may have to be attached to the outside of the container rather than immersed inside. However, you can also obtain thermo-couples or other thermistors which are water resistant and can be immersed directly into liquid.*

Exercise 5-39: *As a further improvement to your home burglar-alarm system (see program 5-7), add a routine to the basic control loop that checks the temperature periodically. If the temperature becomes larger than a set level, say 35 degrees centigrade, then sound the alarm. You have just implemented a fire detector.*

Exercise 5-40: *Another variation: The goal is to hold your soldering iron at the appropriate distance of the thermistor to bring it to a temperature of say 80°C. Modify your program so that it blinks an LED quickly as long as the thermistor's temperature is much less than the desired temperature, then blinks slowly as you approach the desired temperature level. Another LED should also be used to display whether you are over or under the desired temperature.*

SUMMARY

In this chapter, real world applications have been developed, ranging from simple home control to complex industrial control. A variety of input-output devices have been connected to the microprocessor board, ranging from switches and LED's to a DC motor, a thermistor, and a photo-emitter-receiver pair. The selection of devices and techniques presented here should enable you to start solving a large number of actual control problems. For more information on specific interfacing techniques, refer to our reference C207, "Microprocessor Interfacing Techniques". Also, to develop a true programming expertise, experimenting is strongly encouraged.

In the next chapter, actual computer peripherals will be interfaced to the 6502 board.

CHAPTER 6

THE PERIPHERALS

INTRODUCTION

In this chapter, we will connect the 6502 board to actual computer peripherals. The programs in this section have been optimized to demonstrate "elegant" techniques for solving problems, by using the specific resources of the components involved.

First, we will connect a standard 16-key matrix keyboard and make "clever" use of the input-output register capabilities to minimize the number of instructions needed to identify the character and display it. Next, we will manufacture a home-built paper-tape-reader at low cost. In this application, the paper tape can simply be pulled manually through the reader and will be correctly read by the microcomputer. Finally, we will show how simple it is to connect a microprinter (or an ASCII keyboard) to the microcomputer board. At this point, the reader should feel confident that he has acquired the skills required to solve most usual problems encountered in actual applications.

The applications presented here are simple to realize, and useful. The programs are directly applicable to SYM, KIM or AIM65, with minor changes. Practice is, therefore, again encouraged.

All the programs are short, and will provide valuable knowledge even if you do not plan to connect a peripheral. Careful reading of this chapter is recommended to all.

KEYBOARD

We will first connect an external 16-key matrix keyboard (called a hexadecimal keyboard) and identify the key which has been pressed. The keyboard connection is shown on Fig 6-1. It is connected to the 8 bits of the IORA of a 6522. Bits 0 through 3 are connected to the rows, while bits 4 through 7 are connected to the columns. On the diagram, the key at the intersection of row 2 and column 7 has been pressed, connecting the row to the column.

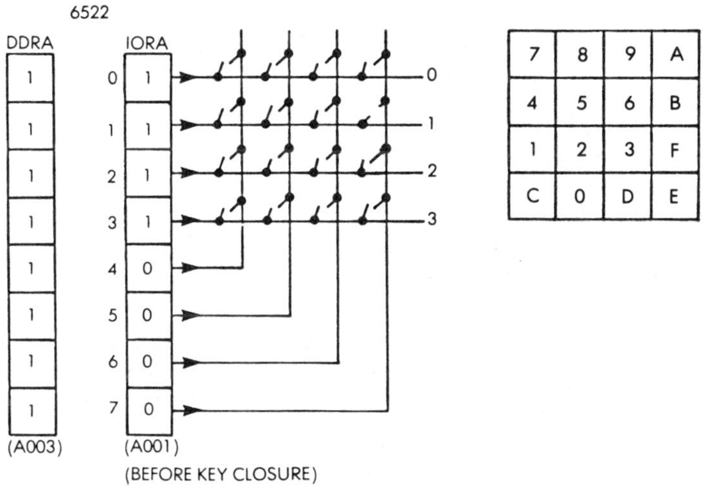

Fig. 6-1: Connecting the Keyboard

The data direction register is configured for all outputs. A special feature of the IORA of the 6522 will be used by this program. The IORA is really a *bi-directional* register. We will condition all rows to be 1's and all columns to be 0's. If a key is pressed, the corresponding row will be grounded by the column connected to it through the switch. When reading back the IORA, the "0" value in the corresponding row will be written into the register. In our example, when reading IORA after the key has been depressed, the resulting value will be "00001011" in binary or "0B" in hexadecimal. Using a "line-reversal technique" (for details, see our references C201 or C207), we will write "11111011" binary or "FB" hexadecimal in IORA. Since row number 2 is "0" (grounded), it will also ground column 7. When reading back the contents of IORA, we will find the final value "01111011" binary or "7B" hexadecimal. At every bit position of IORA where a "0" is present, the corresponding row or column have been interconnected. This technique will not only detect which switch has been pressed, but will also detect errors, such as several keys being depressed at the same time. If more than one key is depressed at any one time, then there will be more than one "0" per nibble (group of 4 bits) in the IORA.

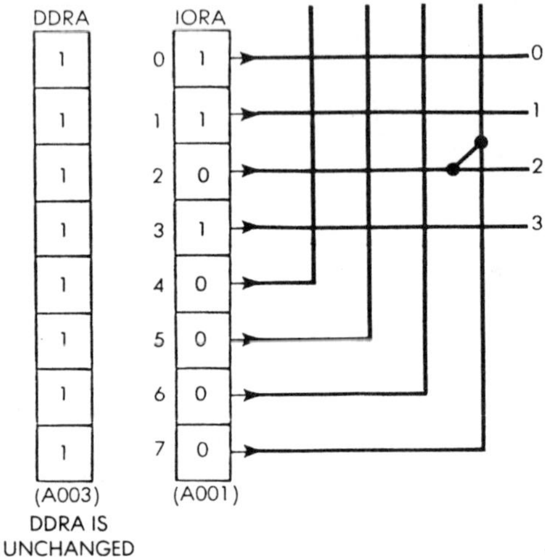

Fig. 6-2: Step 2 -Reading IORA After Key Closure

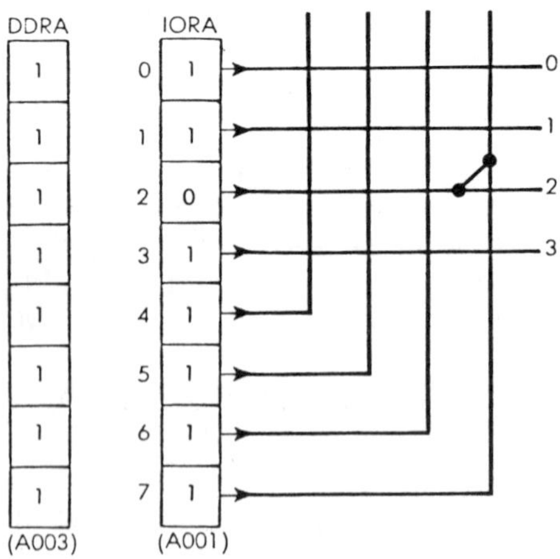

Fig. 6-3: Step 3 -Writing IORA

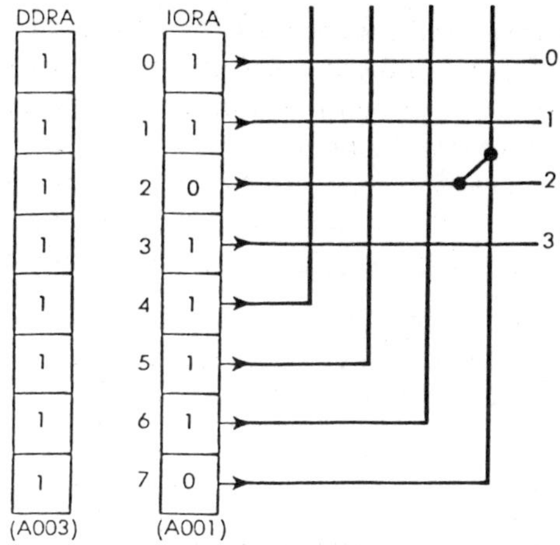

Fig. 6-4: Step 4 -Read back IORA

In order to identify the character corresponding to the key which has been pressed (a hexadecimal character between "0" and "F"), we will simply build a table giving the ASCII representation of the characters for each legal pattern in IORA.

For example, we have just determined that when key "B" is pushed, the pattern "7B" hexadecimal is found in IORA. As an exercise the reader is encouraged to compute the IORA pattern for other characters. The correspondence table is shown on Fig 6-5.

If ever an illegal code is found, it is ignored and the keyboard is scanned again.

Finally, once the ASCII code for the character has been obtained, it can be displayed. As an example here the display routine available as part of the SYM board monitor is used to display the character. Modifications will be suggested at the end of this section to display the characters on other media.

CHARACTER	0	1	2	3	4	5	6	7	8	9	A	B	C	D	E	F
IDCODE	DE	ED	DD	BD	EB	DB	BB	E7	D7	B7	77	7B	EE	BE	7E	7D
ASCII	30	31	32	33	34	35	36	37	38	39	41	42	43	44	45	46

Fig. 6-5: Keyboard Character Codes Table

Note: This program will use 3 monitor routines for convenience: SCAND, HDOUT, ACCESS.

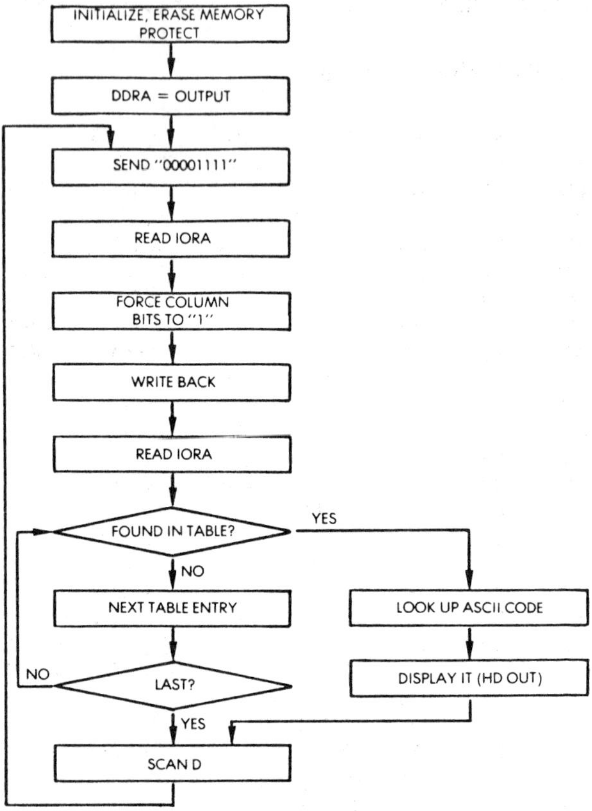

Fig. 6-6: Keyboard Flow Chart

The flow-chart for the program appears on Fig 6-6.

The program is first initialized, then the "0F" (hexadecimal) pattern is sent on IORA. The value of IORA is read back (without changing the DDRA!). This value does not need to be stored in a 6502 register or in the memory, because of the bidirectional feature of the IORA of this component. *It will be latched into the component and remain there.* The four column bits are then forced to a "1", and the new IORA pattern is output. IORA is then read back so that the final bit pattern may be obtained. The pattern in the IO register is then matched against all possible values in the ASCII table of Fig 6-5. If the IORA code does not match the current table entry, the next one is looked up. If none matches, then a branch back to the beginning of the loop occurs.

The program is shown on Fig 6-7.

```
0000  20  86  8B  INIT    JSR   ACCESS
   3  A9  FF              LDA   #$FF
   5  8D  03  A0          STA   DDRA    DDRA is PAD
   8  A2  OF      START   LDX   #$0F
   A  8E  01  A0          STX   IORA    IORA is PA
   D  AD  01  A0          LDA   IORA    IORA is PA
0010  09  F0              ORA   #$F0
   2  8D  01  A0          STA   IORA    IORA is PA
   5  AD  01  A0          LDA   IORA    IORA is PA
   8  D5  30      LOOP    CMP   TAB, X
   A  F0  05              BEQ   DISPL
   C  CA                  DEX
   D  10  F9              BPL   LOOP
   F  30  05              BMI   SCAN
0021  B5  40      DISPL   LDA   ASCT, X
   3  20  00  89          JSR   HDOUT
   6  20  06  89  SCAN    JSR   SCAND
   9  4C  08  00          JMP   START
0030  E7  D7  B7  77 TAB  BYTE  $E7, $D7, $B7, $77, $EB, $DB,
      EB  DB  BB  7B            $BB, $7B, $ED, $DD, $BD,
      ED  DD  BD  7D            $7D, $EE, $DE, $BE, $7E
      EE  DE  BE  7E
0040  37  38  39  41 ASCT BYTE  '7, '8, '9, 'A, '4, '5, '6,
      34  35  36  42            'B, '1, '2, '3, F, 'C, '0,
      31  32  33  46            'D, 'E
      43  30  44  45
```

Fig. 6-7: Keyboard Program (Program 6-1)

The initialization phase removes the memory protection feature, in the case of the SYM board, by using the ACCESS subroutine, then conditions the data direction register of Port A to be all outputs:

```
INIT    JSR   ACCESS
        LDA   #$FF     "11111111"=OUTPUTS
        STA   DDRA
```

The "00001111" pattern is then sent to the data register:

```
START   LDX  #$0F   "00001111"
        STX  IORA
```

It is immediately read back and the columns are forced to all 1's by oring it with the pattern "11110000":

```
        LDA  IORA
        ORA  #$F0   "11110000"
```

The resulting pattern is sent to the data register (IORA):

```
        STA  IORA
```

It is immediately read back and it now contains the final pattern that will be used to determine which key has been pressed:

```
        LDA  IORA
```

The code contained in the accumulator will now be compared in sequence to every entry in the table. Every time we have a table structure, the *indexed addressing* mode is conveniently used to access the elements in sequence. The initial value of the index register if "0F" hexadecimal or "15" decimal. A match will be attempted against the last entry of the table (see Fig 6-7). Then the previous one will be tested. Whenever a match is found a branch occurs to location DISPL:

```
LOOP    CMP  TAB,X
        BEQ  DISPL
        DEX
        BPL  LOOP
```

If the match fails, then the index register X is decremented in anticipation of the next character match. It must be tested against the value "0": When it decrements below "0" and becomes negative, no valid key has been detected and an exit occurs through SCAN:

```
        BMI  SCAN
```

At this point, register X indicates which character has been recog-

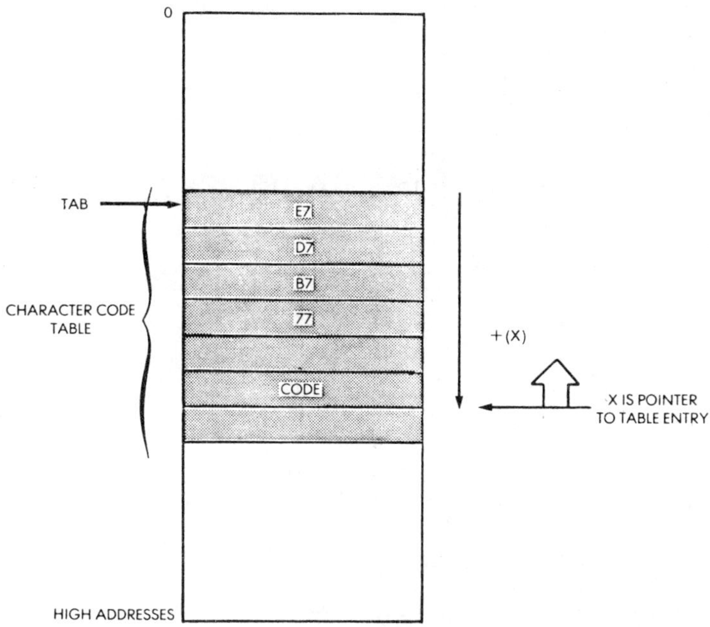

Fig. 6-8: Indexed Addressing for Table Access

nized. It contains a number between "0" and "15". We now want to convert this number to the ASCII code required to display (or print) the character we have recognized:

```
DSPL        LDA   ASCT, X
```

At location DISPL, the accumulator is loaded with the ASCII code corresponding to the value of the character as determined by the value of index register X. Again an *indexed addressing* technique is used for this sequentially ordered data (see Fig 6-9). The subroutine HDOUT (of the SYM) is then used and the character is displayed (SCAND routine of the SYM) before the keyboard scanning resumes:

```
            JSR   HDOUT
SCAN        JSR   SCAND
            JMP   START
```

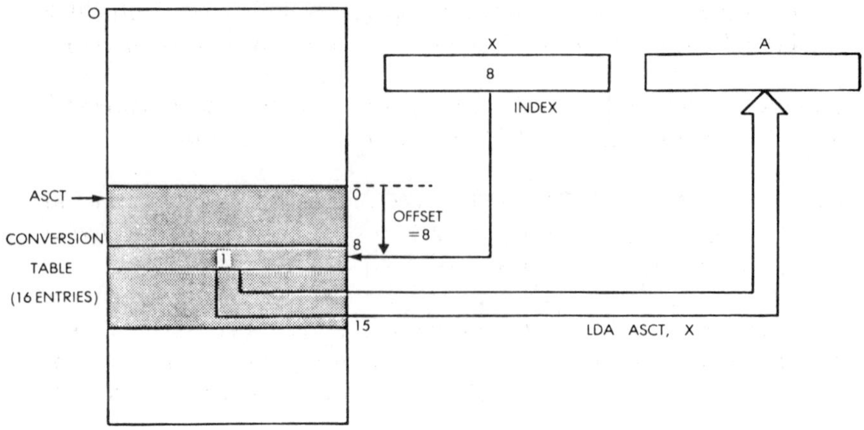

Fig. 6-9: Converting the Character ID # to ASC II

Two tables of constants are used by the program. The first one is called "TAB". The table contains the list of legal bit patterns that may appear in IORA. The value of the index register X at the time it reads one of these entries determines the identity of the key which has been pressed. The second table used is called "ASCT". It contains the ASCII code for each of the digits of the keyboard.

These two tables appear at the end of the program on Fig 6-7. Note that the index register X *does not have to contain the actual hexadecimal digit* corresponding to the key which has been pressed. As long as the two tables are arranged in matching sequence, the proper ASCII code will be extracted for each legal binary pattern found in the table TAB. This is why these two tables on the program are out of the hexadecimal sequence.

***Exercise 6-1:** Rearrange the two tables, TAB and ASCT of Fig 6-7, so that the value of the index register X is always equal to the hexadecimal value of the key which has been pressed on the keyboard.*

***Exercise 6-2:** As an alternative to the above method, relabel the keys of the keyboard, without changing the tables TAB and ASCT, so that the value index register X corresponds to the key which has been pressed.*

Let us suggest now some possible variations so that the digit which has been detected can be displayed to the outside world in other ways:

Exercise 6-3: *Sound the speaker once if character "1" has been pressed. Sound it twice if character "2" has been pressed, and so on.*

Exercise 6-4: *Using the Morse program which has been developed in chapter 4 (see Program 4-3), modify the above program so that it sounds the Morse code corresponding to each key pressed.*

Exercise 6-5: *Modify the above program so that it will sound a note for each key pressed. One key should be dedicated to a silence. Another set of two keys can be used to determine the duration of the note (durations 1, 2, and 4).*

Exercise 6-6: *Write a stored music program. You will first play a tune by hitting the keys of the keyboard in the desired sequence. The first 50 notes (or any other number) of the tune should be memorized in the memory of the system. Then hit a special key, and the program should play back the tune that has just been memorized.*

PAPER TAPE READER OR ASCII KEYBOARD

Connecting a decoded (ASCII) keyboard, or a paper tape reader involves a nearly identical technique. The hardware interface involves 8 data bits (the 7 bit ASCII code plus parity), and an extra status bit indicating that a character is available. A simple interface will be presented here for a "home-built" simplified paper tape reader. The program for a decoded keyboard would be nearly identical.

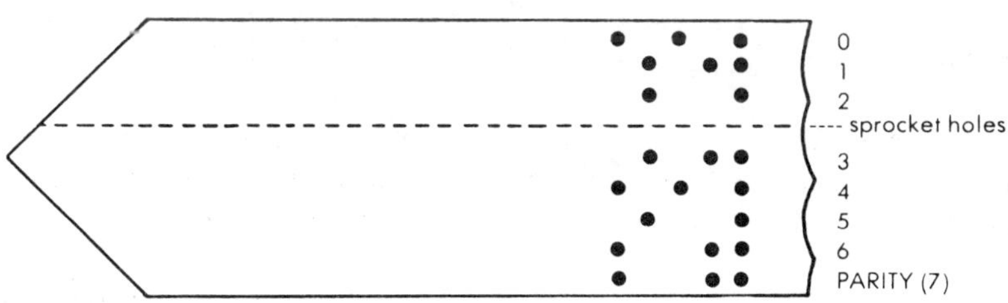

Fig. 6-10: Punched 8-level Paper-tape

Paper tape has traditionally been used to store programs in a reliable and economical form. Each character is represented on the paper tape by a row of holes punched in it (see Fig 6-10). One hole, smaller than the other, is used by the sprocket wheel which positions the paper

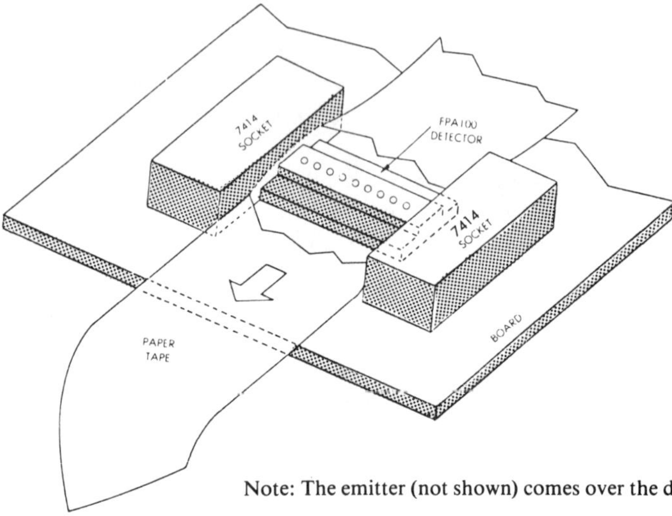

Note: The emitter (not shown) comes over the detector.

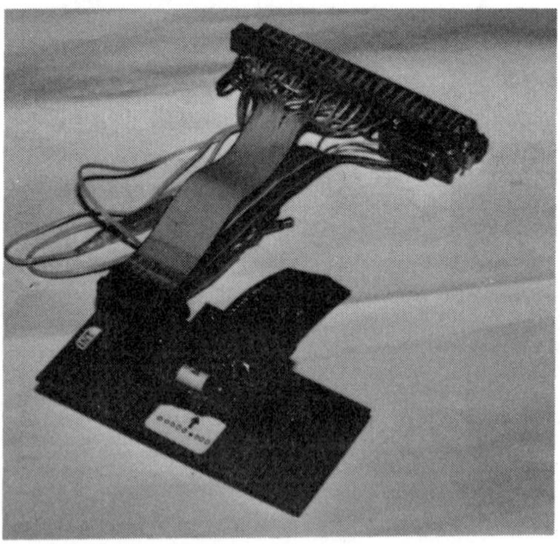

The FPA100 emitter is located on the small board on top. The PTR is connected to the 6502 board via a flat ribbon through the A-connector (top).

Fig. 6-11: Paper Tape Reader Hardware

tape. The other 8 holes (other types of codes exist using less holes) are used to encode the character itself in ASCII format. The paper tape is moved one hole position at a time, and the code corresponding to the hole must be read by the reader. We will use here a pair of photo emitters and detectors FPA100.

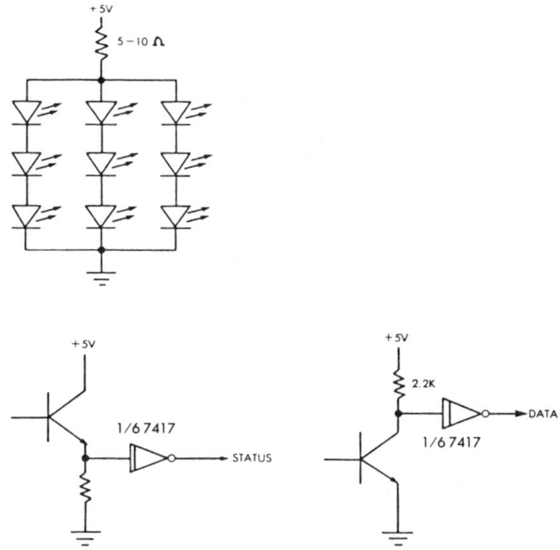

Fig. 6-12: PTR Connection Details

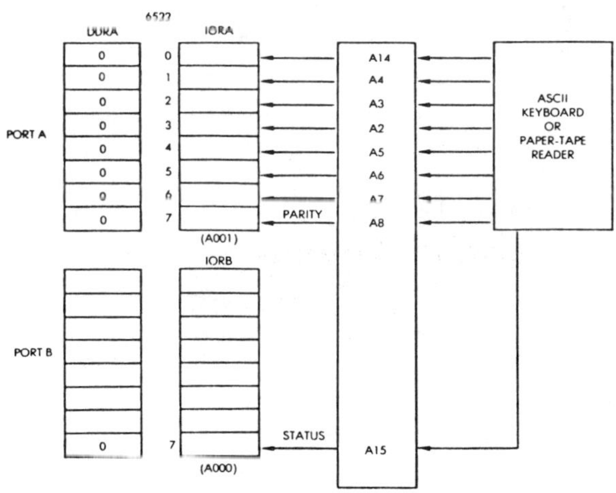

Fig. 6-13: Paper Tape Reader Interface

The light-emitting diodes emit light continuously. When a hole passes in front of the LED, the light will be transmitted and the photo-detector placed on the other side will sense it. This will be a "1". When no light is transmitted, a "0" will be detected. Note that the intensity of the LED's must be adjusted carefully, so that no light goes through the paper tape in the absence of a hole (practical remarks will be presented later). This very low-cost and simple paper-tape-reader can be operated by hand by pulling the paper tape between the two detectors. The program will synchronize itself, as we will see, on the hole normally intended for the sprocket wheel. The hardware diagram appears on Fig 6-11. The detailed connection of the light emmitting diodes and of the hole detectors and the data detector circuits appear on Fig 6-12. The microcomputer interface is shown on Fig 6-13. The IORA of 6522 #1 is used as input for these data bits. The IORB of port B of the same 6522 is used to read the status bit into its position 7.

The signals are conditioned by Schmitt triggers (7414). The two sockets for the 7414's are used as guides for the paper tape itself. Thc signal corresponding to the detection of a *sprocket hole* is "0". The signal corresponding to a *data hole* is "1".

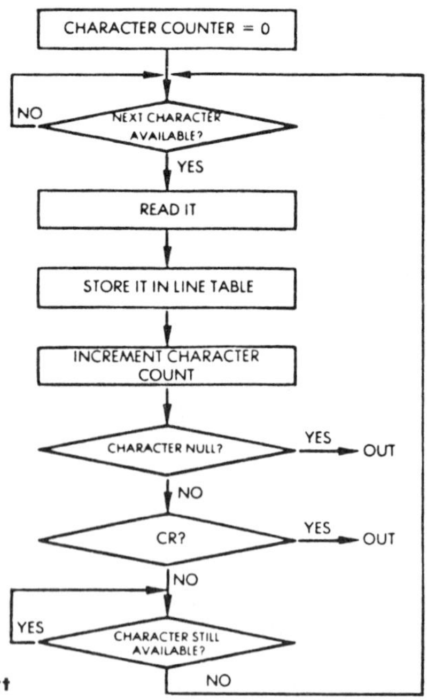

Fig. 6-14: PTR Flow Chart

Note that a single resistor is used in this simple interface to drive all LED's. In practice, individual resistors could be used for each individual LED. The value of the resistor must be adjusted carefully so that just enough light goes through a hole to be detectable by the opposite detector. Otherwise *all 1's* ("11111111") will be detected continuously if the light may go through a normal (fairly transparent) paper tape. If you are experiencing trouble with the value of this resistor, you may consider using initially *black* paper tape, or at least very opaque tape, to eliminate this problem.

The flow-chart for the program is shown on Fig 6-14. A character counter will be used to count the number of characters coming in. The program remains in a waiting loop until the next character becomes available. This will be detected by the presence of a sprocket hole over the corresponding detector. Once the status signal indicates the availability of the character, it should be read quickly. It is read and stored in a line table in the memory. The character counter is then incremented.

By convention, the reading operation will be terminated either by a "NULL" character (nothing punched on the tape), or else an explicit "carriage-return" character (CR). The program, therefore, checks for the NULL character or "CR", and, if they are found, it exits. If they are not found, it can go back to the beginning of the loop. However, before going back to the beginning of the loop, the program must wait until the status information has been reset. Once the "character-available" signal has disappeared, it can go back to the beginning of the loop and wait for the next character to become available.

The memory-map corresponding to this program is shown on Fig 6-15. The program appears on Fig 6-16.

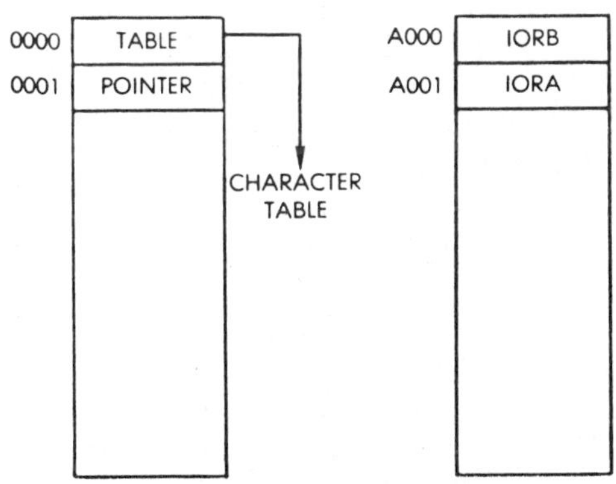

Fig. 6-15: PTR Memory Map

```
0002  A0  00        KBPT  LDY  #0
   4  2C  00  A0    TS    BIT  IORB        IORB is PB
   7  30  FB              BMI  TS
   9  AD  01  A0          LDA  IORA        IORA is PA
   C  91  00              STA  ($00), Y
   E  C8                  INY
   F  C9  00              CMP  #0
0011  F0  0B              BEQ  RET
   3  C9  8D              CMP  #$8D
   5  FO  07              BEQ  RET
   7  2C  00  A0    TE    BIT  IORB        IORB is PB
   A  10  FB              BPL  TE
   C  30  E6              BMI  TS
   E  60            RET   RTS
```

Fig 6-16: PTR/Keyboard Program (Program 6-2)

The program assumes that DDRA and DDRB have been initialized with the proper values. Otherwise extra lines of initialization must be added to the beginning of this program. Register Y is used as the character counter and is initialized to the value "0":

```
KBPT        LDY    #0
```

Next, the value of the status line must be tested, in o. der to determine whether a character is available. It is connected to IOkB bit 7 in order to facilitate its detection:

```
TS          BIT    IORB
            BMI    TS
```

Bit 7 is a preferred bit position to connect a status signal, since it is a bit position which can be tested in one instruction: bit 7 is the "sign" bit. It sets the "N" flag in the status register, which can be tested directly for "positive" and "negative" ("0" or "1"). Here, it is tested by the BMI (branch on minus) instruction. As long as the signal is

"1", no character is available. When it becomes "0", a character is available. The accumulator can then be loaded with the data present on the data lines:

LDA IORA READ DATA 1

The 8-bit character obtained from the paper-tape-reader must then be stored at an appropriate memory location. It is assumed here that the starting address of the line buffer has been deposited at memory location "00, 01." An *indirect addressing* technique will be used in order to access the first element of the table. In addition, the addressing mode will be *indexed* by the value of Y, in order to access successively all elements of the table. The corresponding instruction is:

STA ($00),Y

Let us examine this indirect indexed instruction here. The *indirection* specifies: "go to memory address "00" and use its contents as an address (Step 1 on Fig 6-17).

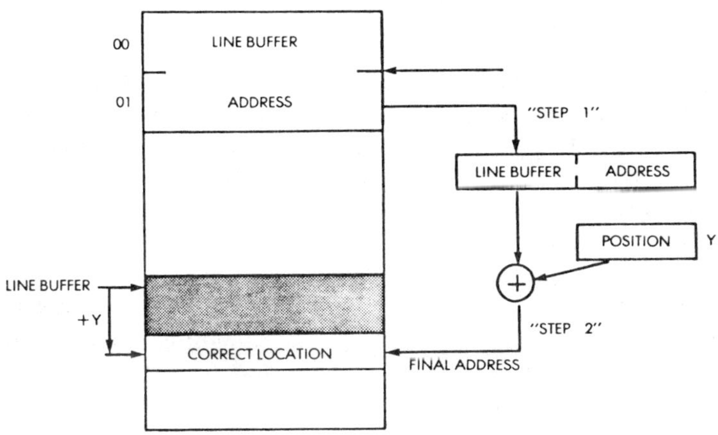

Fig. 6-17: Indirect Indexed Access: STA ($00), Y

Register Y is then used as an index: its contents are added to the base address to provide the final address (Step 2 on Fig 6-17). The contents of Y are the displacement within the line-buffer table, i.e., the pointer to the current entry.

The character counter is then incremented, thus pointing to the next available location in the line buffer, in anticipation of the next character:

```
            INY
```

The character in the accumulator must now be tested for "NULL" or for a "carriage return," to check whether the end of a line has been reached. This is accomplished by the next four instructions:

```
            CMP   #0      NULL?
            BEQ   RET     IF YES, EXIT
            CMP   #$8D    CR?
            BEQ   RET     IF YES, EXIT
```

Finally (refer to the flow-chart of Fig 6-14), we must wait for the "character-ready" signal to disappear before testing it again, or else we would read twice the same character. This is accomplished by the next 3 instructions:

```
TE          BIT   IORB    TEST READY SIGNAL
            BPL   TE
            BMI   TS
```

Finally, the subroutine terminates with the usual return instruction:

```
RET         RTS
```

Exercise: 6-7: *In addition to storing the character in a table, generate through the speaker the Morse code corresponding to the character being read. Be careful to generate the Morse code quickly enough so that you do not lose characters on input. Alternatively you may decide to pull the paper very slowly so that you have enough time to generate the Morse output between two successive characters. Or as another possible solution, you may decide to generate the Morse code only at the end of the line when all the characters have been read. This is definitely the safest solution but it defers the enjoyment of verifying that each character is being correctly read!*

Exercise 6-8: *Connect eight LEDs on the PTR board, and light them with the 6502, as each character is recognized.*

Exercise 6-9: *Sound an alarm if the parity bit is incorrect. (The parity bit insures that the total number of bits for a given character is even or odd, depending on the convention used. You must verify this.)*

MICROPRINTER

Many small microprinters use electrosensitive paper, and print 20 characters across, using a dot matrix to form the characters. Examples are Olivetti (various models) or Matsuhita. The bare printer requires a small interface which will sent the appropriate signals to the printing head, move the paper and manage the mechanical resources of the printer mechanism. Once equipped with such a basic interface, *the microprinter can be connected to any microprocessor equipped with a PIO* (a programmable input/output port). Such a printer will be used here and will be connected to the 6502 system via a 6522 and a 6532 port. Differences may exist if you are using a printer with a different interface. However, the logic of the program should be essentially similar.

The program will print a 20-character line at a time. It will supply the "start print" signal, then send the 20 characters in sequence. In order to send a character, the program waits for the printer interface to supply a "character request signal." In response to this signal, the

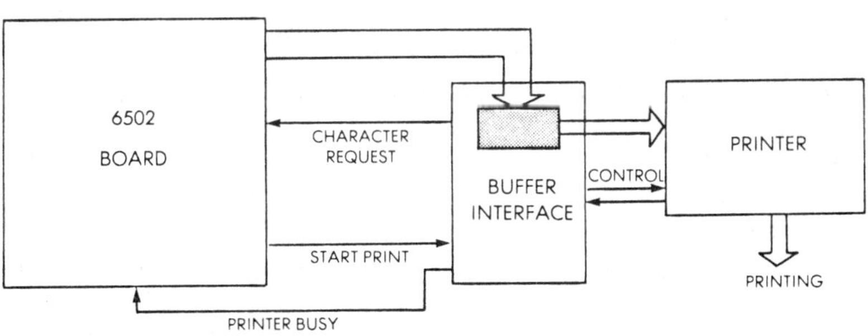

Fig. 6-18: Basic Printer Interface

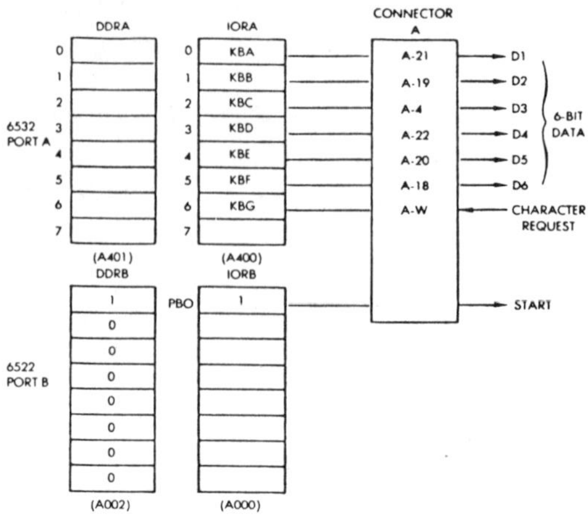

Fig. 6-19: Printer Connection

program must supply the characters, or else the previous character stored in the interface buffer will be printed by error. The character will be supplied on the 6 data lines. A 6 bit character representation is used (see Fig 6-18).

The hardware connection for the printer appears in Fig 6-19. Port A of the 6532 is used and bit 0 of Port B of the 6522 is also used. The IORA of the 6532 supplies the 6 data lines and receives on bit 6 the "character request," as indicated on the illustration. Bit 0 of the IORB of the 6522 is used to generate the "start" signal. In addition, the printer interface normally supplies a "printer busy" signal. It will be ignored here and replaced by a software delay routine of 30 milliseconds. A flow-chart for the program appears on Fig 6-20.

The data-direction registers for the two PIOs are initialized. A start pulse is generated to start the printer. The program then checks the "character request" line. The program waits at this point until a level change indicates that a character is requested. It gets the next character from one of the memory locations where the 20 character line is stored (see Fig 6-21). The character is then sent to the printer. Once the character has been sent, the program waits for the "character request" signal to disappear. It increments the character counter and checks to see whether it has reached the value "20." If it has not

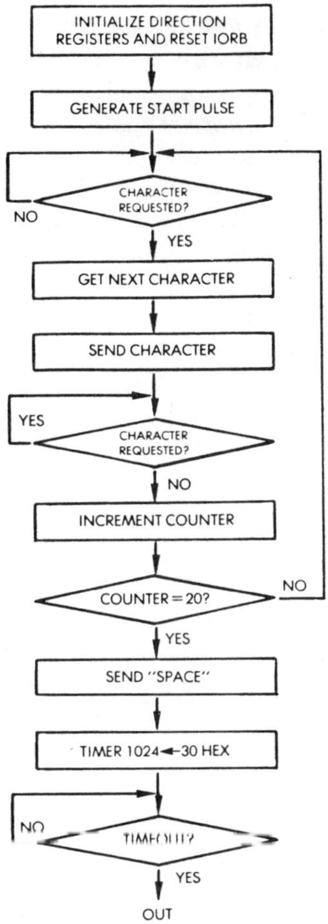

Fig. 6-20: Flow Chart for Printer Program

reached the value "20," another character must be sent to the printer and the loop is re-entered. Once the 20 characters have been sent to the printer, a "space" code is sent to the printer to terminate the line, causing a line feed and a carriage return to be generated. (A different convention may be used by a different interface.) Then a delay of 48 milliseconds must be provided for the mechanical elements of the printer to position themselves for the next line. The internal timer of the 6532 is used for this purpose and the timer word corresponding to the 1024 times factor is used here. The 1024 factor corresponds to a delay of 1024 microseconds or approximately 1 millisecond per delay unit in the timer word. This word is loaded with "30" hexadecimal = "48" decimal. Once it times out, the program exits.

The program is shown on Fig 6-22. The memory map for the printer program is shown on Fig 6-21. The two memory locations "00" and "01" contain the pointer to the location of the first character in the memory. In order to use this program, the user should load the value "01" at memory location "A002" (DDRB), and "00" in memory location "A000" (IORB) before turning the printer on. The memory locations used by the input/output devices appear on the right of Fig 6-19. Let us examine the program.

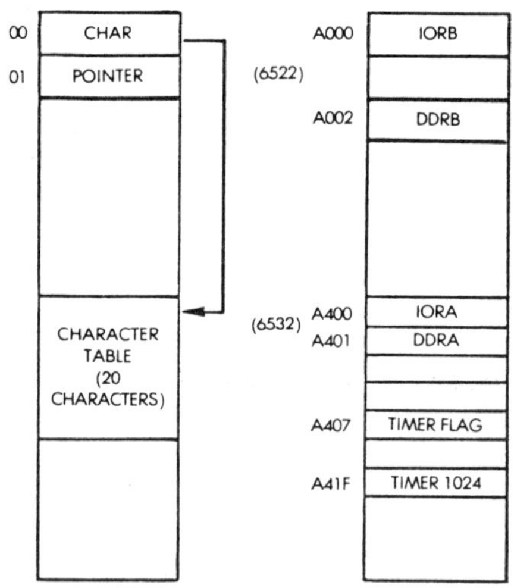

Fig. 6-21: Printer Memory Map

```
0200   A9    3F                  LINE    LDA    #$3F        Configure Port A
   2   8D    01     A4                   STA    IORA
   5   A0    01                          LDY    #1          Send start signal
   7   8C    00     A0                   STY    IORB
   A   88                                DEY
   B   8C    00     A0                   STY    IORB        "0" output
   E   2C    00     A4       TST1    BIT    IORA        Read status
0211   70    FB                          BVS    TST1        Char request?
   3   B1    00                          LDA    ($00),Y     Load character
   5   8D    00     A4                   STA    IORA        Print it
   8   2C    00     A4       TST2    BIT    IORA        Check status
   B   50    FB                          BVC    TST2
   D   C8                                INY                Next character
   E   C0    14                          CPY    #$14        20th?
0220   D0    EC                          BNE    TST1
   2   A9    20                          LDA    #$20        Space/character
   4   8D    00     A4                   STA    IORA
   7   A9    30                          LDA    #$30        Delay constant
   9   8D    1F     A4                   STA    T1024       Timer X1024
   C   2C    07     A4       TTIM    BIT    TIMFLG      Timer status?
   F   10    FB                          BPL    TTIM
0231   60                                RTS
0000   50    00                          WORD   BUFFER
0050   30    31/32  33/34    BUFFER  BYTE   '0, '1, '2, '3, '4, '5, '6, '7,
     35/36   37/38  39/40                   '8, '9, 'W, 'A, 'B, 'C, 'D,
     41, 42  43, 44 45, 46                  'E, 'F, 'G, 'H, 'I
     47/48   49
```

IORA is PA

IORB is PB

Fig. 6-22: Printer Program (Program 6-3)

The data direction register A is first initialized:

```
LINE      LDA   #$3F
          STA   IORA
```

A start pulse is then generated by depositing the value "0000001" in the IORB:

```
          LDY   #1        "00000001"
          STY   IORB
```

IORB is then set to all 0 outputs:

```
        DEY             Y = "00000000"
        STY     IORB
```

We must then check the "character request" line. If this line is a "1", we keep looping. When it becomes a "0", we will get the next character:

```
TST1    BIT     IORA    READ STATUS
        BVS     TST1
```

It should be remembered that the "BIT" instruction will test a given memory location without disturbing its contents. It will copy bits 6 and 7 respectively in the "V" and "N" flags. We are interested here in testing the value of bit 6 (refer to the printer connection on Fig 6-19). The BVS instruction will test the value of the overflow flag "V", which has been set to be identical to the value of bit 6 of IORB. Its value is therefore the value of the "character-request" line. The next character is obtained from the 20 character table stored at the memory address contained in locations "00" and "01". An indirect access instruction will result in accessing the first entry of this table. For generality, we want this segment of the program to be able and retrieve any entry within the table. As in any table organization, *indexed addressing* will, therefore, be used. Register Y is used here as the index register. It contains initially the value "00" which will be incremented through the value 19 before we exit from the loop. An indexed indirect addressing technique is used here:

```
        LDA     ($00),Y
```

The indexed indirect access is illustrated on Fig 6-23. The contents of memory location "0001" are first accessed. They are then used as the address of the base of the table to accessed. The contents of register Y will be added to the contents of memory location 0001 and this final address will be used as the address of the data to be fetched (see Fig 6-21). This data is the ASCII code for the character to be printed. It is sent to IORA:

```
        STA     IORA
```

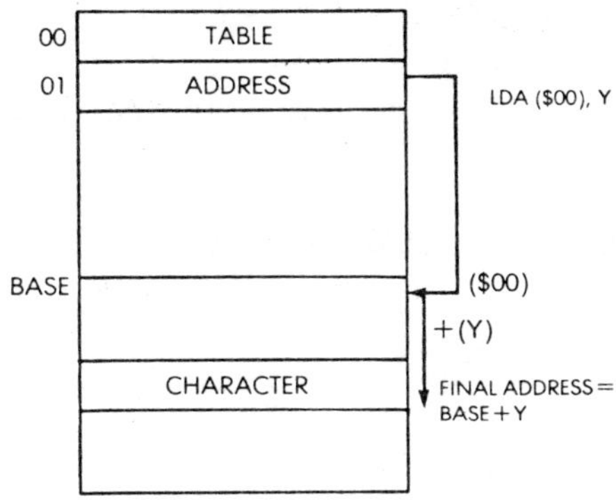

Fig 6-23: Indexed Indirect Access

Once the character has been sent, we must wait for the character request line to become "1" again. A two-instruction loop is used exactly as above:

```
TST2    BIT   IORA
        BVC   TST2
```

The character counter (register Y) is then incremented:

```
        INY
```

and tested against the limit value "20" decimal = "14" hexadecimal. As long as the limit value is not reached we re-enter the loop:

```
        CPY   #$14
        BNE   TST1
```

The code for the required "space" character is then output on IORA:

```
        LDA   #$20
        STA   IORA
```

Finally, we must guarantee the minimal delay between 2 successive line printings. The 1,024 factor is used for the timer. The final 48 ms delay is obtained by simply loading the appropriate memory location with the constant specifying the number of milliseconds (refer to Fig 6-19 for the printer memory map):

```
        LDA   #$30     DECIMAL = 48
        STA   T1024
```

The timer flag is then checked continuously until it becomes "1", indicating a timeout:

```
TTIM    BIT   T1MFLG
        BPL   TTIM
```

The actual printout for the sample 20 character line indicated in the program appears on Fig 6-24:

```
0123456789@ABCDEFGHI
```

Fig 6-24 : Actual 20-Character Printout

Exercise 6-10: *Connect the printer and the paper-tape reader. The printer should print the contents of the papertape at the end of every line.*

SUMMARY

In this chapter, actual peripherals have been interfaced both from a hardware and software standpoint to the microcomputer board. Full use has been made of the specific capabilities of the PIO registers, and of the addressing techniques provided by the 6502 in order to optimize the programs. The reader should now have acquired all the skills required for realizing his own applications programs in most usual cases.

CHAPTER 7

CONCLUSIONS

This book has systematically introduced the hardware and software techniques required to connect an actual 6502 board to the outside world. The input-output chips have first been described, along with usual 6502 boards. Then application programs of increasing complexity have been presented in chapters 4, 5, and 6. At this point, the reader should feel confident that he can connect his own 6502 board to usual input-output devices and solve the hardware and software interfacing problems associated with this. In fact, the author believes that, with the skills acquired now, the reader should be in a position to start solving almost any applications problems of usual complexity. There are naturally cases where specific interfacing problems exist and the reader is encouraged to consult reference C207 "Microprocessor Interfacing Techniques" for that purpose. If at this point, the reader has skipped the exercises, it is strongly suggested that he go back to chapters 4, 5, and 6 and solve all exercises proposed in these chapters, first on paper, then on a real microcomputer board.

The Next Step

If you have not built any applications board yet, the next logical step is to go to your local electronics store and purchase the few low-cost components required by the applications proposed here. You should then try to write some programs by yourself, without consulting this book, and make sure you have acquired the skills required to solve these problems. Use your imagination and you can invent many other possible applications, using the same limited hardware, or else additional simple input-output devices.

For the reader interested in more complex programming techniques required to implement complex algorithms, a third volume in this series will be published, called "6502 Games". In this volume, much more complex algorithms are introduced, and described, which will allow the reader to play a variety of games ranging from mind-bender to magic squares. The hardware required for these games is minimal (one 16-key keyboard, 15 LED's and one loudspeaker).

It has been found that the time required by each person to learn how to program varies very significantly from one person to the next. However, the next logical step after reading any programming book should be the same: practice. It is hoped that the contents of this book will have brought you the skills for such successful practice.

APPENDIX A

A 6502 ASSEMBLER IN BASIC

INTRODUCTION

Developing short programs for the 6502 may be done on paper, and the programs may then be entered on a 6502 board. However, if longer programs are to be developed (say more than a few dozen instructions), or else if a large number of small programs is to be developed, the convenience of an assembler becomes of significant importance. Since it is assumed that most readers seriously interested in applying a 6502 to real applications will start developing such programs, this book includes the full listing of an assembler for the 6502 written in BASIC for those who do not already have access to a 6502 assembler.

The advantage of an assembler for the 6502 written in BASIC is that it can be run on any computer equipped with BASIC which may be accessible to the user. The version of BASIC used in this program is the one available on Hewlett-Packard computers. It can be characterized as a subset of most microcomputer BASICs in that it does not include the features found on the latter ones. Using this assembler on a computer having a different BASIC will involve a translation process. However, the translation effort should be moderate, in view of the fact that most popular BASICs available on microcomputers include many more features than the one which has been used for this assembler. This assembler is therefore essentially upwardly compatible. In fact, a user who is good at programming in his BASIC will probably be capable of effecting a significant reduction in the number of instructions used for this assembler.

This assembler has been used to assemble a large number of programs for the 6502 and has performed successfully. To the best of our knowledge, it is therefore a reliable product. However, it is included here for educational purposes only and not warranted for any purpose whatsoever. A Microsoft BASIC version of this assembler will be published in the near future for readers interested in this particular version.

A complete listing of the assembler is shown in this section, and a sample output demonstrating its operation is shown below.

All the programs at the end of Chapter Four have been assembled with this assembler.

GENERAL DESCRIPTION

ASM 65 is a complete 6502 mnemonic assembler. It recognizes all industry standard mnemonics, and will produce the standard hexadecimal listings, as shown on the example of Fig A-1.

In addition, this assembler provides the industry standard directives, with only exception the use of "." to indicate current location assignments and references. The directives available are: .BYT, .WORD,.DBYT,.TEXT. The user is referred to any manufacturer's assembler description for the details of these directives.

USING THE ASSEMBLER

The ASM 65 is written in Hewlett-Packard 2000 series F BASIC. A description of the features of this particular BASIC implementation appear later in this section. Few changes should be needed to adapt this interpreter to other versions of BASIC to which the reader would have access.

ASM 65 operates on serial files. A minimum of three files are equipped and four are normally used. They are: the source file, the symbol table file, a temporary file, and optionally a destination file distinct from the source file.

The input file contains the assembly language instructions. It must

```
% CAT SRC
;MEMORY BLOCK MOVE PROGRAM
;MOVES UP TO 255 BYTES FROM A TABLE STARTING AT
;LOC1 TO A TABLE STARTING AT LOC2. LENGTH OF THE
;SECTION TO BE MOVED IS IN MOVLEN.
MOVLEN   =$00
LOC1     =$200
LOC2     =$300
;
         LDX MOVLEN ;LOAD LENGTH OF MOVE TO INDEX
LOOP     LDA LOC1,X ;LOAD BYTE TO BE MOVED
         STA LOC2,X ;STORE BYTE TO BE MOVED
         DEX ;COUNT DOWN
         BPL LOOP ;IF NOT DONE, MOVE NEXT BYTE
         RTS ;DONE
% RUN ASM65
SOURCE FILE ?SRC
OBJECT FILE ?DEST
PRINTOUT ?YES
ASSEMBLY BEGINS...
                ;MEMORY BLOCK MOVE PROGRAM
                ;MOVES UP TO 255 BYTES FROM A TABLE STARTING AT
                ;LOC1 TO A TABLE STARTING AT LOC2. LENGTH OF THE
                ;SECTION TO BE MOVED IS IN MOVLEN.
                MOVLEN   =$00
                LOC1     =$200
                LOC2     =$300
                ;
0000: A6 00              LDX MOVLEN    ;LOAD LENGTH OF MOVE TO INDEX
0002: BD 00 02  LOOP     LDA LOC1,X    ;LOAD BYTE TO BE MOVED
0005: 9D 00 03           STA LOC2,X    ;STORE BYTE TO BE MOVED
0008: CA                 DEX           ;COUNT DOWN
0009: 10 F7              BPL LOOP      ;IF NOT DONE, MOVE NEXT BYTE
000B: 60                 RTS           ;DONE


SYMBOL TABLE:
 MOVLEN     0000          LOC1        0200        LOC2        0300
 LOOP       0002
DONE
```

Fig A1: Using the ASM 65 Assembler

therefore contain ASCII text, and must be structured as per the rules of the assembler syntax (described in the next section). In general, the input lines can be written in free format, with the fields separated by one or more spaces. However, any label must start in column one. Any line without a label may not start in column one.

The assembler will automatically format the comment field on the output file. However it will not format the other fields within the instructions so that the user may tabulate his input statements in any reasonable way for clarity. This feature is intended to improve readability.

The output file is also ASCII text, including the representation of all numbers. The output file may be optionally printed after the second pass of the assembler has been executed. A prompt is printed on the listing, or appears on the screen: "PRINTOUT?" and the user may specify "yes" or "no."

The assembler provides extensive diagnostics and will describe all errors it has identified, then list them on the output.

In this implementation, the error printout may contain various field markers such as operator field limiters ("!"), and the internal unresolved reference delimiter ("**").

The symbol table gives the usual hexadecimal for all symbolic labels used by the program. An example is shown on figure A-2.

```
SYMBOL TABLE:
 MOVLEN      0000           LOC1          0200           LOC2          0300
 LOOP        0002
DONE
```

Fig A-2: The Symbol Table

SYNTAX

Constants

Constants may be expressed in any of the four usual number representations:

• Hexadecimal: the constant must be preceded by a "$". Example: "LDA $20" will load the accumulator from memory address "20" hexadecimal.

• Binary: it must be preceded by a "%". Example: "LDA %11111111" will load the accumulator with all ones.

• Decimal: usual representation. Example "LDA #0" will load the accumulator with the decimal value zero.

•ASCII: must be proceeded by a " ' ". Example: "LDA'A" will load the ASCII code for A into the accumulator.

Arithmetic Expressions

Arithmetic expressions may be used in the operator field, in a label assignment, or in a memory allocation instruction.

The operand in an arithmetic expression may be a number expressed in any representation, or a label, or a "·" (the current location symbol) or any combination of those. The legal operators are "+" and "–·". In the case where more than one operator is used, the arithmetic expression will be evaluated from left to right.

Comments

Comments must be preceded by a ";". They may begin in any column including column one. All comments will be justified in the middle of the output sheet unless they begin in column one.

Memory Assignments

Memory assignments are performed by one or more of the four directives:

.BYT	– Assigns one byte of data to one memory location.
.WORD	– Assigns two bytes of data to two consecutive memory locations, low order byte first.
.DBYT	– Assigns two bytes of data to two consecutive memory locations, high order byte first.
.TEXT	– Converts an ASCII string to hex data, and stores it in consecutive memory locations. The string must be delimited by two identical non-blank characters.

There is no end directive– an end-of-file is used instead.

Example of a memory assignment:

```
.BYT    $2A, WORDCONST
.WORD   2, %10
```

HP2000F BASIC:

Hewlett-Packard BASIC is different from many common mini- and microcomputer BASICs, but is easily adapted. The following is a list of features which differ from most BASICs, or from the Dartmouth standard.

Files

Files are declared in a FILES statement at the beginning of the program and are numbered in the order in which they appear in it. The ASSIGN statement assigns a file specified by its first argument to a file number specified by the second argument. The third argument is a dummy variable. A star appearing in a FILES statement means a file will later be assigned to that file position by an ASSIGN statement. The READ statement reads the file. Its first argument, preceded by a "#", is the file number of the file to be read from. If the record number is one, and there is no semicolon, the statement serves to reset the file pointer to Ø, as in "READ #2, 1". Any arguments after the semicolon are those variables to be read.

The PRINT statement is similar to the read statement. It also has a special form, "PRINT #2,END", which makes an end-of-file marker on the file.

The IF END # THEN statement operates in a way analogous to a vectored interrupt. When an end-of-file occurs on a read, program execution will continue at the line number mentioned after the THEN, instead of causing the program to crash. This will occur even if the computer is not currently executing the statement: i.e., the end-of-file vector need only be specified once, unless it needs to be changed.

Strings

Strings are one dimensional, and can only be dimensioned as such. To assign Ø (zero) length to a string, or clear it, a statement of the type "L$=" " is used. Characters in a string are referenced as follows: to reference a substring within a larger string, the form "T$(a,b)" is used where a and b are expressions signifying respectively the first and last character addresses in the main string of the desired substring. Characters in a string are addressed from left to right, starting at 1. Example: if A$="ABCDE" and the statement "B$=A$(2,3)" is executed, B$ will become "BC".

The form "T$(a)" references all characters in T$ starting with character #a and continuing on to the end of T$.
Example: if A$="12345", A$(3) means the substring "345".

The string functions CHR$ and ASC$, which respectively convert an ASCII decimal number into a one-character string, and a one-character string into its decimal ASCII equivalent are not available, so ASM65 reads a string of ordered ASCII characters from a system file called $ASCIIF, which it then uses for number and string conversion.

MAX returns the maximum of 2 values.
Example: "B = 11 MAX 9" would yield 11.
MIN returns the minimum of 2 values.
LIN when in a print statement adds amount of linefeed specified in its argument to output.

The above definitions are intended only as guidelines for the translation of ASM65 into other versions of BASIC.

Fig A-3: 6502 Assembler Listing
copyright © 1979, Sybex Inc.

```
ASM65

10  REM : ********** 6502 MNEMONIC ASSEMBLER, VERSION 2.0 **********
20  REM
30  REM : WRITTEN IN HP2000F TSS BASIC.
40  REM : CAN BE USED WITH ALL 65XX PROCESSORS AS MADE BY COMMODORE,
50  REM : SYNERTEK, AND ROCKWELL.
60  REM : ALL MNEMONICS AND DIRECTIVES ARE INDUSTRY STANDARD, WITH
70  REM : THE EXCEPTION OF THE USE OF '.' FOR CURRENT ADDRESS.
80  R=10
90  T9=0
100  A=0
110  DIM L$[72],M$[72],O$[72],C$[72],Z$[72],P$[72],T$[72]
120  DIM A$[72],N$[72]
130  DIM I$[72]
140  L=0
150  FILES *,SYMTAB,TEMP,*,$ASCIIF
160  PRINT 'SOURCE FILE ';
170  INPUT T$
180  PRINT 'OBJECT FILE ';
190  INPUT O$
200  ASSIGN T$,1,Q8
210  ASSIGN O$,4,Q8
220  READ #1,1
230  PRINT #2,1
240  PRINT #3,1
250  R8=0
260  PRINT 'PRINTOUT ';
270  INPUT I$
280  IF I$ <> 'NO' THEN 300
290  R8=1
300  PRINT 'ASSEMBLY BEGINS...'
310  C=0
```

```
320  IF  END #1 THEN 2440
330  L$=""
340  I$=""
350  M$=""
360  O$=""
370  C$=""
380  Z$="
390  L=L+1
400  REM*********** SEPARATE TOKENS, STORE LABEL ASSIGNMENTS **********
410  READ #1;I$
420  T5=C
430  IF I$="" THEN 830
440  P=1
450  P$=";"
460  GOSUB 3970
470  IF P1=0 THEN 510
480  IF P1=1 THEN 800
490  C$=I$[P1]
500  I$=I$[1,P1-1]
510  IF I$[1,1]=" " THEN 590
520  GOSUB 3790
530  L$=P$
540  IF L$ <> "." THEN 590
550  M$="."
560  GOSUB 4940
570  L$=""
580  GOTO 860
590  GOSUB 3790
600  M$=P$
610  IF M$[1,3]=".WO" THEN 3110
620  IF M$[1,3]=".TE" THEN 3110
630  IF M$[1,3]=".BY" THEN 3110
640  IF M$[1,3]=".DB" THEN 3110
650  IF M$ <> "" THEN 850
660  C$=C$[1,34]
670  IF LEN(L$) <> 0 THEN 700
680  I$=I$[1,19]
690  GOTO 820
700  GOSUB 3790
710  N$=P$
720  IF LEN(N$) <> 0 THEN 750
730  T1=C
740  GOTO 780
750  GOSUB 4070
760  IF T4=2 THEN 830
770  T1=F1
780  PRINT #2;L$,T1
790  PRINT #2; END
800  I$=I$[1,LEN(I$) MIN 55]
810  Z$[17,17+LEN(I$)]=I$
820  Z$[(LEN(I$)+19 MAX 38) MIN 72]=C$
830  PRINT #3;Z$,T5
840  GOTO 320
850  IF M$[1,1] <> "." THEN 1050
860  P$="="
870  GOSUB 3970
880  IF P1>0 THEN 910
890  PRINT "MISSING '=' IN LINE ";L
900  GOTO 3090
910  P=P1+1
920  GOSUB 3790
930  IF P$[1,1] <> "" THEN 960
940  PRINT "MISSING ARGUMENT IN LINE ";L
950  GOTO 3090
960  N$=P$
```

```
970  GOSUB 4070
980  IF T4 <> 2 THEN 1010
990  PRINT 'ILLEGAL FORWARD REFERENCE IN LINE ';L
1000  GOTO 3090
1010  T1=C
1020  C=F1
1030  IF L$ <> '' THEN 780
1040  GOTO 800
1050  RESTORE 5710
1060  IF M$='' THEN 1140
1070  FOR I=1 TO 56
1080  READ T$
1090  IF T$=M$ THEN 1130
1100  NEXT I
1110  PRINT 'UNKNOWN OPCODE IN LINE ';L
1120  GOTO 3090
1130  O=I
1140  IF L$='' THEN 1170
1150  PRINT #2;L$,C
1160  PRINT #2; END
1170  GOSUB 3750
1180  O$=P$
1190  I$[P-LEN(O$)-1,P-LEN(O$)-1]='!'
1200  REM********** FIND ADDRESSING MODES, LOAD EFFECTIVE ADDRESS **********
1210  IF O$ <> '' THEN 1240
1220  M=1
1230  GOTO 2200
1240  IF O$ <> 'A' THEN 1270
1250  M=2
1260  GOTO 2200
1270  IF O$[1,1] <> '#' THEN 1320
1280  M=3
1290  P=P+1
1300  N$=O$[2]
1310  GOTO 1870
1320  IF M$[1,1] <> 'B' THEN 1460
1330  IF M$='BIT' THEN 1460
1340  M=12
1350  N$=O$
1360  GOSUB 4070
1370  IF T4 <> 2 THEN 1400
1380  A=-200
1390  GOTO 1970
1400  A=F1-C-2
1410  IF A >= 0 THEN 1430
1420  A=256+A
1430  IF ABS(F1-C) <= 127 THEN 1970
1440  PRINT 'BRANCH OUT OF RANGE IN LINE ';L
1450  GOTO 3090
1460  P$='('
1470  P=P-LEN(O$)
1480  GOSUB 3970
1490  P5=P1
1500  P$=','
1510  GOSUB 3970
1520  P6=P1
1530  P7=0
1540  IF  NOT P6 THEN 1610
1550  IF I$[P6+1,P6+1] <> 'X' THEN 1580
1560  P7=1
1570  GOTO 1610
1580  IF I$[P6+1,P6+1]='Y' THEN 1610
1590  PRINT 'BAD ADDRESSING MODE IN LINE ';L
1600  GOTO 3090
1610  IF P5 <> 0 THEN 1780
```

```
1620  GOSUB 3790
1630  N$=P$
1640  IF  NOT P6 OR  NOT P7 THEN 1670
1650  M=5
1660  GOTO 1710
1670  IF  NOT P6 THEN 1700
1680  M=6
1690  GOTO 1710
1700  M=4
1710  GOSUB 4070
1720  A=F1
1730  IF T4 <> 2 THEN 1750
1740  A=-1000
1750  IF ABS(A) <= 255 THEN 1970
1760  M=M+3
1770  GOTO 1970
1780  GOSUB 3790
1790  N$=P$[2]
1800  IF  NOT P6 OR  NOT P7 THEN 1830
1810  M=10
1820  GOTO 1870
1830  IF  NOT P6 THEN 1860
1840  M=11
1850  GOTO 1870
1860  M=13
1870  GOSUB 4070
1880  A=F1
1890  IF (M <> 10 AND M <> 11) OR A <= 255 THEN 1920
1900  PRINT "VALUE TOO LARGE FOR ZERO PAGE IN LINE ";L
1910  GOTO 3090
1920  IF T4 <> 2 THEN 1970
1930  A=-1000
1940  IF M=13 THEN 1970
1950  A=-200
1960  REM********** PRINT OPCODES & EA ON FILE **********
1970  IF A >= 0 THEN 2070
1980  Z$[10,11]="**"
1990  C=C+1
2000  IF M <> 12 THEN 2020
2010  Z$[11,11]="R"
2020  W9=A+256
2030  IF W9 >= 0 THEN 2200
2040  Z$[13,14]="**"
2050  C=C+1
2060  GOTO 2200
2070  R=16
2080  I=A
2090  GOSUB 4940
2100  T$=A$
2110  A$="000"
2120  A$[4]=T$
2130  IF (M >= 3 AND M <= 6) OR (M >= 10 AND M <= 12) THEN 2180
2140  Z$[13,14]=A$[LEN(A$)-3,LEN(A$)-2]
2150  Z$[10,11]=A$[LEN(A$)-1]
2160  C=C+2
2170  GOTO 2200
2180  Z$[10,11]=A$[LEN(A$)-1]
2190  C=C+1
2200  R=16
2210  I=T5
2220  GOSUB 4940
2230  T$="000"
2240  T$[4]=A$
2250  Z$[1,4]=T$[LEN(T$)-3]
2260  RESTORE 5140
```

```
2270  FOR I=1 TO (O-1)*13+M
2280  READ T$
2290  NEXT I
2300  IF T$ <> "  " THEN 2370
2310  IF M>6 OR M<4 THEN 2350
2320  M=M+3
2330  C=T5
2340  GOTO 1970
2350  PRINT "ILLEGAL ADDRESSING MODE IN LINE ";L
2360  GOTO 3090
2370  Z$[7,8]=T$
2380  Z$[5,5]=":"
2390  C=C+1
2400  Z$[17,17+LEN(I$)]=I$
2410  Z$[(19+LEN(I$)) MAX 38]=C$[1,72-(19+LEN(I$) MAX 38)]
2420  PRINT #3;Z$,T5
2430  GOTO 320
2440  REM*********** SECOND PASS: RESOLVE FWD REFERENCES **********
2450  PRINT #2; END
2460  PRINT #3; END
2470  READ #2,1
2480  L=0
2490  READ #3,1
2500  PRINT #4,1
2510  IF  END #3 THEN 2870
2520  P=1
2530  READ #3;I$,T5
2540  L=L+1
2550  IF I$="" THEN 2850
2560  P$="!"
2570  GOSUB 3970
2580  IF P1=0 OR P1=17 THEN 2610
2590  P=P1
2600  I$[P,P]=" "
2610  IF I$[10,10] <> "*" THEN 2850
2620  GOSUB 3790
2630  N$=P$
2640  IF N$[1,1] <> "(" THEN 2660
2650  N$=N$[2]
2660  GOSUB 4070
2670  IF T4 <> 2 THEN 2700
2680  PRINT "IRRESOLVABLE FWD REF / BAD LABEL IN LINE ";L
2690  GOTO 3090
2700  I=F1
2710  IF I$[11,11] <> "R" THEN 2750
2720  I=F1-T5-2
2730  IF I >= 0 THEN 2750
2740  I=I+256
2750  R=16
2760  GOSUB 4940
2770  T$=A$
2780  A$="000"
2790  A$[4]=T$
2800  IF I$[13,14] <> "**" THEN 2840
2810  I$[13,14]=A$[LEN(A$)-3,LEN(A$)-1]
2820  I$[10,11]=A$[LEN(A$)-1]
2830  GOTO 2850
2840  I$[10,11]=A$[LEN(A$)-1]
2850  PRINT #4;I$
2860  GOTO 2510
2870  PRINT #4; END
2880  IF R8=1 THEN 3080
2890  IF  END #4 THEN 2940
2900  READ #4,1
2910  READ #4;I$
```

```
2920  PRINT I$
2930  GOTO 2910
2940  READ #2,1
2950  PRINT LIN(2);"SYMBOL TABLE:"
2960  IF  END #2 THEN 3080
2970  FOR I6=1 TO 3
2980  READ #2;O$,T5
2990  R=16
3000  I=T5
3010  GOSUB 4940
3020  T$="0000"
3030  T$[LEN(T$)+1]=A$
3040  PRINT TAB((I6-1)*25+1);O$;TAB((I6-1)*25+13);T$[LEN(T$)-3];
3050  NEXT I6
3060  PRINT
3070  GOTO 2970
3080  END
3090  PRINT "<"I$">"
3100  END
3110  REM*********** PROCESS MEMORY LOADS **********
3120  Q7=1
3130  IF M$[2,3] <> "TE" THEN 3260
3140  IF Q7 <> 1 THEN 3190
3150  GOSUB 3750
3160  P=P-LEN(P$)
3170  O$=I$[P,P]
3180  P=P+1
3190  IF P <= 72 THEN 3220
3200  PRINT "BAD DELIMITER IN LINE ";L
3210  GOTO 3090
3220  P$[1]="'"
3230  P$[2,2]=I$[P,P]
3240  IF P$[2,2]=O$ THEN 320
3250  GOTO 3280
3260  GOSUB 3790
3270  Z$="
3280  P=P+1
3290  IF LEN(P$)=0 THEN 320
3300  N$=P$
3310  GOSUB 4070
3320  IF T4 <> 2 THEN 3350
3330  PRINT "BAD LABEL IN MEMORY ASSIGNMENT OF LINE ";L
3340  GOTO 3090
3350  R=16
3360  I=F1
3370  GOSUB 4940
3380  T$=A$
3390  A$="000"
3400  A$[4]=T$
3410  IF M$[2,2] <> "W" THEN 3460
3420  Z$[10,11]=A$[LEN(A$)-3,LEN(A$)-2]
3430  Z$[7,8]=A$[LEN(A$)-1]
3440  C=C+2
3450  GOTO 3560
3460  IF M$[2,2]="D" THEN 3530
3470  IF F1<256 THEN 3500
3480  PRINT "NUMBER TOO LARGE IN MEMORY ASSIGNMENT OF LINE ";L
3490  GOTO 3090
3500  Z$[7,8]=A$[LEN(A$)-1]
3510  C=C+1
3520  GOTO 3560
3530  Z$[7,8]=A$[LEN(A$)-3,LEN(A$)-2]
3540  Z$[10,11]=A$[LEN(A$)-1]
3550  C=C+1
3560  I=T5
```

```
3570  R=16
3580  GOSUB 4940
3590  T$="000"
3600  T$[4]=A$
3610  Z$[1,4]=T$[LEN(T$)-3]
3620  Z$[5,5]=":"
3630  IF Q7 <> 1 THEN 3700
3640  IF LEN(L$)=0 THEN 3670
3650  PRINT #2;L$,T5
3660  PRINT #2; END
3670  Z$[17,17+LEN(I$)]=I$
3680  Z$[(19+LEN(I$)) MAX 38]=C$[1,72-(19+LEN(I$)) MAX 38]
3690  GOTO 3710
3700  Z$=Z$[1,15]
3710  Q7=0
3720  PRINT #3;Z$,T5
3730  T5=C
3740  GOTO 3130
3750  REM ***** ROUTINE TO ISOLATE TOKEN *****
3760  REM : STARTS LOOKING FOR TOKEN AT P, PUTS IT IN P$, AND
3770  REM : UPDATES P. IF ENTERED HERE, STOPS SCAN AT ' '.
3780  T9=1
3790  REM : IF ENTERED HERE, STOPS SCAN AT ' ', ',', ')', '='.
3800  FOR I1=P TO LEN(I$)
3810  IF I$[I1,I1] <> " " THEN 3830
3820  NEXT I1
3830  P$=""
3840  FOR I2=I1 TO LEN(I$)
3850  IF I$[I2,I2]=" " THEN 3920
3860  IF T9=1 THEN 3900
3870  IF I$[I2,I2]="," THEN 3920
3880  IF I$[I2,I2]=")" THEN 3920
3890  IF I$[I2,I2]="=" THEN 3920
3900  P$[LEN(P$)+1]=I$[I2,I2]
3910  NEXT I2
3920  P=I2
3930  IF LEN(P$) <> 0 THEN 3950
3940  P=P+1
3950  T9=0
3960  RETURN
3970  REM ***** FIND SYMBOL ROUTINE *****
3980  REM : RETURNS P1=SYMLOC IF IT IS FOUND, P1=0
3990  REM : IF SYMBOL NOT FOUND
4000  FOR I=P TO LEN(I$)
4010  IF I$[I,I]=P$[1,1] THEN 4050
4020  NEXT I
4030  P1=0
4040  RETURN
4050  P1=I
4060  RETURN
4070  REM ***** NUMERIC STRING INTERPRETER *****
4080  REM : SIMPLIFIES STRINGS OF LABELS AND NUMERIC EXPRESSIONS
4090  REM : OF NUMBERS IN ANY BASE, PLUS ASCII CONSTANTS.
4100  F1=W=0
4110  A$=""
4120  FOR I=1 TO LEN(N$)
4130  IF N$[I,I]="+" THEN 4180
4140  IF N$[I,I]="-" THEN 4180
4150  IF N$[I,I]=")" THEN 4610
4160  A$[LEN(A$)+1]=N$[I,I]
4170  NEXT I
4180  IF A$ <> "." THEN 4210
4190  F2=C
4200  GOTO 4480
4210  IF A$[1,1]>"Z" THEN 4350
4220  IF A$[1,1]<"A" THEN 4350
```

```
4230  READ #2,1
4240  IF  END #2 THEN 4330
4250  READ #2;T$,T1
4260  IF T$ <> A$ THEN 4240
4270  F2=T1
4280  T4=3
4290  IF  END #2 THEN 4320
4300  READ #2;T$,T1
4310  GOTO 4300
4320  GOTO 4480
4330  T4=2
4340  RETURN
4350  IF A$[1,1] <> "'" THEN 4390
4360  A$=A$[2]
4370  GOSUB 4640
4380  GOTO 4480
4390  B=10
4400  IF A$[1,1] <> "%" THEN 4430
4410  B=2
4420  GOTO 4450
4430  IF A$[1,1] <> "$" THEN 4460
4440  B=16
4450  A$=A$[2]
4460  GOSUB 4750
4470  F2=F
4480  IF W=2 THEN 4510
4490  F1=F1+F2
4500  GOTO 4520
4510  F1=F1-F2
4520  IF I >= LEN(N$) THEN 4610
4530  T$="+-"
4540  FOR W=1 TO LEN(T$)
4550  IF T$[W,W]=N$[I,I] THEN 4590
4560  NEXT W
4570  PRINT "ILLEGAL OPERATOR IN LINE ";L
4580  GOTO 3090
4590  A$=""
4600  GOTO 4170
4610  T4=0
4620  RETURN
4630  REM ***** ASCII CHARACTER TO NUMBER CONVERTER *****
4640  A$=A$[1,1]
4650  F2=0
4660  READ #5,1
4670  READ #5;T$
4680  FOR I=1 TO 72
4690  IF A$[1,1]=T$[I,I] THEN 4740
4700  F2=F2+1
4710  NEXT I
4720  F2=F2-8
4730  GOTO 4670
4740  RETURN
4750  REM ***** MULTI-RADIX STRING TO NUMBER CONVERTER *****
4760  REM : B IS BASE OF NUMBER IN A$, F IS PRODUCT.
4770  F=0
4780  I1=0
4790  FOR I2=LEN(A$) TO 1 STEP -1
4800  RESTORE 4910
4810  FOR N=0 TO B-1
4820  READ F$
4830  IF F$=A$[I2,I2] THEN 4870
4840  NEXT N
4850  PRINT "BAD NUMBER IN LINE ";L
4860  GOTO 3090
4870  F=F+N*B^I1
```

```
4880  I1=I1+1
4890  NEXT I2
4900  RETURN
4910  DATA "0","1","2","3","4","5","6","7","8","9","A","B","C","D"
4920  DATA "E","F","G","H","I","J","K","L","M","N","O","P","Q","R","S"
4930  DATA "T","U","V","W","X","Y","Z"
4940  REM ***** MULTI-RADIX NUMBER TO STRING CONVERTER
4950  REM : I IS INPUT NUMBER, R IS BASE THAT A$ WILL BE AS PRODUCT.
4960  A$=""
4970  T=I
4980  FOR N=20 TO 0 STEP -1
4990  IF T/R^N >= 1 THEN 5020
5000  NEXT N
5010  N=N-1
5020  Q=INT(T/R^N)
5030  IF Q <= R-1 THEN 5050
5040  Q=0
5050  T=T-Q*R^N
5060  RESTORE 4910
5070  FOR S=0 TO Q
5080  READ T$
5090  NEXT S
5100  A$[LEN(A$)+1]=T$
5110  IF N>0 THEN 5010
5120  RETURN
5130  REM *************** OPCODE TABLE ***************
5140  DATA "  ","  ","69","65","75","  ","6D","7D","79","61","71","  ","  "
5150  DATA "  ","  ","29","25","35","  ","2D","3D","39","21","31","  ","  "
5160  DATA "  ","0A","  ","06","16","  ","0E","1E","  ","  ","  ","  ","  "
5170  DATA "  ","  ","  ","  ","  ","  ","  ","  ","  ","  ","  ","90","  "
5180  DATA "  ","  ","  ","  ","  ","  ","  ","  ","  ","  ","  ","B0","  "
5190  DATA "  ","  ","  ","  ","  ","  ","  ","  ","  ","  ","  ","F0","  "
5200  DATA "  ","  ","  ","24","  ","  ","2C","  ","  ","  ","  ","  ","  "
5210  DATA "  ","  ","  ","  ","  ","  ","  ","  ","  ","  ","  ","30","  "
5220  DATA "  ","  ","  ","  ","  ","  ","  ","  ","  ","  ","  ","D0","  "
5230  DATA "  ","  ","  ","  ","  ","  ","  ","  ","  ","  ","  ","10","  "
5240  DATA "00","  ","  ","  ","  ","  ","  ","  ","  ","  ","  ","  ","  "
5250  DATA "  ","  ","  ","  ","  ","  ","  ","  ","  ","  ","  ","50","  "
5260  DATA "  ","  ","  ","  ","  ","  ","  ","  ","  ","  ","  ","70","  "
5270  DATA "18","  ","  ","  ","  ","  ","  ","  ","  ","  ","  ","  ","  "
5280  DATA "D8","  ","  ","  ","  ","  ","  ","  ","  ","  ","  ","  ","  "
5290  DATA "58","  ","  ","  ","  ","  ","  ","  ","  ","  ","  ","  ","  "
5300  DATA "B8","  ","  ","  ","  ","  ","  ","  ","  ","  ","  ","  ","  "
5310  DATA "  ","  ","C9","C5","D5","  ","CD","DD","D9","C1","D1","  ","  "
5320  DATA "  ","  ","E0","E4","  ","  ","EC","  ","  ","  ","  ","  ","  "
5330  DATA "  ","  ","C0","C4","  ","  ","CC","  ","  ","  ","  ","  ","  "
5340  DATA "  ","  ","  ","C6","D6","  ","CE","DE","  ","  ","  ","  ","  "
5350  DATA "CA","  ","  ","  ","  ","  ","  ","  ","  ","  ","  ","  ","  "
5360  DATA "88","  ","  ","  ","  ","  ","  ","  ","  ","  ","  ","  ","  "
5370  DATA "  ","  ","49","45","55","  ","4D","5D","59","41","51","  ","  "
5380  DATA "  ","  ","  ","E6","F6","  ","EE","FE","  ","  ","  ","  ","  "
5390  DATA "E8","  ","  ","  ","  ","  ","  ","  ","  ","  ","  ","  ","  "
5400  DATA "C8","  ","  ","  ","  ","  ","  ","  ","  ","  ","  ","  ","  "
5410  DATA "  ","  ","  ","  ","  ","  ","4C","  ","  ","  ","  ","  ","6C"
5420  DATA "  ","  ","  ","  ","  ","  ","20","  ","  ","  ","  ","  ","  "
5430  DATA "  ","  ","A9","A5","B5","  ","AD","BD","B9","A1","B1","  ","  "
5440  DATA "  ","  ","A2","A6","  ","B6","AE","  ","BE","  ","  ","  ","  "
5450  DATA "  ","  ","A0","A4","B4","  ","AC","BC","  ","  ","  ","  ","  "
5460  DATA "  ","4A","  ","46","56","  ","4E","5E","  ","  ","  ","  ","  "
5470  DATA "EA","  ","  ","  ","  ","  ","  ","  ","  ","  ","  ","  ","  "
5480  DATA "  ","  ","09","05","15","  ","0D","1D","19","01","11","  ","  "
5490  DATA "48","  ","  ","  ","  ","  ","  ","  ","  ","  ","  ","  ","  "
5500  DATA "08","  ","  ","  ","  ","  ","  ","  ","  ","  ","  ","  ","  "
5510  DATA "68","  ","  ","  ","  ","  ","  ","  ","  ","  ","  ","  ","  "
5520  DATA "28","  ","  ","  ","  ","  ","  ","  ","  ","  ","  ","  ","  "
```

```
5530  DATA "  ","2A","  ","26","36","  ","2E","3E","  ","  ","  ","  ","
5540  DATA "  ","6A","  ","66","76","  ","6E","7E","  ","  ","  ","  ","
5550  DATA "40","  ","  ","  ","  ","  ","  ","  ","  ","  ","  ","  ","
5560  DATA "60","  ","  ","  ","  ","  ","  ","  ","  ","  ","  ","  ","
5570  DATA "  ","  ","E9","E5","F5","  ","ED","FD","F9","E1","F1","  ","
5580  DATA "38","  ","  ","  ","  ","  ","  ","  ","  ","  ","  ","  ","
5590  DATA "F8","  ","  ","  ","  ","  ","  ","  ","  ","  ","  ","  ","
5600  DATA "78","  ","  ","  ","  ","  ","  ","  ","  ","  ","  ","  ","
5610  DATA "  ","  ","  ","85","95","  ","8D","9D","99","81","91","  ","
5620  DATA "  ","  ","  ","86","  ","96","8E","  ","  ","  ","  ","  ","
5630  DATA "  ","  ","  ","84","94","  ","8C","  ","  ","  ","  ","  ","
5640  DATA "AA","  ","  ","  ","  ","  ","  ","  ","  ","  ","  ","  ","
5650  DATA "A8","  ","  ","  ","  ","  ","  ","  ","  ","  ","  ","  ","
5660  DATA "BA","  ","  ","  ","  ","  ","  ","  ","  ","  ","  ","  ","
5670  DATA "8A","  ","  ","  ","  ","  ","  ","  ","  ","  ","  ","  ","
5680  DATA "9A","  ","  ","  ","  ","  ","  ","  ","  ","  ","  ","  ","
5690  DATA "98","  ","  ","  ","  ","  ","  ","  ","  ","  ","  ","  ","
5700  REM *************** MNEMONIC TABLE ***************
5710  DATA "ADC","AND","ASL","BCC","BCS","BEQ","BIT","BMI","BNE"
5720  DATA "BPL","BRK","BVC","BVS","CLC","CLD","CLI","CLV","CMP","CPX","C
5730  DATA "DEC","DEX","DEY","EOR","INC","INX","INY","JMP","JSR","LDA","L
5740  DATA "LDY","LSR","NOP","ORA","PHA","PHP","PLA","PLP","ROL","ROR","R
5750  DATA "RTS","SBC","SEC","SED","SEI","STA","STX","STY","TAX","TAY","T
5760  DATA "TXA","TXS","TYA"
5770  END
```

APPENDIX B

MULTIPLICATION GAME: THE PROGRAM

```
                    ;***** MULT *****
                    ;
                    N       =$00
                    P       =$01
                    NSAVE   =$02
                    PSAVE   =$03
                    T       =$04
                    D       =$9D
                    X       =$200
                    Y       =$201
                    RESUL   =$202
                    ASAVE   =$240
                    XSAVE   =$241
                    YSAVE   =$242
                    PA      =$1700
                    PAD     =$1701
                    TIMER   =$1707
                    ;
                            .=$20
0020: A5 00         START   LDA N
0022: 85 02                 STA NSAVE
0024: A5 01                 LDA P
0026: 85 03                 STA PSAVE
0028: A9 01                 LDA #$01
002A: 8D 01 17              STA PAD
002D: 20 50 02      M1      JSR SOUND
0030: 20 90 00              JSR DL250
```

```
0033: C6 00              DEC N
0035: D0 F6              BNE M1
0037: A2 14              LDX #$14       ;2 SECOND
0039: 20 9E 00           JSR TIME10     ;.1 SEC SUBROUTINE
003C: 20 50 02  M2       JSR SOUND
003F: 20 90 00           JSR DL250
0042: C6 01              DEC P
0044: D0 F6              BNE M2
0046: A9 00     AGAIN    LDA #0
0048: 85 04              STA T
004A: AD 00 17  POL      LDA PA
004D: 30 FB              BMI POL
004F: E6 04     PLUS1    INC T          ;KEY DOWN?
0051: AD 00 17  M3       LDA PA
0054: 10 FB              BPL M3
0056: A0 1E              LDY #$1E       ;KEY UP?
0058: A2 01     M4       LDX #1
005A: 20 9E 00           JSR TIME10
005D: AD 00 17           LDA PA
0060: 10 ED              BPL PLUS1
0062: 88                 DEY
0063: 10 F3              BPL M4
                ;ANSWER COMPLETE: RESULT IN T
0065: A6 02              LDX NSAVE
0067: A4 03              LDY PSAVE
0069: 20 10 02           JSR MULTI      ;RESULT IN A
006C: C5 04              CMP T
006E: F0 0D              BEQ BRAVO
                ;WRONG ANSWER
0070: A0 10              LDY #$10
0072: 20 50 02  M5       JSR SOUND
0075: 20 90 00           JSR DL250
0078: 88                 DEY
0079: D0 F7              BNE M5
007B: F0 C9              BEQ AGAIN
                ;CORRECT ANSWER
007D: A0 20     BRAVO    LDY #$20
007F: 20 50 02  M6       JSR SOUND
0082: 88                 DEY
0083: D0 FA              BNE M6
0085: 00                 BRK
                ;
                       .=$90
0090: 98        DL250    TYA
0091: A2 3D              LDX #$3D
0093: A0 00     DL2      LDY #0
0095: C8        DL1      INY
0096: D0 FD              BNE DL1
0098: E8                 INX
0099: D0 F8              BNE DL2
009B: A8                 TAY
009C: 60                 RTS
                ;
                       .=$9E
009E: 86 9D     TIME10   STX D          ;DURATION IN 1/10 SEC
00A0: A9 62     TO       LDA #$62       ;98 BASE TEN
00A2: 8D 07 17           STA TIMER      ;TIMER 1024
00A5: AD 07 17  T1       LDA TIMER
00A8: 10 FB              BPL T1
00AA: C6 9D              DEC D
00AC: D0 F2              BNE TO
00AE: 60                 RTS
                ;
                       .=$210
0210: 8E 00 02  MULTI    STX X
```

```
0213: 8C 01 02          STY Y
0216: A0 08             LDY #8
0218: A9 00             LDA #0
021A: 4E 00 02   ONE    LSR X
021D: 90 04             BCC TWO
021F: 18                CLC
0220: 6D 01 02          ADC Y
0223: 4A         TWO    LSR A
0224: 6E 02 02          ROR RESUL
0227: 88                DEY
0228: D0 F0             BNE ONE
022A: AD 02 02          LDA RESUL
022D: 60                RTS
                 ;
                        .=$250
0250: 8D 40 02   SOUND  STA ASAVE
0253: 8E 41 02          STX XSAVE
0256: 8C 42 02          STY YSAVE
0259: A9 00             LDA #0
025B: A2 80             LDX #$80
025D: A0 00      CL2    LDY #0
025F: C8         CL1    INY
0260: D0 FD             BNE CL1
0262: 49 01             EOR #1
0264: 8D 00 17          STA PA
0267: E8                INX
0268: D0 F3             BNE CL2
026A: AD 40 02          LDA ASAVE
026D: AE 41 02          LDX XSAVE
0270: AC 42 02          LDY YSAVE
0273: 60                RTS

SYMBOL TABLE:
 N          0000      P          0001      NSAVE      0002
 PSAVE      0003      T          0004      D          009D
 X          0200      Y          0201      RESUL      0202
 ASAVE      0240      XSAVE      0241      YSAVE      0242
 PA         1700      PAD        1701      TIMER      1707
 START      0020      M1         002D      M2         003C
 AGAIN      0046      POL        004A      PLUS1      004F
 M3         0051      M4         0058      M5         0072
 BRAVO      007D      M6         007F      DL250      0090
 DL2        0093      DL1        0095      TIME10     009E
 T0         00A0      T1         00A5      MULTI      0210
 ONE        021A      TWO        0223      SOUND      0250
 CL2        025D      CL1        025F
DONE
```

APPENDIX C
PROGRAM LISTINGS
(Chapter 4, Part 1)

```
LCC       CODE       LINE

0000                 ;THIS IS A SUBROUTINE WHICH  ACCEPTS ASCII CHARACTERS
0000                 ;IN THE RANGE 2CH TO 5AH (PLUS 20H FOR SPACE) AND PLAYS
0000                 ;THEIR MORSE CODE EQUIVILENT ON A SPEAKER HOOKED UP TO
0000                 ;PB7, 6522-U25.  IT ALSO TURNS ON AND OFF PBO, 6522-
0000                 ;U25, AND WITH A SUITABLE DRIVER, THIS BIT CAN KEY A
0000                 ;TRANSMITTER.   A MAIN PROGRAM WILL CALL THIS SUBROUTINE
0000                 ;WITH THE ASCII CHARACTER IN THE ACCUMULATOR.
0000                 ;EXAMPLES OF THE MAIN PROGRAM WOULD BE ONE THAT
0000                 ;GETS INPUT FROM A!TERMINAL AND SENDS MORSE CODE OUT
0000                 ;THROUGH THIS PROGRAM, OR A PROGRAM WHICH RANDOMIZES
0000                 ; A SERIES A CHARACTERS AND SENDS THEM FOR CODE PRACTICE.
0000                 ;THE FORMAT FOR THE MORSE CODE CAHRACTERS IN THE TABLE
0000                 ;IS : MOVING FROM LEFT TO RIGHT , THE FIRST HIGH
0000                 ;BIT (A ONE) IS THE START BIT, AND AFTER THIS .
0000                 ;EACH ONE IS A DASH, AND EACH ZERO IS A DOT.
0000                 SPEED=$F0
0000                 COUNT=$F1
0000                 CHAR=$F2
0000                         .=$300
0300: C9 20          MORSE   CMP #$20          ;IF A SPACE, DO SPACE ROUTINE
0302: F0 67                  BEQ SPACE
0304: C9 2C                  CMP #$2C         ;SEE IF ASCII CODE
0306: 90 4E                  BCC EXIT          ;     IS LESS THEN 2CH, AND RETURN IF SO.
0308: C9 5B                  CMP #$5B          ;SEE IF ASCII CODE IS OVER
030A: B0 4A                  BCS EXIT          ;      5AH, AND RETURN IF SO
030C: AA                     TAX               ;PUT CODE IN INDEX REGISTER
030D: BD 45 03               LDA TABLE-$2C,X   ;GET MORSE CHARACTER
0310: A0 08                  LDY #$8           ;NUMBER OF BITS TO BE ROTATED FROM ACCUMULATOR
0312: 84 F1                  STY COUNT
0314: 0A             STARTB  ASL A
0315: C6 F1                  DEC COUNT
0317: 90 FB                  BCC STARTB        ;SHIFT A UNTIL START BIT FOUND
0319: 85 F2                  STA CHAR
031B: A5 F2          NEXT    LDA CHAR
031D: 0A                     ASL A             ;NOW SHIFT OUT MORSE CODE (1=DASH, 0=DOT)
031E: 85 F2                  STA CHAR
0320: A0 01                  LDY #$1           ;DOT= 1 TIME PERIOD, DEFAULT TO DOT
0322: 90 02                  BCC SEND          ;IF CARRY CLEAR, DOT
0324: A0 03                  LDY #$3           ;ELSE DASH    (3 TIME PERIODS)
```

Program 4-1: Morse (Fig 4-31 in text)

```
                           ; THIS SECTION SENDS A HIGH OUTPUT FOR (Y REGISTER ) NU
                           ;OF TIME PERIODS, AND THEN A LOW FOR 1 TIME PERIOD.
0326: A9 C0        SEND    LDA #$C0
0328: 8D 0B A0             STA $A00B       ;SET TIMER  MODE TOFREE RUNNING MODE
032B: A9 00                LDA #$0         ; THIS VALUE,
032D: 8D 06 A0             STA $A006
0330: A9 04                LDA #$04        ; AND THIS VALUE DETERMINE THE TONE
0332: 8D 07 A0             STA $A007       ;       OF THE OUTPUT (APPROX 1000HZ)
0335: 8D 05 A0             STA $A005       ;THIS STARTS TONE
0338: A9 01                LDA #$1         ;TURN ON OUTPUT BIT-PB0
033A: 8D 00 A0             STA $A000
033D: 20 57 03             JSR DELAY       ;DELAYFOR ELEMENT TIME PERIOD
0340: A9 00                LDA #$0
0342: 8D 0B AC             STA $A00B       ;TURN OFF TONE
0345: 8D 00 AC             STA $A000       ;TURN OFF OUTPUT BIT (PB0)
0348: A0 01                LDY #$01
034A: 20 57 03             JSR DELAY       ;DELAY FOR 1 TIME PERIOD(SPACE BETWEEN ELEMENTS)
034D: C6 F1                DEC COUNT       ;DECREMENT COUNT -SEE IF 8 BITS WERE ROTATED
034F: D0 CA                BNE NEXT        ;  IF NOT, DO ANOTHER ELEMENT
0351: A0 02        FINISH  LDY #$2         ;DELAY FOR 3(TWO HERE PLUS PREVIOUS SPACE
0353: 20 57 03             JSR  DELAY      ;   AT END OF LAST ELEMENT) TIME PERIODS(SPACE BET
0356: 60           EXIT    RTS
                           ; THIS DELAYS FOR (Y REGISTER) *SPEED*.005 SECONDS
0357: 98           DELAY   TYA
0358: 0A                   ASL A
0359: 0A                   ASL A
035A: A8                   TAY
035B: A5 F0        D3      LDA SPEED
035D: A2 FA        D2      LDX #$FA
035F: CA           D1      DEX
0360: D0 FD                BNE D1
0362: 38                   SEC
0363: E9 01                SBC #$1
0365: D0 F6                BNE D2          ;DELAY FOR 7 TIME PERIODS
0367: 88                   DEY             ;    (SPACE BETWEEN WORDS)
0368: D0 F1                BNE D3          ;RETURN FROM MORSE PROGRAM
036A: 60                   RTS
036B: A0 07        SPACE   LDY #$7
036D: 20 57 03             JSR DELAY
0370: 60                   RTS
```

Program 4-1: Morse (Continued)

```
0077  0371: 73        TABLE   .BYTE $73,$31,$6A,$32,$3F,$2F
0077  0372: 31
0078  0373: 6A
0078  0374: 32
0078  0375: 3F
0078  0376: 2F
0078  0377: 27                .BYTE $27,$23,$21,$20,$30,$38
0078  0378: 23
0079  0379: 21
0079  037A: 20
0079  037B: 30
0079  037C: 38
0079  037D: 3C                .BYTE $3C,$3E,$01,$01,$01,$01
0079  037E: 3E
0080  037F: 01
0080  0380: 01
0080  0381: 01
0080  0382: 01
0080  0383: 01                .BYTE $01,$4C,$01,$05,$18,$1A
0080  0384: 4C
0081  0385: 01
0081  0386: 05
0081  0387: 18
0081  0388: 1A
0081  0389: 0C                .BYTE $0C,$02,$12,$0E,$10,$04
0081  038A: 02
0082  038B: 12
0082  038C: 0E
0082  038D: 10
0082  038E: 04
0082  038F: 17                .BYTE $17,$0D,$14,$07,$06,$0F
0082  0390: 0D
0083  0391: 14
0083  0392: 07
0083  0393: 06
0083  0394: 0F
0083  0395: 16                .BYTE $16,$1D,$0A,$08,$03,$09
0083  0396: 1D
0084  0397: 0A
0084  0398: 08
```

Program 4-1: Morse (Continued)

```
0399: 03
039A: 09
039B: 11                .BYTE $11,$0B,$19,$1B,$1C
039C: 0B
039D: 19
039E: 1B
039F: 1C

SYMBOL TABLE:
 SPEED       00F0         COUNT       00F1         CHAR        00F2
 MORSE       0300         STARTB      0314         NEXT        031B
 SEND        0326         FINISH      0351         EXIT        0356
 DELAY       0357         D3          035B         D2          035D
 D1          035F         SPACE       036B         TABLE       0371
```

Program 4-1: Morse (Continued)

```
LOC    CODE        LINE

                   ;FIRST LOAD A7 IN LOCATION A67E, AND 03 IN A07F
0000               ;THIS IS A REAL TIME CLOCK ROUTINE WHICH MAINTAINS
0000               ;THE CURRENT TIME IN THE LOCATIONS SEC (00F6), MIN
0000               ;(00F5), AND HOUR (00F4) [24 HOUR TMEE]. IT IS BRANCHED TO
0000               ;BY THE TIME OUT OF THE INTERRUPT TIMER, WHICH
0000               ;CAUSES AN INTERRUPT AND BRANCH TO THE CLOCK
0000               ;ROUTINE TWENTY TIMES PER SECOND. THE CLOCK ROUTINE
0000               ;AND INTERVAL TIMER MUST BE INITIALIZED FIRST. THE
0000               ;CODE 'INIT' DOES THIS, AND IT MUST BE BRANCHED TO TO
0000               ;START THE CLOCK. TO INITIALIZE, PUT THE CURRENT TIME
0000               ;THE CLOCK ROUTINE WILL BE STARTED IN SEC, MIN, AND
                   ;HOUR, THEN ISSUE THE COMMAND 'GO 0390 CR' AT THAT
                   ;EXACT TIME. NOTHING ELSE MUST BE DONE.
0000               COUNT=$00F7           ;COUNTER FOR TWENTIETHS OF A SEC
0000               SECS=$00F6            ;CURRENT TIME
0000               MIN = $00F5
0000               HOUR = $00F4
0000               ACR = $A00B           ;TIMER MODE REGISTER
0000               T1LL = $A006          ;LOW ORDER TIMER CONSTANT
0000               T1HC = $A005          ;HIGH ORDER TIMER CONSTANT
0000                       * = $0390
0390   A9 14       INIT    LDA #$14              ;SET TO FIRST TWENTY
0392   85 F7               STA COUNT             ;COUNTS
0394   8D 0B A0            STA ACR               ;SET BITS 8 AND 7 LOW
                                                 ;IN ACR
0397   A9 C0               LDA #$C0              ;;SET BITS 8 AND 7 HIGH IN
0399   8D 0E A0            STA $A00E             ;THE INTERRUPT ENABLE
                                                 ;REGISTER (TO ENABLE
                                                 ;INTERRUPTS FROM TIMER 1)
039C   A9 50               LDA #$50              ;STORE C350 IN TIMER
039E   8D 06 A0            STA T1LL              ;  (DELAY CONSTANT FOR
03A1   A9 C3               LDA #$C3              ;  50 MS)
03A3   8D 05 A0            STA T1HC              ;THIS STARTS TIMER
03A6   60                  RTS                   ;RETURN TO MONITOR
03A7   08          CLOCK   PHP                   ;SAVE STATUS
03A8   48                  PHA
03A9   F8                  SED
03AA   A9 50               LDA #$50              ;STORE C350 IN TIMER
03AC   8D 06 A0            STA T1LL              ;  (DELAY CONSTANT FOR
03AF   A9 C3               LDA #$C3              ;  50 MS)
03B1   8D 05 A0            STA T1HC              ;THIS STARTS TIMER
03B4   C6 F7               DEC COUNT             ;DECREMENT COUNT OF
                                                 ;TWENTY
03B6   D0 31               BNE EXIT              ;EXIT IF WE HAVE NOT
                                                 ;COUNTED TO TWENTY YET
03B8   A9 14               LDA #$14              ;ELSE RESTORE COUNT—
03BA   85 F7               STA COUNT             ;A FULL SECOND HAS PASSED
03BC   A9 01               LDA #$01
03BE   18                  CLC
03BF   65 F6               ADC SECS              ;ADD 1 TO SEC
03C1   85 F6               STA SECS
03C3   C9 60               CMP #$60              ;SEE IF 60 SECONDS
03C5   D0 22               BNE EXIT              ;IF NOT, EXIT
03C7   A9 00               LDA #$00              ;ELSE RESET SECONDS TO 0
03C9   85 F6               STA SECS
03CB   A9 01               LDA #$01
03CD   18                  CLC
```

Program 4-2: Time of Day (Fig 4-37 in text)

```
03CE   65 F5          ADC MIN      ;AND ADD 1 TO MINUTES
03D0   85 F5          STA MIN
03D2   C9 60          CMP #$60     ;SEE IF 60 MINUTES
03D4   D0 13          BNE EXIT     ;IF NOT, EXIT
03D6   A9 00          LDA #$00
03D8   85 F5          STA MIN      ;ELSE RESET MINUTES TO 0
03DA   A9 01          LDA #$01
03DC   18             CLC
03DD   65 F4          ADC HOUR     ;AND ADD 1 TO HOUR
03DF   85 F4          STA HOUR
03E1   C9 24          CMP #$24     ;SEE IF 24 HOURS
03E3   D0 04          BNE EXIT     ;IF NOT, EXIT
03E5   A9 00          LDA #$00
03E7   85 F4          STA HOUR     ;ELSE RESET HOUR TO 0
03E9   68       EXIT  PLA          ;RESTORE STATUS
03EA   28             PLP
03EB   40             RTI

ERRORS = 0000 <0000>

SYMBOL TABLE

SYMBOL   VALUE

ACR      A00B     CLOCK    03A7     COUNT    00F7     EXIT     03E9
HOUR     00F4     INIT     0390     MIN      00F5     PLS      03EA
SECS     00F6     T1HC     A005     T1LL     A006

END OF ASSEMBLY
```

Program 4-2: Time of Day (continued)

```
LOC    CODE       LINE

0000              ;THIS IS A SIMPLE HOME CONTROL ROUTINE WHICH RUNS
0000              ;THROUGH A LOOP. EACH TIME THROUGH IT DISPLAYS THE
0000              ;CURRENT TIME AND BRANCHES TO A NUMBER OF USER
                  SUBROUTINES
0000              ;WHICH SERVICE DEVICES.
0000              ;EXAMPLES:
0000              ;1) A SUBROUTINE COULD CHECK THE CURRENT TIME AND
0000              ;   TURN ON A LIGHT IF THE TIME WERE RIGHT.
0000              ;2) A SUBROUTINE COULD MONITOR THE STATUS OF AN
0000              ;   ALARM SYSTEM AND TAKE APPROPRIATE ACTION IF AN
0000              ;   INTRUDER WERE DETECTED.
0000              DDRB=$AC02
0000              IORB=$AC00
0000              HOUR=$00F4
0000              MIN=$00F5
0000              OUTBYT=$82FA
0000              SCAND=$8906
0000                     *=$0200
0200   D8         CONTRL CLD                 ;
0201   A9 OF             LDA #$0F            ;SET DATA DIRECTION
0203   8D 02 AC          STA DDRB            ;REGISTER TO OUTPUT FOR
                                             RELAYS
0206   A9 00             LDA #$00
0208   8D 00 AC          STA IORB            ;TURN OFF RELAYS
020B   A5F4       LOOP   LDA HOUR            ;THIS IS THE MAIN CONTROL
                                             LOOP
020D   20 FA 82          JSR OUTBYT          ;OUTPUT CURRENT HOUR TO
                                             DISPLAY
0210   A5 F5             LDA MIN
0212   20 FA 82          JSR OUTBYT          ;OUTPUT CURRENT MINUTE
                                             TO DISPLAY
0215   20 06 89          JSR SCAND           ;REFRESH (LIGHT) DISPLAY
                                             WITH TIME
0218   EA                .BYTE $EA,$EA,$EA
0219   EA
021A   EA
021B   EA                .BYTE $EA,$EA,$EA
021C   EA
021D   EA
021E   EA                .BYTE $EA,$EA,$EA
021F   EA
0220   EA
0221   EA                .BYTE $EA,$EA,$EA
0222   EA
0223   EA
0224   EA                .BYTE $EA,$EA,$EA
0225   EA                                    ;THE USER CAN PLACE
                                             JUMPS TO
0226   EA                                    ;SUBROUTINES HERE TO SER-
                                             VICE DEVICES
0227   EA                .BYTE $EA,$EA,$EA
0228   EA
0229   EA
022A   EA                .BYTE $EA,$EA,$EA
022B   EA
022C   EA
022D   EA                .BYTE $EA,$EA,$EA
022E   EA
```

Program 4-3: Home Control (Fig 4-38 in text)

```
0036    022F    EA
0037    0230    EA                      .BYTE $EA,$EA,$EA
0037    0231    EA
0037    0232    EA
0038    0233    EA                      .BYTE $EA,$EA,$EA

0038    0234    EA
0038    0235    EA
0039    0236    4C 0B 02                JMP LOOP
0040    0239

ERRORS = 0000<0000>

SYMBOL TABLE

SYMBOL   VALUE

CONTRL   0200    DDRB    AC02    HOUR     00F4    IORB    AC00
LOOP     020B    MIN     00F5    OUTBYT   82FA    SCAND   8906

END OF ASSEMBLY
```

Program 4-3: Home Control (continued)

```
LOC     CODE        LINE

0000                ;THIS IS A PROGRAM WHICH DIALS PRE STORED
0000                ;TELEPHONE NUMBERS. IT PRODUCES A TWO TONE OUTPUT
0000                ;THROUGH A SPEAKER HOOKED UP IN CONFIGURATION 2
0000                ;(TWO TONES—SEE SPEAKER). THESE TONES WILL ACTIVATE
0000                ;A STANDARD TOUCH TONE PHONE WHEN THE SPEAKER IS
0000                ;PLACED DIRECTLY OVER THE MOUTH PIECE OF THE TELE-
0000                ;PHONE. TO USE THE PROGRAM, PLACE THE PHONE
0000                ;NUMBER(S) ANYWHERE IN MEMORY, ONE DIGIT PER BYTE,
0000                ;AND ENDING WITH OF (HEX). FOR EXAMPLE, THE NUMBER
0000                ;555-1212 WOULD BE 05 05 05 01 02 01 02 0F (ALL HEX) IN
0000                ;MEMORY. THEN PLACE THE ADDRESS OF THE NUMBER,
0000                ;LOW BYTE FIRST, IN THE LOCATIONS 00C0 AND 00C1.
0000                ;THEN EITHER GO TO THIS ROUTINE FROM THE MONITOR
                    ;OR JSR TO IT FROM ANOTHER PROGRAM.
0000                NUMPTR = $00C0       ;THIS POINTS TO THE ADDRESS OF
                                         ;THE TELEPHONE NUMBER
0000                ONDEL = $40          ;THIS IS THE DELAY CONSTANT FOR
                                         ;THE TIME WHEN THE
0000                OFFDEL = $20         ;DELAY CONSTANT FOR THE TIME
                                         ;WHEN THE TONES ARE 0
0000                DELCON = $FF         ;GENERAL PURPOSE DELAY
                                         ;CONSTANT
0000                ACR1 = $A00B         ;THESE ARE THE TIMER MODE
                                         ;REGISTERS (TIMER 1)
0000                ACR2 = $AC0B         ;(TIMER 2)
0000                T1CH = $A005         ;THIS IS THE TIMER 1 COUNTER
                                         ;(HIGH BYTE)
0000                T1LH = $A007         ;TIMER 1 LATCH (HIGH BYTE)
0000                T1LL = $A004         ;   (LOW BYTE)
0000                T2CH = $AC05         ;SAME AS TIMER 1 — FOR TIMER 2
0000                T2LH = $AC07
0000                T2LL = $AC04
0000                        * = $0300
0300    A0 00       PHONE   LDY #$00           ;INDEX FOR DIGITS OF
                                               ;PHONE NUMBER
0302    B1 C0       DIGIT   LDA (NUMPTR)Y      ;GET DIGIT
0304    C8                  INY
0305    C9 0F               CMP #$0F           ;SEE IF END OF PHONE
                                               ;NUMBER
0307    D0 01               BNE NOEND
0309    60                  RTS                ;RETURN IS SO (TO
                                               ;MONITOR OR CALLING
                                               ;PROGRAM)
030A    0A EA EA    NOEND   ASL A              ;MULTIPLY NUMBER BY
                                               ;FOUR TO INDEX TABLE
030D    0A EA EA            ASL A              ;   (EACH TABLE ENTRY IS
                                               ;   4 BYTES)
0310    AA                  TAX                ;X = INDEX FOR TABLE
0311    A9 C0               LDA #$C0
0313    8D 0B A0            STA ACR1           ;SET TIMER MODE TO FREE
                                               ;RUNNING ON BOTH TIMERS
0316    8D 0B AC            STA ACR2
0319    BD 5D 03            LDA TABLE,X        ;GET LOW ORDER, FIRST
                                               ;TONE
031C    8D 04 A0            STA T1LL           ;STORE IN TIMER 1
031F    E8                  INX
0320    BD 5D 03            LDA TABLE,X        ;GET HIGH ORDER, FIRST
                                               ;TONE
```

Program 4-4: Phone Dialer (Fig 4-41 in text)

```
0323    8D 07 A0                 STA T1LH          ;STORE TIMER 1
0326    8D 05 A0                 STA T1CH          ;THIS STARTS TIMER 1
                                                   ;GOING
0329    E8                       INX
032A    BD 5D 03                 LDA TABLE,X       ;GET LOW ORDER, SECOND
                                                   ;TONE
032D    8D 04 AC                 STA T2LL          ;STORE IN TIMER 2
0330    E8                       INX
0331    BD 5D 03                 LDA TABLE,X       ;GET HIGH ORDER, SECOND
                                                   ;TONE
0334    8D 07 AC                 STA T2LH          ;STORE IN TIMER 2
0337    8D 05 AC                 STA T2CH          ;THIS STARTS TIMER 2
                                                   ;GOING
033A    A2 40                    LDX #ONDEL        ;GET TONES-ON DELAY
                                                   ;CONSTANT
033C    20 55 03        ON       JSR DELAY         ;DELAY WHILE TONE IS ON
033F    CA                       DEX
0340    D0 FA                    BNE ON
0342    A9 00                    LDA #$00
0344    8D 0B A0                 STA ACR1          ;TURN BOTH TIMERS OFF
0347    8D 0B AC                 STA ACR2
034A    A2 20                    LDX #OFFDEL       ;GET TONES-OFF DELAY
                                                   ;CONSTANT
034C    20 55 03        OFF      JSR DELAY         ;DELAY WHILE TONE IS OFF
034F    CA                       DEX
0350    D0 FA                    BNE OFF
0352    4C 02 03                 JMP DIGIT         ;GO BACK FOR NEXT DIGIT
                                                   ;OF PHONE NUMBER
0355                    ;
0355                    ;THIS IS A SIMPLE DELAY ROUTINE FOR THE TONE ON AND
                        ;OFF PERI
0355                    ;
0355    A9 FF           DELAY    LDA #DELCON       ;GET DELAY CONSTANT
0357    38              WAIT     SEC               ;DELAY FOR THAT LONG
0358    E9 01                    SBC #$01
035A    D0 FB                    BNE WAIT
035C    60                       RTS
035D                    ;
035D                    ;THIS IS A TABLE OF THE CONSTANTS FOR THE TONE
035D                    ;FREQUENCIES FOR EACH TELEPHONE DIGIT. THE
035D                    ;CONSTANTS ARE TWO BYTES LONG, LOW BYTE FIRST.
035D                    ;
035D    13              TABLE    .BYTE $13,$02,$76,$01    ;TWO TONES FOR '0'
035E    02
035F    76
0360    01
0361    CD                       .BYTE $CD,$02,$9E,$01    ;TWO TONES FOR '1'
0362    02
0363    9E
0364    01
0365    CD                       .BYTE $CD,$02,$76,$01    ;     '2'
0366    02
0367    76
0368    01
0369    CD                       .BYTE $CD,$02,$53,$01    ;     '3'
036A    02
036B    53
036C    01
036D    89                       .BYTE $89,$02,$9E,$01    ;     '4'
036E    02
```

Program 4-4: Phone Dialer (continued)

```
0082   036F   9E
0082   0370   01
0083   0371   89          .BYTE $89,$02,$76,$01   ;   '5'
0083   0372   02
0083   0373   76
0083   0374   01
0084   0375   89          .BYTE $89,$02,$53,$01   ;   '6'
0084   0376   02
0084   0377   53
0084   0378   01
0085   0379   4B          .BYTE $4B,$02,$9E,$01   ;   '7'
0085   037A   02
0085   037B   9E
0085   037C   01
0086   037D   4B          .BYTE $4B,$02,$76,$01   ;   '8'
0086   037E   02
0086   037E   76
0086   0380   01
0087   0381   4B          .BYTE $4B,$02,$53,$01   ;   '9'
0087   0382   02
0087   0383   53
0087   0384   01
0088   0385               .END

ERRORS = 0000 <0000>

SYMBOL TABLE

SYMBOL   VALUE

ACR1     A00B     ACR2     AC0B     DELAY    0355     DELCON   00FF
DIGIT    0302     NOEND    030A     NUMPTR   00C0     OFF      034C
OFFDEL   0020     ON       033C     ONDEL    0040     PHONE    0300
T1CH     A005     T1LH     A007     T1LL     A004     T2CH     AC05
T2LH     AC07     T2LL     AC04     TABLE    035D     WAIT     0357

END OF ASSEMBLY
```

Program 4-4: Phone Dialer (continued)

APPENDIX D

HEXADECIMAL CONVERSION TABLE

HEX	0	1	2	3	4	5	6	7	8	9	A	B	C	D	E	F	00	000
0	0	1	2	3	4	5	6	7	8	9	10	11	12	13	14	15	0	0
1	16	17	18	19	20	21	22	23	24	25	26	27	28	29	30	31	256	4096
2	32	33	34	35	36	37	38	39	40	41	42	43	44	45	46	47	512	8192
3	48	49	50	51	52	53	54	55	56	57	58	59	60	61	62	63	768	12288
4	64	65	66	67	68	69	70	71	72	73	74	75	76	77	78	79	1024	16384
5	80	81	82	83	84	85	86	87	88	89	90	91	92	93	94	95	1280	20480
6	96	97	98	99	100	101	102	103	104	105	106	107	108	109	110	111	1536	24576
7	112	113	114	115	116	117	118	119	120	121	122	123	124	125	126	127	1792	28672
8	128	129	130	131	132	133	134	135	136	137	138	139	140	141	142	143	2048	32768
9	144	145	146	147	148	149	150	151	152	153	154	155	156	157	158	159	2304	36864
A	160	161	162	163	164	165	166	167	168	169	170	171	172	173	174	175	2560	40960
B	176	177	178	179	180	181	182	183	184	185	186	187	188	189	190	191	2816	45056
C	192	193	194	195	196	197	198	199	200	201	202	203	204	205	206	207	3072	49152
D	208	209	210	211	212	213	214	215	216	217	218	219	220	221	222	223	3328	53248
E	224	225	226	227	228	229	230	231	232	233	234	235	236	237	238	239	3584	57344
F	240	241	242	243	244	245	246	247	248	249	250	251	252	253	254	255	3840	61440

5		4		3		2		1		0	
HEX	DEC	HEX	DEC	HEX	DEC	HEX	DEC	HEX	DEC	HEX	DEC
0	0	0	0	0	0	0	0	0	0	0	0
1	1,048,576	1	65,536	1	4,096	1	256	1	16	1	1
2	2,097,152	2	131,072	2	8,192	2	512	2	32	2	2
3	3,145,728	3	196,608	3	12,288	3	768	3	48	3	3
4	4,194,304	4	262,144	4	16,384	4	1,024	4	64	4	4
5	5,242,880	5	327,680	5	20,480	5	1,280	5	80	5	5
6	6,291,456	6	393.216	6	24,576	6	1,536	6	96	6	6
7	7,340,032	7	458,752	7	28,672	7	1,792	7	112	7	7
8	8,388,608	8	524,288	8	32,768	8	2,048	8	128	8	8
9	9,437,184	9	589,824	9	36,864	9	2,304	9	144	9	9
A	10,485,760	A	655,360	A	40,960	A	2,560	A	160	A	10
B	11,534,336	B	720,896	B	45,056	B	2,816	B	176	B	11
C	12,582,912	C	786,432	C	49,152	C	3,072	C	192	C	12
D	13,631,488	D	851,968	D	53,248	D	3,328	D	208	D	13
E	14,680,064	E	917,504	E	57,344	E	3,584	E	224	E	14
F	15,728,640	F	983,040	F	61,440	F	3,840	F	240	F	15

APPENDIX E

ASCII CONVERSION TABLE

HEX		0	1	2	3	4	5	6	7
	BITS	000	001	010	011	100	101	110	111
0	0000	NUL	DLE	SPACE	0	@	P	–	p
1	0001	SOH	DC1	!	1	A	Q	a	q
2	0010	STX	DC2	"	2	B	R	b	r
3	0011	ETX	DC3	#	3	C	S	c	s
4	0100	EOT	DC4	$	4	D	T	d	t
5	0101	ENQ	NAK	%	5	E	U	e	u
6	0110	ACK	SYN	&	6	F	V	f	v
7	0111	BEL	ETB		7	G	W	g	w
8	1000	BS	CAN	(	8	H	X	h	x
9	1001	HT	EM	)	9	I	Y	i	y
A	1010	LF	SUB	*	:	J	Z	j	z
B	1011	VT	ESC	+	;	K	[	k	{
C	1100	FF	FS	,	<	L	\	l	¦
D	1101	CR	GS	–	=	M	]	m	}
E	1110	SO	RS	.	>	N	∧	n	~
	1111	SI	US	/	?	O	←	o	DEL

THE ASCII SYMBOLS

NUL —Null
SOH —Start of Heading
STX —Start of Text
ETX —End of Text
EOT —End of Transmission
ENQ —Enquiry
ACK —Acknowledge
BEL —Bell
BS —Backspace
HT —Horizontal Tabulation
LF —Line Feed
VT —Vertical Tabulation
FF —Form Feed
CR —Carriage Return
SO —Shift Out
SI —Shift In
DLE —Data Link Escape
DC —Device Control
NAK —Negative Acknowledge
SYN —Synchronous Idle
ETB —End of Transmission Block
CAN —Cancel
EM —End of Medium
SUB —Substitute
ESC —Escape
FS —File Separator
GS —Group Separator
RS —Record Separator
US —Unit Separator
SP —Space (Blank)
DEL —Delete

APPENDIX F

6502 INSTRUCTIONS (ALPHABETIC)

ADC	Add with carry
AND	Logical AND
ASL	Arithmetic Shift Left
BCC	Branch if carry clear
BCS	Branch if carry set
BEQ	Branch if result = 0
BIT	Test bit
BMI	Branch if minus
BNE	Branch if not equal to 0
BPL	Branch if plus
BRK	Break
BVC	Branch if overflow clear
BVS	Branch if overflow set
CLC	Clear carry
CLD	Clear decimal flag
CLI	Clear interrupt disable
CLV	Clear overflow
CMP	Compare to accumulator
CPX	Compare to X
CPY	Compare to Y
DEC	Decrement memory
DEX	Decrement X
DEY	Decrement Y
EOR	Exclusive OR
INC	Increment memory
INX	Increment X
INY	Increment Y
JMP	Jump
JSR	Jump to subroutine
LDA	Load accumulator
LDX	Load X
LDY	Load Y
LSR	Logical shift right
NOP	No operation
ORA	Logical OR
PHA	Push A
PHP	Push P status
PLA	Pull A
PLP	Pull P status
ROL	Rotate left
ROR	Rotate right
RTI	Return from interrupt
RTS	Return from subroutine
SBC	Subtract with carry
SEC	Set carry
SED	Set decimal
SEI	Set interrupt disable
STA	Store accumulator
STX	Store X
STY	Store Y
TAX	Transfer A to X
TAY	Transfer A to Y
TSX	**Transfer *SP* to *X***
TXA	Transfer X to A
TXS	Transfer X to SP
TYA	Transfer Y to A

INDEX

AN INTRODUCTION TO PERSONAL AND BUSINESS COMPUTING

RODNAY ZAKS
250 pp, 125 illustr. ref C200

No computer background is required.

This is a basic introductory text on microcomputers. Its main goal is to answer the question: "What do I need for...?" in specific detail. No previous technical background is assumed. The author addresses progressively all the essential topics of interest to the microcomputer user (as opposed to the designer). How a system works. Which modules are required for which function. How much memory is needed. Which peripheral should be used. The cost. The software. Differences between existing microcomputers. Is a mini-BASIC sufficient? The real cost of a business system. Its limitations. Can you really manage a mialing list on a floppy disk? Packages and other programs. The traps for the hobbyist. Application techniques. New systems and facilities.

The book is designed to educate the reader in all the aspects of a system, from the selection of the microcomputer to the required peripherals.

CONTENTS:

1- THE MICROCOMPUTER ERA. 2- USING THE SYSTEM. 3- BASIC DEFINITIONS: The CPU. The buses. The memory. Input-output. A microprocessor system. 4- HOW IT WORKS. 5- PROGRAMMING IT: Programming languages. Flow-charting. Information representation. Developing a program. 6- BASIC AND APL: Automating loops. Subroutines. User defined functions. Lists and arrays. A business tabulation. How complete is your Basic? Business Basic. How fast is your Basic? The limitations of Basic. Alternatives to Basic. APL. Natural language. 7- BUSINESS COMPUTING: Applications of computers in business. Word processing. The requirements of a business system: accounts receivable, accounts payable, inventory, update, mailing list. Custom business programs. Buying the system: a summary. 8- SELECTING A SYSTEM: Selection criteria. Peformance. Benchmarks. The important criteria. 9- THE PERIPHERALS: The keyboard. The CRT display. Displaying text on a display. Dumb vs intelligent. Thermal and electrosensitive printer. Band printer. The Selectric. The daisy wheel printer. Matrix printer. The line printer. Superprinter. Printers for business. Disks. The floppy disk. The minifloppy. Increasing the storage. One or two disks? Tapes. Future bulk storage. The light pen. The joystick. The mouse. Rand tablet. Voice input. Voice output. 10- SELECTING A MICROCOMPUTER: A microhistory of computers. Commerical microcomputers. Single board microcomputes. The KIMI, NECTK80. Minimal cost home system: Videobrain, Bally, PET, TRS80. General purpose microcomputers. Apple II, Altair, Imsai, Sol, Cromemco, etc. Small business systems. 11- ECONOMICS OF A BUSINESS SYSTEM: The real cost of a system. The hidden costs. When to buy. Time sharing. 12- HOW TO FAIL WITH A BUSINESS SYSTEM: Hardware failures. Techniques for enhanced reliability. Software failures. Procedures: data accuracy, enforcing control, check digits, data security, computer-shock. 13- HELP: Obtaining information. Magazines. Clubs and computer stores. Education. Computer shows. Overseas. Microcomputer magazines. 14- TOMORROW.

MICROPROCESSORS

From chips to systems

RODNAY ZAKS

420 pp, 200 illustr, ref C201

The basic text on microprocessors for everyone with a technical or scientific background. This is an educational book, designed to teach step by step all the fundamentals of microprocessors. It is the result of the author's experience in teaching microprocessor design to more than 2 000 persons. It has been qualified by virtually every reader as « easy to read », « truly educational ». It is being used at leading universities worldwide.

CONTENTS :

1 - FUNDAMENTAL CONCEPTS : Introduction - Principles of Operation - Buses - A Pocket Calculator - The Memory - Memory Organization - Basic Microprocessor Definitions - Manufacturing a Microprocessor - LSI Technologies - Brief History of Microprocessors - Silicon Valley - Advantages of Microprocessors - Summary.

2 - INTERNAL OPERATION OF A MICROPROCESSOR : The Constraints of LSI - Standard Microprocessor Architecture - A Case Study : The 8080 - The Four Main Architectures.

3 - SYSTEM COMPONENTS : The Microprocessor Families - The Memory - Input-Output Techniques - UART - PIO - I/O Management Chips - Peripheral Controller Chips - Typical Microprocessor I/O Devices.

4 - COMPARATIVE MICROPROCESSOR EVALUATION : Functional Elements of an MPU - Classifying Microprocessors - 4-Bit Microprocessors - 4-Bit 1-Chip Microcomputers - 8-Bit Microprocessors - 8-Bit 1-Chip Microcomputers - 16-Bit Microprocessors - 16-Bit 1-Chip Microcomputers - Bit-Slice Processors - Comparison Summary - Microprocessor Selection - Summary.

5 - SYSTEM INTERCONNECT : Standard System Architecture - Assembling a CPU. Connecting the Address Bus - Connecting the Memory - Connecting the Input-Output - System Interconnect - Conclusion.

6 - MICROPROCESSOR APPLICATIONS : Application Areas - Computer Systems - Industrial Systems - Consumer Applications - Special Applications - Building A Microprocessor Application - A Front-Panel Controller - A Paper-Tape Reader-Punch Controller - Analog Input-Output - Case Studies - Personal Computing.

7 - INTERFACING TECHNIQUES : Scope - Keyboard - LED Display - Teletype - Floppy-Disk - CRT - Multimicroprocessors - Bus Standards.

8 - MICROPROCESSOR PROGRAMMING : Definitions - Internal Representation of Information - External Representation of Information - Instruction Formats - Assembly Language Programming - A Multiplication - Simulating Digital Logic - Limitations of Programmed Logic - Microprocessor Controlled Music - Advantages of Programming - Summary.

9 - SYSTEM DEVELOPMENT : Development - Developing a Program - Fundamental Choices - Development Tools - Summary.

10 - THE FUTURE : Introduction - The Yield - Technological Evolution - Component Evolution - Social Impact.

PROGRAMMING THE 6502
RODNAY ZAKS
300 pp, 200 illustr, ref C202

This book is an educational text designed to teach programming, using the 6502 (other books in this series cover the 8080 and Z80). It does not require any prior programming knowledge, yet can be used to advantage by anyone wishing to familiarize himself with the 6502.

It has been designed as a progressive, step by step course, with exercises in the text designed to test the reader at every step. The author has taught programming to over 1000 persons, and the pedagogy of the book is a direct result of his experience.

It covers all essential aspects of programming, as well as the advantages and disadvantages of the 6502 and should bring the reader to the point where he can start writing complete applications programs. This text is a companion volume to the 6502 Applications Book.

CONTENTS:

1- BASIC CONCEPTS: What is Programming? Flow-Charting-Information representation: Internal and external. Representing Programs and Data.

2- 6502 HARDWARE ORGANIZATION: System Architecture. Internal Organization of the 6502. The Instruction Execution Cycle. Fetching and Next Instruction. 6502 Registers. The Stack.

3- BASIC PROGRAMMING TECHNIQUES: Arithmetic Programs: addition, subtraction. BCD arithmetic. Multiplication. Division. Subroutines.

4- THE 6502 INSTRUCTION SET: Classes of instructions: data transfers, data processing, test and branch, input-output, control. Instructions available on the 6502.

5- ADDRESSING TECHNIQUES. Addressing modes: Implicit, immediate, absolute, direct, relative, indexed (pre- and post), indirect. Combination Modes. Sample Programs.

6- INPUT-OUTPUT TECHNIQUES: Basic Input-Output: Generate a Signal-Delay Generation. Sensing Pulses. Parallel and Serial Transfer. Communication with I/O devices: handshaking, LED, Teletype. Input-Output scheduling: polling, interrupts, break.

7- INPUT-OUTPUT DEVICES: The standard PIO, the 6530, 6522, 6532.

8- APPLICATION EXAMPLES: Clearing Memory, Reading Characters, Testing a Character, Bracket Testing, Parity Generation, Code Conversion, Largest Element, Sum of a Table, Checksum, Counting the Zeroes.

9- DATA STRUCTURES: Pointers. Lists: Sequential, directories, linked, queue, stack, circular, trees, doubly linked. Searching and sorting.

10- PROGRAM DEVELOPMENT: Programming Choices. Software support-Development Sequence. Hardware Alternatives. Hardware Resources. The Assembler. Macros. Other facilities.

11- CONCLUSION

MICROPROCESSOR INTERFACING TECHNIQUES

(2ND EXPANDED EDITION)

AUSTIN LESEA and **RODNAY ZAKS**

416 pp, 320 illustr. ref C207

Microprocessor interfacing is no longer an art. It is a set of techniques, and in some cases just a set of components. This comprehensive book introduces the basic interfacing concepts and techniques, then presents in detail the implementation details, from hardware to software. It covers all the essential peripherals, from keyboard to floppy disk, as well as the standard buses (S100 to IEEE 488) and introduces the basic troubleshooting techniques.

CONTENTS :

1 - INTRODUCTION : Concepts, basic techniques, microprocessor control signals.

2 - ASSEMBLING THE CENTRAL PROCESSING UNIT : Introduction, system architecture, addressing. The 8080 system, the 6800 system, the Z-80. Dynamic RAM interface. The 8085.

3 - BASIC INPUT-OUTPUT : memory vs I/O mapping. Parallel Input-Output : techniques and chips (PIO). Serial Input-Output : program and UART. The three input-output control methods : polling, interrupts, DMA. Useful circuits.

4 - INTERFACING THE PERIPHERALS keyboards, bounce, encoding, rollover. LED displays Teletype. Paper - tape reader. Line printer. Magnetic-stripe credit-card reader. Cassette interface. CRT display. CRTC. Floppy disk. FDC. CRC.

5 - ANALOG - DIGITAL CONVERSION : Conceptual D/A, practical A/D, real products, the A/D, sampling theorem, successive approximation, integration, direct comparison conversion. ADC and DAC. Interfacing D/A's and A/D's. Data collection subsystem, scaling, offset, conclusions.

6 - BUS STANDARDS : Parallel : S100, 6800, IEEE - 488, CAMAC. Serial : EIA-RS 232 C, RS 422, RS 423, synchronous formats.

7 - CASE-STUDY : A 32 - CHANNEL MULTIPLEXER : Introduction, specifications, architecture, software, CPU module, RAM module, USART Module, Host interface module, conclusion.

8 - DIGITAL TROUBLE-SHOOTING The problems. What goes wrong : components, noise, software ; the tools and the methods : VOM, DVM, oscilloscope, logic probes, signature analysis, emulation, simulation, logic-state analyzers. Case-study : trouble history. The perfect bench.

9 - CONCLUSION - EVOLUTION : The new chips, one-chip systems. Plastic software.

APPENDIX A : Manufacturers APPENDIX B : S100 Manufacturers

PUBLICATIONS LIST
(Also available in other languages)

1 - TEXTS

C200 -Introduction to Personal and Business Computing
C201 -Microprocessors
C202 -Programming the 6502
C208 -Programming the 8080*
C280 -Programming the Z80
D302 -6502 Applications Book
G402 -6502 Games Book*
D380 -Z80 Applications Book*
C207 -Microprocessor Interfacing Techniques
IMD -International Microprocessor Dictionary (10 languages)
X1 -Microprocessor Lexicon
Z10 -Microprogrammed APL Implementation
and more

2 - SELF-STUDY COURSES

Each course includes audio-cassettes plus a special book.

S1 -Introduction to Microprocessors (2.5 hrs)
S2 -Programming Microprocessors (2.5 hrs)
S3 -Designing a Microprocessor System (2.5 hrs)
S10 -Introduction to Personal & Business Computing (2.5 hrs)
SB1 -Microprocessors (12 hrs)
SB2 -Microcomputer Programming (10 hrs)
SB3 -Military Microprocessor Systems (6 hrs)
SB5 -Bit-slice (6 hrs)
SB6 -Industrial Applications (4.5 hrs)
SB7 -Microprocessor Interfacing Techniques (6 hrs)

3 - COURSES ON VIDEO-CASSETTES

V1 -Microprocessors (12 hrs)
V3 -Military Microprocessor Systems (6 hrs)
V5 -Bit-slice (6 hrs)
V7 -Microprocessor Interfacing Techniques (6 hrs)

4 - SEMINAR TRAINING BOOKS

B1 - Microprocessors, 550 pp.
B2 - Microprocessor Programming and Microprogramming, 500 pp.
B3 - Military Microprocessor Systems, 350 pp.
B5 - Bit-slice, 300 pp.
B6 - Industrial Microprocessor Systems, 300 pp.
B7 - Microprocessor Interfacing Techniques, 350 pp.
B9 - Microprocessor Troubleshooting
S1 - Introduction to Microprocessors, 100 pp.
S2 - Programming Microprocessors, 150 pp.
S3 - Designing a Microprocessor System
S4 - Microprocessor Applications
S5 - Equipment Selection and Evaluation
S6 - Super Speed : Bit-slice

* To be published

FOR A COMPLETE CATALOGUE OF OUR PUBLICATIONS

SYBEX

USA:
2020 Milvia St.
Berkeley, CA 94704
Tel: 415/848-8233

EUROPE:
18 rue Planchat
75020 - Paris, France
Tel: (1) 370 32 75

About SYBEX

SYBEX is specialized in high-level education and training and provides seminars in the microprocessor field worldwide. More than 5000 persons have graduated from SYBEX microprocessor seminars in the U.S.A., Europe, Japan and other countries. SYBEX books have been derived directly from this extensive experience in education. Many are accompanied by self-study courses on cassettes and videotapes. Special courses and video-cassettes can also be prepared. SYBEX texts on microprocessors ("C" series) are used at educational institutions worldwide and are available in foreign translations.